Solution Architectures

Brian Matsik

New Riders
201 West 103rd Street, Indianapolis, Indiana 46290

MCSD Fast Track: Solution Architectures

Copyright © 1999 by New Riders Publishing

All rights reserved. No part of this book shall be reproduced, stored in a retrieval system, or transmitted by any means, electronic, mechanical, photocopying, recording, or otherwise, without written permission from the publisher. No patent liability is assumed with respect to the use of the information contained herein. Although every precaution has been taken in the preparation of this book, the publisher and author assume no responsibility for errors or omissions. Neither is any liability assumed for damages resulting from the use of the information contained herein.

International Standard Book Number: 0-7357-0029-X

Library of Congress Catalog Card Number: 99-63019

Printed in the United States of America

First Printing: September 1999

03 02 01 00 99   7 6 5 4 3 2 1

Interpretation of the printing code: The rightmost double-digit number is the year of the book's printing; the rightmost single-digit number is the number of the book's printing. For example, the printing code 99-1 shows that the first printing of the book occurred in 1999.

Trademarks

All terms mentioned in this book that are known to be trademarks or service marks have been appropriately capitalized. New Riders Publishing cannot attest to the accuracy of this information. Use of a term in this book should not be regarded as affecting the validity of any trademark or service mark.

Solution Architectures is a registered trademark of Microsoft Corporation.

Warning and Disclaimer

Every effort has been made to make this book as complete and as accurate as possible, but no warranty or fitness is implied. The information provided is on an "as is" basis. The author and the publisher shall have neither liability nor responsibility to any person or entity with respect to any loss or damages arising from the information contained in this book.

Publisher
David Dwyer

Executive Editor
Mary Foote

Acquisitions Editor
Stacey Beheler

Development Editor
Rob Tidrow

Managing Editor
Sarah Kearns

Project Editor
Jennifer Chisholm

Technical Editors
Mike Draganza
Eeraj Qaisar

Copy Editor
Cliff Shubs

Indexer
Virginia Bess

Proofreader
John Rahm

Compositor
Ron Wise

Contents at a Glance

INTRODUCTION

PART I	WHAT'S IMPORTANT TO KNOW ABOUT EXAM 70-100
1	Analyzing Business Requirements 11
2	Developing Data Models 69
3	Developing the Conceptual and Logical Design for an Application 103
4	Designing a User Interface and User Services 135
5	Defining the Technical Architecture for a Solution 163
	Objective Review Notes 173

PART II	INSIDE EXAM 70-100
6	Fast Facts Review 195
7	Hotlist of Exam-Critical Concepts 215
8	Sample Scenario and Sample Test Questions 249
9	Insider's Spin on Exam 70-100 269
10	Did You Know? 287

INDEX   291

Table of Contents

Part I What's Important to Know About Exam 70-100

1 Analyzing Business Requirements 11

Project Scope 12
  Defining the Problem 15
  Determining the Expected Results 15
  Existing Applications 16
  Expected Lifetime 16
  Project Budget 18
    Time and Labor 18
    Total Cost 19
    Benefit Trade-Offs 20
    Feature Selection 20
    Creating the Feature List 21
    Avoiding Feature Creep 22

Business Requirements 22
  Business Goals 23
  Customer Requirements 24
  Reading Between the Lines 24
  Establishing the Type of Problem 25
  TCO and ROI 26
    Minimizing Total Cost of Ownership 26
    Increasing Return on Investment 27
  Current Infrastructure Design 30
  Incorporating the Platform and Infrastructure into the Solution 30
  Analyzing the Impact of New Technology 30
  Establishing the Application Environment 31
  Establishing a Schedule 32

Human Factors 32
  Identifying Users 33
  Training 35
  Local and Remote Users 36
  Localization Issues 38

Integration with Existing Applications 39
   Legacy Applications and Hardware 39
      Migration to a New System 40
      Creating and Using Middleware 40
   Connectivity 42
   Data Conversion and Character Translation 43

Business Methodologies and Limitations 43
   Current Business Practices 44
   Business and Organizational Structure 44
   Customer's Needs 46

Security 46
   Security Models 46
      System 47
      Server/Machine 47
      User 47
      Group 47
      File 48
      Database 48
   Identifying Roles 49
   Auditing 49
   Fault Tolerance 51
      Hardware Fault Tolerance 51
      Disk Duplexing and Mirroring 51
      Disk Striping 52
      RAID 52
      Software Fault Tolerance 54

Performance 54
   Bandwidth 54
   Peak Usage 56
   Online/Offline Hours 56
   Response Time 57
      Physical Response Time 57
      Perceived Response Time 58
      Transaction Processing 58

Maintainability 59
   Application Distribution and Upgrades 59
   Support 61
   Future Planning 62

Availability 63
   Geographic Scope 63
   Operational Timelines 63
   Impact of Downtime 64

Scalability 65
  Planning for Growth 65
  Organizational Changes 66
  Expanding Data 67
What Is Important to Know 68

2 Developing Data Models 69

Logical Design 70
  Entities, Attributes, and Relationships 70
  Entities 71
  Attributes 73
  Relationships 76
  Keys 77
    Primary Keys 77
    Foreign Keys 80
  One-to-One 81
  One-to-Many 82
  Many-to-Many 83
  Generating the Model 85
  Primary and Foreign Keys 89
  Normalization and Denormalization 90
  First Normal Form 91
  Second Normal Form 91
  Third Normal Form 95
  Denormalization 98

Physical Design Considerations 99
What Is Important to Know 101

3 Developing the Conceptual and Logical Design for an Application 103

Application Models 104
  Application Types 104
  SDI 104
  MDI 105
  Console 106
  Service 107
  Web-Based Applications 108
  Interface Pros and Cons 110
  Client/Server Architecture 111
  Single Tier 113
  Single Tier/File Server 113
  Thin Client/Terminal 114
  Two Tier 115
  Three Tier 116
  n-Tier 117

An Introduction to COM   119
Interfaces   120
Properties   121
Methods   123
Events   124
Object Organization   126
User   126
Business   127
Data   128
Object Models   128

Encapsulating Databases   130

Key Terms   132

What Is Important to Know   133

4 Designing a User Interface and User Services   135

User Interface Basics   136
Using the Windows Common Control Library   137
Toolbars   137
Tabstrips   137
Treeview   138
Listview   138
Trackbar   139
Progress bar   140
Keeping a Clean Interface   141
Navigation   143
Menus   144
Application Assistance   147
Input Validation   147
Visual Cues   149
Formatting Input   151

User Feedback   152
Status Bars   152
ToolTips   153
What's This Help   153
Wizards   154

Help Files   155
Standard   155
HTML Help   155

Errors   156
Presenting Errors   156
Do's and Don'ts of Error Handling   158

Prototyping   159
Key Terms   160
What Is Important to Know   161

5 Defining the Technical Architecture for a Solution   163

Identifying Appropriate Technologies   164

Data Storage and Design   165
   Architecture   166
   Performance Considerations   167
   Reporting   168

Feasibility Testing   168
   Meeting the Business Requirements   169
   Meeting the Use Cases   169
   Falling Short of the Solution   169

Deployment   170

What Is Important to Know   172

Objective Review Notes   173
Analyzing Business Requirements   175
Developing Data Models   180
Developing the Conceptual and Logical Design for an Application   183
Designing a User Interface and User Services   187
Defining the Technical Architecture for a Solution   189

Part II   Inside Exam 70-100

6 Fast Facts Review   195
What to Study   196
Analyzing Business Requirements   196
Developing Data Models   202
Developing the Conceptual and Logical Design for an Application   203
Designing a User Interface for a Solution   207
Defining the Technical Architecture for a Solution   211

7 Hotlist of Exam-Critical Concepts 215

Products, Tools, and Technologies 216
   Development Tools 216
      Visual Basic 216
      Visual C++ 218
      Visual FoxPro 219
      Visual InterDev 220
      Visual J++ 222
      Visual SourceSafe 223
   Database Servers 224
      SQL Server 224
      Access 225
   Data Connection Services 226
      ODBC 226
      ADO 227
      DAO 228
      RDO 228
      OLE DB 229
   Networking and Infrastructure 229
      Windows 3.11 229
      Windows 95/98 230
      Windows NT 230
      Workstation 230
      Server 231
      AS/400 231
      Networking 232
      LAN 232
      WAN 232
      Network Speeds 232
      RAS/VPN 233
      Internet 234
      Internet Information Server 234
      Mainframe Computing 234
      Microsoft SNA Server 235
      CICS 235
   Other 236
      Microsoft Transaction Server 236
      Microsoft Exchange Server 237

Key Terms and Definitions 238

Other Key Technology Information 245
   Development Tools Comparison 245
   Database Comparison 247

8 Sample Scenario and Sample Test Questions 249

Sample Scenario-Based Questions 250

Background 251

Problem Statements 251
- Salesperson 251
- Order-Entry Specialist 252
- Information Technology Manager 252

Current Systems 252
- Customers 252
- Salesperson 252
- Information Technology Manager 253

Environments 253
- Information Technology Manager 253
- Chief Information Officer 253
- Network Administrator 253

Envisioned System 254
- Sales Manager 254
- Order-Processing Manager 254
- Network Administrator 254

Security 254
- Sales Manager 254
- Order Processing Manager 255

Performance 255
- Sales Manager 255
- System Administrator 255
- Information Technology Manger 255

Maintainability 256
- Network Administrator 256
- Information Technology Manager 256

Availability 256
- Order-Entry Manager 256
- Information Technology Manager 256

Sample Test Questions 257

Answers and Explanations 263

9 Insider's Spin on Exam 70-100   269
Build List and Reorder   271
Create a Tree   271
Drop and Connect   273
Get into Microsoft's Mind-Set   275
Understand the Exam's TimeFrame   276
Get Used to Answering Questions Quickly   278
Taking the Test   279
Where the Questions Come From   284
Different Flavors of Questions   285

10 Did You Know?   287

Index   291

About the Author

Brian Matsik is currently the president and senior consultant at Object Oriented Consulting Services in Charlotte, North Carolina. Brian has been working with Microsoft Visual Basic since version 2.0 for Windows and 1.0 for DOS. He has worked for many organizations in the Charlotte area, consulting in Windows client/server development, version control/source management, and Visual Basic/COM architecture design. He spends his spare time trying to keep a golf ball out of the woods and chatting on IRC. He can frequently be found on #MCSE as NC_MCSD.

About the Technical Reviewers

Mike Draganza is a Microsoft Certified Solution Developer. He lives in Costa Mesa (Orange County), CA with his wife Robin and two kids Natalie, 10, and Lauren, 8. When he is not programming or reading about programming, he enjoys tennis and golf. He currently works as a contract programmer for Boeing. His programming experience runs the gamut of Windows technologies: COM and ATL, ActiveX, MFC, and Win32.

Eeraj J. Qaisar has a degree in Chemical Engineering from AMU - Aligarh (India). He is also a MCSD with product specialization in VB5.0 and SQL Server 6.5. He currently works for MediaServ.com—a Microsoft Certified Solutions Partner as a solutions consultant. He can be reached at eeraj@hotmail.com.

Dedications

To my mother, the first woman that I ever loved.

To Tracy, the last woman that I will ever love.

Acknowledgments

I would like to thank my future wife, Tracy, for all of the support that she has given me over the past few months. I know that between my consulting work and this book she has started to wonder who the strange, yet familiar looking, man in her house is and how he got a key. I don't know how she puts up with me, but she does and I love her for it.

I would also like to thank my father, John, for introducing me to my first TRS-80 model 2 and Timex Sinclair 1000. I've come a long way since my very first BASIC applications. I wouldn't have been the techie that I am without his guidance and assistance. Thanks for everything.

I can't forget Duane and Kipp for not giving me a hard time about missing out on all of the golf while putting this book together. Well, the book is done and it's time to hit the links again—I'll be in the woods looking for my ball if anyone needs me.

Of course I can't forget the people at New Riders. Thanks to Amy for getting this started and Stacey for getting it finished. Thanks to Rob and Eeraj for going through the tech review process with me and helping me though my first book.

Finally, I can't forget all of the great people that I have worked with and learned from over the years: Harry Kendall, Bobby Allen, John Ramminger, Brian Nash, Geoff White, and Brad Mabe. Each of you have been a part of my success and growth over the years. I hope to work with each of you again in the future.

Tell Us What You Think!

As the reader of this book, *you* are our most important critic and commentator. We value your opinion and want to know what we're doing right, what we could do better, what areas you'd like to see us publish in, and any other words of wisdom you're willing to pass our way.

As the Executive Editor of the Certification team at New Riders Publishing, I welcome your comments. You can fax, email, or write me directly to let me know what you did or didn't like about this book—as well as what we can do to make our books stronger.

Please note that I can't help you with technical problems related to this book, and that due to the high volume of mail I receive, I might not be able to reply to every message.

When you write, please be sure to include this book's title and author, as well as your name and phone or fax number. I will carefully review your comments and share them with the author and editors who worked on the book.

Fax: 317-581-4663

Email: certification@mcp.com

Mail: Mary Foote
Executive Editor
Certification Group
Macmillan Computer Publishing
201 West 103rd Street
Indianapolis, IN 46290 USA

Introduction

WHO SHOULD READ THIS BOOK

The Solutions Architecture study guide in the *MCSD Fast Track* series is designed to assist in preparing for the 70-100 Analyzing Requirements and Defining Solution Architectures certification exam. This exam is a core requirement for the Microsoft Certified Solution Developer (MCSD) certification.

This exam and this book are geared toward developers who have at least three years experience developing client/server applications. You should have had some exposure to database design, client/server architectures, and application development.

HOW THIS BOOK HELPS YOU

This book covers some of the key topics of enterprise development. You might already be familiar with many of these items but have forgotten their details, or you might not have had a high level of exposure to them. The book is designed to review this information and utilize your study time by focusing only on the key topics that will be covered on the exam.

HOW TO USE THIS BOOK

When you are ready to take the test, use this guide to quickly review and assess your skills.

When you have completed the exercises and understand the new format of the 70-100 exam, then you are ready to register to take the exam. You can use this guide as a quick reference right before exam time to commit important terms and concepts to memory, as well as cross check any final misunderstandings.

About the 70-100 Exam

The 70-100 Solutions Architecture exam is a new type of exam from Microsoft. This is not a product-specific exam like the Microsoft Visual Basic and Microsoft Visual C++ exams. There is no coding in the exam. All questions are based on concepts, methodologies, design standards, and industry-wide product knowledge.

The 70-100 exam is geared toward developers with several years experience. This is one of the first "real world" Microsoft exams that does not present a series of fact-based right or wrong answers. A given question can have literally hundreds of correct answers. Also introduced are new types of questions called *scenario-based questions*.

These scenario-based questions present you with a long case study that is followed by several questions. The exam also introduces new question types that look for ordered list answers or have you draw a database or data flow model, as well as answer a hierarchical organization problem.

This book covers not only the key topics to pass the exam, but also more exam-specific detail than some of the previous Fast Track books covered. You will find that this book spends almost as much time on the exam as it does on the concepts. This is a peculiar exam, and you need not only to know *what* to answer, but *how* to answer.

What the Solutions Architecture (70-100) Exam Covers

The 70-100 Solutions Architecture exam is designed to test developers on their ability to analyze problems, determine solutions, and interact with end users and clients. This is not a coding test as with the Visual Basic and Visual C++ exams; rather, this exam covers the "soft skills" that developers should have.

You will be tested on your ability to implement Microsoft solutions in a given environment, as well as your overall knowledge of Microsoft products. You will need to know items such as which database to use (Microsoft SQL Server or Microsoft Access) and which languages should be used (Microsoft Visual Basic, Microsoft Visual C++, or other Microsoft languages). Along with this, you will need to know how Microsoft products interact and function together.

This test is intended for developers with several years experience implementing and using these products. Keep in mind that the syllabus recommends that the developer should have a minimum of two years experience in the following areas:

- Analyzing customer needs and creating specifications documents for client/server solutions in multiple business domains
- Process modeling, data modeling, component design, and user interface design
- Designing, developing, and implementing a client/server solution
- Knowledge of the functionality of both Microsoft Office and Microsoft Back Office applications
- Integration of new systems and applications into legacy environments
- Developing Microsoft Windows and Web applications

This test is designed to see how you think as a developer. Unlike previous exams where there was only one correct answer, the 70-100 exam can have many correct answers that vary from "completely correct" to "partially correct." This makes the exam even more difficult because there are few bullet point items that you can study to prepare for it. This is not as much of a fact-based exam as it is a process and analysis exam.

The main sections that are covered in this book are as follows:

- Analyzing Business Requirements
- Developing Data Models
- Developing the Conceptual and Logical Design for an Application
- Designing a User Interface and User Services
- Defining the Technical Architecture for a Solution
- Deriving the Physical Design

Analyzing Business Requirements

This section requires that you be able to determine the business requirements for a given scenario. It requires knowledge of planning, application methodologies, and general software design principles.

Objectives for Analyzing Business Requirements

- Analyze the scope of a given problem
- Analyze the extent of the business requirement
- Analyze security requirements for a given problem
- Analyze performance requirements
- Analyze maintainability requirements
- Analyze human factors
- Analyze the requirements for integrating a solution with existing applications
- Analyze existing methodologies and limitations of a business
- Analyze scalability requirements

Developing Data Models

This section covers the ability to design an effective data model from a given scenario. Knowledge of relationships, physical and logical designs, and normalization of data are necessary skills for this portion of the exam.

Objectives for Developing Data Models

- Specify the relationships between entities
- Develop a conceptual data model using standard normalization techniques
- Identify the key components of a data model
- Identify appropriate levels of denormalization
- Choose the foreign key that will enforce relationships between entities and will ensure referential integrity
- Convert a logical data model to a physical data model

DEVELOPING THE CONCEPTUAL AND LOGICAL DESIGN FOR AN APPLICATION

This section tests your ability to take a logical design and create the physical components of the design. The logical design must be designed through the given scenarios. Knowledge of object-oriented design and analysis will be tested.

Objectives for Developing the Conceptual and Logical Design for an Application

- Construct a conceptual design, taking into account business processes, task sequences, and environment models.
- Given the conceptual design, derive the components of the logical design.
- Given a business scenario, identify which solution type is appropriate. Solution types are single-tier and *n*-tier.
- Incorporate business rules into your object designs.
- Assess the impact of the design with respect to maintainability, security, extensibility, and scalability.

Designing a User Interface and User Services

This section focuses on designing a user interface that is user friendly and follows existing business standards. Prior knowledge of interface design and Windows application standards are beneficial to correctly working through the interface issues on the exam.

Objectives for Designing a User Interface and User Services

- Identify the proper interface design for the current business situation
- Determine the method of input validation to be used
- Evaluate and identify key user assistance interfaces such as online help, tooltips, and HTML help
- Establish the means of data output
- Construct a user interface based on current Windows application design standards, business requirements, and organizational standards

Defining the Technical Architecture for a Solution

This section wraps up some of the key areas of focus covered in other sections and introduces some product and technology specific decision processes. Knowledge of technology and product standards, feasibility testing, and architecture types will assist in completing this section.

Objectives for Defining the Technical Architecture for a Solution

- Identify which architecture type is appropriate for a given solution
- Identify the appropriate technologies to be implemented within a solution
- Choose an appropriate data storage architecture
- Test the feasibility of a proposed technical architecture
- Develop an appropriate deployment strategy

DERIVING THE PHYSICAL DESIGN

This section covers the final phase of the development cycle by taking the logical models and implementing the physical solution. Final assessments on the design pertaining to security, maintainability, and extensibility are analyzed, and the final business objects are created for the application.

Objectives for Deriving the Physical Design

- Assess the potential impact of the physical design on performance, maintainability, extensibility, scalability, availability, and security
- Evaluate whether access to a database should be encapsulated in an object
- Design the properties, methods, and events of components

PART I

WHAT'S IMPORTANT TO KNOW ABOUT EXAM 70-100

MCSD Fast Track: Solution Architectures was written as a study aid for people preparing for Microsoft Certification Exam 70-100. This book is intended to help reinforce and clarify information with which the student is already familiar. This series is not intended to be a single source for exam preparation, but rather a review of information and a set of practice tests to help increase the likelihood of success when taking the actual exam.

Part I of this book is designed to help you make the most of your study time by presenting concise summaries of information that you need to understand to succeed on the exam. Each chapter covers a specific exam objective area as outlined by Microsoft:

1. Analyzing Business Requirements

2. Developing Data Models

3. Developing the Conceptual and Logical Design for an Application

4. Designing a User Interface and User Services

5. Defining the Technical Architecture for a Solution

   Objective Review Notes

About the Exam

Exam Number	70-100
Minutes	180
Questions	Varies (4-5 Testlets)
Passing Score	*
Scenario	Yes
Single Answer Questions	Yes
Multiple Answer with Correct Number Given	Yes
Multiple Answer without Correct Number Given	Yes
Build List and Reorder	Yes
Create a Tree	Yes
Drop and Connect	Yes
Objective Categories	6

* At the time of publication, this information was unavailable.

OBJECTIVES

- Analyze the scope of a project.
- Analyze the extent of a business requirement.
- Analyze security requirements
- Analyze performance requirements.
- Analyze maintainability requirements.
- Analyze extensibility requirements. Solutions must be able to handle the growth of functionality.
- Analyze availability requirements.
- Analyze human factor requirements.
- Analyze the requirements for integrating a solution with existing applications.
- Analyze existing methodologies and limitations of a business.
- Analyze scalability requirements.

CHAPTER 1

Analyzing Business Requirements

Analyzing the business requirements of a solution is the first step in the process of creating and implementing a customer solution. During this phase of development, the following items should be completed or addressed:

- Establish a business case for the project
- Determine cost and budget
- Identify and set priorities
- Manage personnel

The process of establishing the business case for a project enables you to identify the problems and propose a resolution. Without a clear goal or target, the project will struggle to achieve any level of success.

Costs and budgeting lay the groundwork for the total cost of the project. Costs, such as hardware and software, are to be itemized and identified. The total budget is to include additional items, such as support costs, labor, training, and any other additional overhead costs.

Identifying the priorities of a project helps to further refine the goal of the project. Individual features and functionality will be identified and set into milestones. These milestones will gauge the progress of the project and set a timeline for the completion of the project.

The creation of the development teams is the next important step in starting an enterprise application. Team members should be selected by their skillsets and placed into specific roles within the team. A well-organized team consists of both generalists (the jack-of-all-trades) and specialists, such as architects and database administrators (or DBAs).

PROJECT SCOPE

The first phase of development according to the Microsoft Solution Framework (MSF) is the vision/scope process, which identifies the nature and establishes the outcome of the project. Questions, such as "What are the existing systems" and "What needs to be accomplished," are completed during vision/scope. This is a critical time in the development process because this phase lays the groundwork for every other step in the process.

> **NOTE: Microsoft Solution Framework**—MSF is the development model used internally at Microsoft and implemented externally by Microsoft Consulting Services and Microsoft Certified Solution Providers.

If the true scope of the project is not properly identified, the project will suffer because the resolution will not fit the problem. Many projects fail to deliver an adequate solution because the project was either planned improperly or the problem was not properly identified.

When analyzing the project scope, you must consider several things:

- What are the existing applications and tools?
- What are the anticipated environmental and infrastructure changes?
- What is the expected lifetime of the project?
- What is the budget of the project?
- What are the time constraints for the project?

Identifying existing applications identifies key systems being used and is used in later stages of planning when dealing with integration or detailed system analysis. You should always note the importance of an existing system and costs involved with replacing systems. High-cost systems help to dictate how the solution will be implemented because these systems might force the team to work around difficult integration or access issues.

Anticipating the environmental and infrastructure changes also plays a major role in application development because the time involved with an infrastructure change might be used to the team's advantage. For instance, a project is planned for six months, but the internal network, as well as WAN (wide area network) connections, are to be upgraded to handle a higher bandwidth. In this case, the known increase in bandwidth allows for more options when developing the new systems.

Another major factor that directs the development and the design of a solution is the expected lifetime. If the project consists of several fixes to key functionality until new systems are fully implemented, the development approach would be different than if you were developing a new system from the ground up. The focus on maintainability changes, depending on the lifetime of a system. Obviously, on a "throw-away" project, maintenance is not an issue, but the speed of implementation is. Likewise, a long-term application has a major focus on maintainability and a minor focus on rapid development. Know what the lifetime is and use it to your advantage in planning and design.

Project budget is the largest limiting factor in any project, both enterprise and desktop. If the budget only supports the implementation of 50% of the total functionality, then either the project scope or the budget must change. If the project and the budget do not agree, the project could fail (after reaching or exceeding the budget) or go far over budget. Either case does not provide an adequate solution. Every project should meet both the design goals and the allotted budget.

The budget also affects the tools you can use. A small project with a limited budget might not allow for the addition of both Microsoft SQL Server and Microsoft Exchange, so the tools must be modified and the development plan must be adjusted. Instead of SQL Server, look at implementing a Microsoft Access solution (for a small workgroup), and instead of an enterprise application like Exchange, look at more cost-effective solutions that fit the project size.

As if fitting a large project into a small budget were not enough, you also need to meet the proposed schedule. A project that meets the budget but misses the implementation by six months is still not a fully successful project. Meet the time constraints and the financial constraints while providing the most functionality you can, and you will have a successful project. Not an easy task, but it can be done. Proper planning and the use of milestones and versioned releases allows a team to deliver a product faster and allows for implementation sooner. Versioned releases and milestones are covered later.

Defining the Problem

The problem definition phase of requirement analysis gives the development team the ability to define the functional areas the process will encompass. This phase should look at high-level issues dealing with the business problem and attempt to place the general parameters around the process.

For example, the business problem might focus around the accounting department, but you will need to determine which components of that department are in need of focus. If the problem turns out to be centered on the payroll system, you need not be concerned with the accounts receivable or accounts payable systems.

To define the problem, you should create a problem statement that outlines the problem with the basic parameters you have defined. The following is an example of the problem statement you would come up with.

> "The current payroll system does not expose enough interfaces to allow for quick and error-free data entry."

This problem statement could be a sentence or a few paragraphs, depending on the size of the project. If you are creating an enterprise application, several problem statements can be created because there might be several general business problems that need to be resolved.

Determining the Expected Results

The next step that should be accomplished after the problem definition phase should be the solution definition phase. This is similar to the above, but rather than defining the problem, you will define the high-level solution.

Again, create a statement that outlines the resolution. In the previous example with the payroll system issues, a resolution statement might read:

> "The payroll system will be enhanced with new data entry screens that will capture a specific subset of the employee data for faster and more reliable data entry."

As with the problem statement, your resolution statement may be a sentence or several paragraphs.

These statements come in handy during the development process when you start defining the specific issues of the problems and the resolutions. The problem and resolution statements act as a vision statement to keep you on track and focused on the overall goals of the development process.

Existing Applications

When analyzing the existing applications within a project, it is important to consider the platforms that the existing applications utilize. The application platform becomes important in later stages of planning and development because individual platforms require unique approaches and can limit the tools you can utilize.

When dealing with existing applications, it is important to note the limitations and the extensibility of the applications. You might discover that the existing applications can be used in new ways with APIs or libraries, or you might realize that the existing applications are actually contributing to the problem.

Another important issue with existing applications deals with the data processing mechanism of each application. Integrating a real-time order entry system and a batch inventory system presents unique challenges and problems.

> **NOTE**
> **Batch**—A batch system uses transactions to update data. These transactions are run in groups (or batches), usually at night. Mainframe systems are often batch systems.

Expected Lifetime

Solution lifetime is a commonly overlooked part of the vision/scope process. Analyzing and defining the lifetime of a given solution is a driving factor in the design and architecture of the development process.

For instance, a short-term solution calls for less extensibility and a shorter development time. On the other hand, a long-term solution focuses around both maintainability and extensibility, but requires more time to complete (see Figure 1.1).

If the lifetime of the solution is planned to be long-term, an additional focus on extensibility and modular design should be placed on the development process. This planning allows the application to grow and change as technology and tools change. For instance, an application that was written even two years ago did not have the Internet in mind as an application design model. Today, the emphasis is on Internet and intranet development. If the application was written to allow for extensibility and used modular design, the application can be slowly migrated to the new medium of the Internet without forcing a rewrite of the entire application. Planning for the unknown technology changes in long-life applications pays off major dividends in the future.

As the expected lifetime of the application increases, the time expended on development should increase as well. Never sacrifice quality in application development. Instead, limit the features that are implemented or the additional time to make the application scalable or extensible.

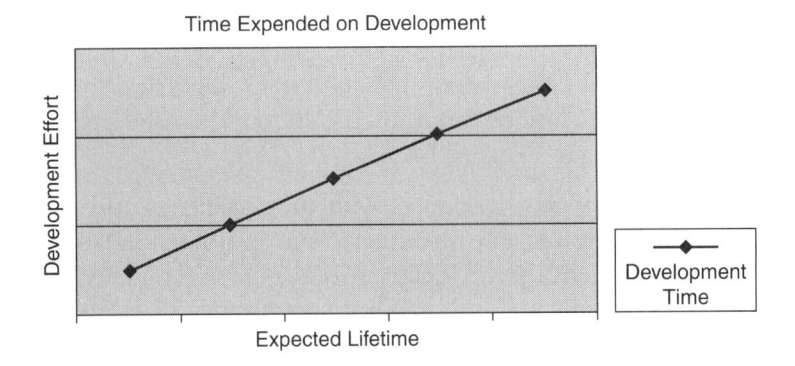

FIGURE 1.1
Time expanded on development.

Project Budget

One of the most critical and dreaded of the vision/scope items is the budget. This is the biggest deciding factor in the solution and design. Large books have been written on the topic of budgeting, and several schools of thought exist concerning the budgeting process in general. This chapter will address the key areas of managing a budget rather than the keys to creating the budget. The discussion of cost management is important and drastically reduces the number of trees required to cover this topic.

Several items need to be addressed when dealing with budgeting and managing costs:

- Time and labor
- Total cost
- Benefit trade-offs

Time and Labor

Cost is one of the most important aspects of a project because it can get out of control faster than any other. Time and labor typically consume the majority of all project-related cost, so it is logical that time and labor be watched more than other areas. This is not to say that a project should look to find the cheapest labor; on the contrary, a project should look to find the most cost-effective labor.

For instance, a team of ten developers with four architects and three database wizards is not cost effective due to the major redundancy in skillsets. The opposite end of the spectrum is a team of ten generalists; this gives too much overlap of skills and not enough specialization.

When putting a project together, it is important to assemble a team that has a mix of specialists and generalists. Such a team is leaner and more cost effective, allowing the project to better manage time and labor costs.

The final point with time and labor deals with experienced/expensive labor versus inexperienced/inexpensive labor. Costs cannot be contained by using inexpensive labor because the experienced senior architect or database analyst can complete more work in less time than a small team of junior generalists. Time and labor costs cover the life of the project, so it is important to look at how experience, though more costly, can reduce the overall project development time and reduce long-term costs.

Total Cost

Total cost involves not only the budget-eating time and labor costs, but other smaller costs that can easily skyrocket the overall development costs if not properly contained.

Here is a list of some of the obvious and not-so-obvious costs involved with a project budget:

- Hardware (servers, workstations, upgrades)
- Software (operating systems, database servers, third-party systems)
- Downtime
- Training
- Maintenance
- IT staff augmentation

The above items can increase total cost if not properly contained.

Training and downtime are often overlooked budget items. End-user training might not consist simply of training on the new application, but might include training costs due to upgrading existing applications to new versions or newly installed operating systems. Major infrastructure changes decrease overall productivity due to the learning curve of the new system. Major changes require an additional analysis of training and learning time of several aspects of new system implementation.

Downtime is an additional cost that is commonly overlooked because it is not a hard cost, which means you cannot see or touch downtime. For instance, an online bookseller that has $24,000 worth of sales per day might require six hours of downtime. This equates to $6,000 of hidden costs due to the inability of customers to place orders through the system. Additional future revenue might be lost if customers have a pleasant experience with the online competition. This downtime cost is usually looked at in terms of six hours and not $6,000 dollars.

Staff augmentation is also an important cost to keep in mind because it is not directly a development cost. Staff augmentation typically happens after development and is not necessarily budgeted under development because it is simultaneously a staffing cost and a long-term cost. A news system might require a full-time DBA, an additional network administrator, and two maintenance developers. This might amount to an $200,000 more per year in additional staff, which is an important cost to remember when you begin looking at the total cost of ownership of a system.

Benefit Trade-Offs

When creating an application, you must define what must be created. To have a successful project, you must be able to identify the most important components and use that information to generate a milestone for your project. By trading one feature for another, you will be able to release an application faster and monitor the development process in a more accurate manner. This section deals with how to handle benefit trade-offs.

Feature Selection

One of the major development processes (and arguably one of the more painful) is the feature-selection process. After you complete the planning phases and before you begin the development, you need to analyze the features that are planned for the first release. What you will typically find is a laundry list of features that will inevitably destroy a budget and never deliver a product within a reasonable period of time.

At this point in the process, you need to identify the priorities and benefits of the features. Then, after a list of features and benefits is generated, you must make a final selection of what will be put into the released application.

This process is part of the Microsoft Solution Framework (which is detailed later). MSF is designed around versioned releases. Versioned releases would be in the release sense (1.0, 1.1, 1.5, 2.0). Versioned releases enable you to implement the most important and beneficial features in a product while developing a timeline that would allow for a rapid deployment of an application. Thus, you can have the application in a working form in three months and plan on a new release every four to six weeks after that. Each subsequent release would add a new enhancement to the product while still allowing for the live implementation of the application.

The bottom line to this process is that you implement all of the features in the same overall timeframe as you would by trying to implement all features at once with the following benefits:

- Productivity is increased because the application is deployed to the desktop in a more rapid fashion.
- Progress can be tracked more easily because versioned releases allow the client to "see" the milestones.
- Incremental testing reduces overall bug maintenance on a near logarithmic scale.
- Enhancements and additional features can be implemented without impacting the overall timeline and/or budget.

Creating the Feature List

Creating the feature list is a relatively simple process, but generating the feature order is much more complex. Your feature list should be an overall listing of items, such as application requirements, business processes, and user-suggested features.

The feature list should be laid out so that the following fields are defined:

- Classification (user interface, business rules, infrastructure)
- Priority (1 = cannot implement application without; 5 = nice feature to have—no impact on usability)
- Ease of implementation (1 = extremely hard—major architecture and design work; 5 = easy—less than one programmer day to implement and test)
- Source (business requirement, end user suggestion, previous application feature)

These items are general suggestions. You can create additional classifications or fields, but the important issue is the ability to classify the need, cost, and source.

After the feature list is generated, it should be sorted with the highest priority ranked at the top. All groups should be included in this process—developers, users, administrators, testers, and so on. It is important to reach agreement on the classification and ordering of features for several reasons:

- Buyoff from all groups instills a sense of ownership and responsibility across all roles.

- Importance and need are relative—a feature that is easy to implement might not have the staff to support its implementation.

- Larger features can be broken into smaller items, and a brainstorming session might reveal issues that have not been considered.

When the list is finally organized and sorted, a release point should be identified. This point on the feature chart is where the cutoff would be for the first release. This allows for the setting of the first release milestone and sets all expectations concerning the functionality of the application. At this point, it should be made clear that no new features are to be implemented or added. This avoids a problem in the development process known as "feature creep."

Avoiding Feature Creep

Feature creep is the process of adding new features to an application that affect the project budget and/or schedule. Feature creep is a major reason why many software projects do not meet their budget, schedule, or expected results. By identifying the critical components to an application by using a feature list to determine the items included in a first version release, you aid in avoiding feature creep. The feature list sets the boundaries for a release and should not be changed in middevelopment. The focus encouraged by the feature list allows the project to stay on schedule and gives the development team specific priorities.

BUSINESS REQUIREMENTS

Gathering the business requirements is the process of determining the application requirements and the current environment. During this process, you should begin to create a high-level application design that describes the business process and environment, as well as the general application specifications. You're in danger in this phase of overanalyzing the design to the point that too many details pile up, and the requirements might change that force the entire design to change. Underanalyzing during this phase is counterproductive because many important details might be missed, forcing you to make middevelopment changes to the design or worse—implementing an application that does not solve the problem.

Business Goals

Setting the business goals should be the first step in analyzing the business requirements for a system. The business objectives, strategies, and overall goals should be addressed.

Identify key business processes and generate a business process diagram to draw a form of flowchart of how the business operates. The following items should be identified and diagrammed:

- Management processes
- Cross-functional and cross-group processes
- Logical processes (business flows such as an order process or class registration process)
- Interactions between groups

This business process design gives a graphical representation of a business and identifies redundant or missing processes. Diagramming helps to generate a system that is designed around processes and focuses on the users.

This phase should incorporate representatives of all groups within an organization. Management, development, support, and users should all be represented because each group might have its own internal processes and have different understandings of outside processes. This leads to a better, more complete understanding of the business and builds a consensus among individuals as to the structure and organization of the business.

Some key questions should be addressed during this process:

- What are the business needs?
- Will a solution change the business structure or organization?

- What are the redundant systems and processes that can be changed, merged, or enhanced?
- What are the key strengths and weaknesses of the current structure and processes?
- How tolerant is the business to change?

Customer Requirements

A customer-focused application goes to great lengths to assist the users and add value to their tasks. Systems should be designed so that productivity and usability are increased. Focus on user tasks and how users interact with other business processes. Streamline their current tasks, eliminate overlap, and automate redundant processes.

Keep in mind that the user is not simply the person who operates the software—the user is the client as a whole. Consider the perspectives of management, end-users, support, and so on when determining whether a feature adds value or does not even meet a business need.

In order to create a customer-focused application, you should be able to answer a few questions:

- What do the users need to do and what do they really do?
- Does the solution add value to their jobs or increase productivity?
- What is the technical level of the users?
- Which user tasks can be streamlined or automated?

Reading Between the Lines

When establishing the business requirements, it is important to read between the lines of the problem to determine what the solution should be. The problem might not necessarily be with the inventory system, but with the process behind the system. The solution does not always lie within the problem; sometimes you need to look deeper into the process to find the real issues.

With legacy systems, infrastructures might be part of the problem, just as the business organization or system implementation might be part of the problem. Most enterprise systems are comprised of several applications interacting at once. These complex interactions can cause problems that will propagate through the entire system, causing additional problems that need to be resolved to properly implement a solution.

Once again, a complete business process design should help in identifying some of these problem areas. After a potential problem has been defined, go back to the users and gather more input. Never make assumptions about an existing system. You will sometimes find that a system is used in a way that is not consistent with the design, so looking at the application will not reveal the problem, whereas analyzing the implementation of the system will.

Establishing the Type of Problem

Establishing the problem for a given situation dictates that you read between the lines and use deductive reasoning to identify the problem and propose a solution. Sometimes the problem is hidden or masked by other issues. The customer might know that there are problems with the synchronization between the order entry system and the inventory system, but he or she might not know why. The answer to the problem might be with the application, business process, or other factors, and the problems among them might appear completely unrelated. You need to be able to pinpoint the cause of the problem so that you can begin developing the appropriate solution.

Key areas of focus for establishing the problem are:

- Infrastructure—hardware, software, network protocols
- Application design—limited scalability, high cost of maintenance
- Object design—high overhead, business object logic problems, poor data consistency
- Tools—limitation of the development environment, high learning curve
- Technology—support applications that are too old and have reached their usable life or applications that are too new and untried in the marketplace

When the problem has been determined, a solution can begin to form. It is important to go through the motions of creating the solution. Proper planning is important in any project, and rushed development only causes new problems. Poor planning and limited design work become a zero sum game when the dust settles at the end of the project. This means that a properly planned project might take six months to release, whereas a poorly designed project might take two months to release and another four months to fix all of the problems. The major overall difference between a properly planned and a poorly planned project is cost. A poorly planned project never comes in under budget.

Two questions should be answered during this phase: what and where. The "what" is the definition of the problem that you will use throughout the development process. All project planning, design, and implementation will be centered on the "what." The "where" defines the specific part of the existing application, business process, organization, or limitation that is the cause of the "what." Over time, the "where" and "what" will form the project plan and vision that is used until the completion of the process.

TCO and ROI

Total cost of ownership (TCO) and return on investment (ROI) are currently popular topics within the realm of enterprise development. As applications become larger and more complex, costs must be controlled and long-term investments minimized. TCO and ROI attempt to handle these long-term costs and manage costs in the implementation of features by determining the items that are most cost effective for the project.

Minimizing Total Cost of Ownership

The total cost of ownership (TCO) describes the overall costs of development, training, implementation, support, maintenance, and administration. TCO is an important area to focus on because many hidden costs might make the solution less cost effective than it appears. A given solution might have a low cost of development, but that solution might require daily administration, drastically increased training, or costly maintenance due to the design.

There are two types of TCO costs: budgeted and unbudgeted. The budgeted TCO costs include items such as hardware, software, support, and development, whereas unbudgeted costs would be end-user costs and downtime costs. Unbudgeted costs are important to keep in mind due to your limited ability to plan and budget them properly. When dealing with TCO, try to identify the processes or issues that might affect the unbudgeted costs and try to plan additional controls around those items to reduce potential budget problems.

Proper application development and infrastructure planning reduces the TCO for a project by:

- Decreasing maintenance costs
- Decreasing administration costs
- Minimizing training costs
- Limiting downtime
- Increasing productivity

> **NOTE**
>
> **MSF Definition of TCO**—A comprehensive model designed to help the enterprise understand the total cost of owning and using IT component assets over time.

Increasing Return on Investment

Return on investment (ROI) is a critical process when analyzing business requirements. Nearly every project is faced with a project "wish list" that must be pared down in order to develop a timely and accurate solution.

For instance, take the following situation where ROI must be analyzed.

1. Implementing a new order validation process reduces the number of incorrect shipments by 50%. For this given situation, assume that all incorrect shipments are lost sales. In any given month, 2% of all orders are returned due to incorrect shipping instructions. Monthly shipments are $50,000. Implementing this fix would cost $8,000.

2. Implementing a change in the accounts payable module would allow the company to pay its invoices in a more timely manner and would allow the company to take advantage of prepayment discounts. The average discount is 2% for early payment, and 20% of our payees give this discount. Accounts payable payments are typically $20,000 per month. The cost to implement this change would be $1,500.

At first glance, the second option appears to be the best "bang for the buck," or to have the highest ROI. In actuality, the first option has the higher ROI. Item number one would take 16 months to recover the cost of development, whereas the second option would take almost 19 months to recover the costs. Here is how we arrive at this recovery time:

Fix 1: Implementing this would recover the cost of the incorrect shipments. This is 2% of all orders per month, and we do $50,000 per month in sales. So, $50,000 × 2% = $1000, but this fix would only cut that in half to $500 per month. The fix costs $8,000 so can find the recovery time by taking $8,000 ÷ $500 = 16 months.

Fix 2: If 20% of payees allow a 2% early payment discount and our accounts payable is $20,000 per month then we know that we are talking about $20,000 × 20% × 2% = $80. The price of the fix is $1,500 so the recovery time would be $1,500 ÷ $80 = 18.75 months.

The moral of the story: Never rely on the cost of implementation alone. Determine what you are saving, how much the implementation costs, and what the recovery time is.

You will see instances where implementing a system change is not the most cost-effective means of solving a problem. It is sometimes necessary to bypass a development change and implement a process change or increase headcount to achieve the most cost-effective solution. Additional code is not always the answer.

The chart shown in Figure 1.2 gives an example of cost recovery in a ROI calculation. The proposed solution would cost $5,000 to implement while recovering $500 per month. The costs would be fully recovered in 10 months, thus giving the ROI baseline. In order for another proposed solution to be considered a higher ROI, it would have to recover costs in less than 10 months.

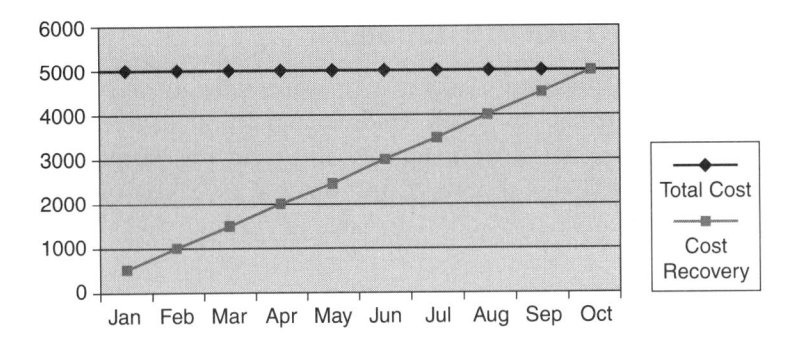

FIGURE 1.2
A cost recovery graph.

When dealing with ROI, take the following steps:

1. Estimate the cost of the issue and determine the overall cost impact of keeping the current issue unchanged.

2. Propose a solution (or series of solutions) that would satisfy the need.

3. Determine the time it would take to recover the costs of the proposed solution.

A solution that has a price tag of $10,000 is rather small on a large-scale client/server project. But, if the proposed cost recovery is 24 months, the solution does not have a high ROI, and resources could possibly be allocated to another issue that would provide a higher ROI for the project.

The method of calculating the ROI is as follows:

1. Determine the overall cost of the suggested solution.

2. Determine the amount of money per period (week, month, year) that implementing the solution would save.

3. Divide the labor savings into the total cost to give the time to recover costs.

Always run a ROI calculation when dealing with multiple proposed solutions. Some items might at first glance appear to be the automatic pick, but running all of the solutions through the ROI calculation reveals the true winner.

Current Infrastructure Design

Diagramming and documenting existing systems not only provides additional documentation to the customer, it aids in application planning and design. Knowing where hardware is located and what the hardware is capable of handling is vitally important information, especially in large businesses where the entire operation is connected through a WAN.

Incorporating the Platform and Infrastructure into the Solution

The incorporation of existing platforms into an enterprise application can be a tricky problem. Analyzing and documenting the capabilities of existing systems enables you to better leverage existing technology and reduce the duplication of work.

If, for instance, the business has a significant investment in a series of older servers that cannot easily be replaced due to cost, try to leverage the hardware in the application. One server might not be capable of handling the entire application's needs, but, collectively, the servers might make up a very powerful network. Utilize some of the servers as dedicated processors for intense business objects, thus creating a series of object servers. The remaining servers might be able to individually handle applications such as Exchange and SQL Server.

Sometimes, the existing infrastructure might not be integrated into the solution, and new plans must be made to acquire the necessary equipment. If the client would like to be directly connected to the Internet but there are no routers or dedicated lines, they must be acquired in order to implement the solution.

Analyzing the Impact of New Technology

Implementing a large-scale technology change might be the best theoretical solution, but it might not be the best practical solution. A wholesale change in the technology and infrastructure of a business can bring such high costs and force such fundamental changes in the business model that the solution is not financially feasible. It is important to identify these limitations in the approaches that could be taken when implementing a solution. The planning phases should answer the following questions:

- Will a change in infrastructure or technology affect the business model?
- What changes will the budget accept?
- Can existing tools and technologies be leveraged to reduce cost?
- Can the current infrastructure handle large-scale changes to items such as operating systems, servers, and network protocols?
- Is a migration of technology necessary?

Establishing the Application Environment

Establishing the application environment includes analyzing the existing hardware and software platforms, as well as the planned infrastructure. Some systems are more fault tolerant than others, while the TCO of some platforms is lower.

For instance, a large-scale financial has certain requirements due to the transaction processing and fault tolerance needs, whereas an inventory and order entry system have completely different requirements.

Several technology areas need to be considered when establishing the environment:

- Server architecture
- Database servers
- Object methodologies
- Internet servers
- Transaction and message servers

Each of these environments will play a key role in the solution that you create. Be familiar with each technology and know how each can and cannot interact together.

Establishing a Schedule

After the problem has been defined and a solution has been presented, a schedule must be created. This is one of the more complex topics when putting a project together because there is no exact science to scheduling. Many factors affect the creation of a project schedule:

- Team size
- Budget
- Complexity of the problem

Just as budgeting has volumes of books on the topic, scheduling has its share of documentation. The key to effective scheduling is using milestones and key development points to use as a target and as a gauge of the current status of the process. Breaking a large problem into smaller, more manageable tasks allows for a more accurate picture of the expected schedule.

Human Factors

Users should be one of the primary focuses (if not the most important) of the development process. Users must be identified and worked with in order to present a solution that not only solves the business problems from a technical level, but addresses these problems on a practical level. A solution might be able to solve every problem within a business environment, but if the users cannot implement the features of the application, the project has not been a success.

Be sensitive to the needs of the users and know how their needs coincide with the business requirements. You should know basic information about the users and their situations:

- Who are the users?
- Will they need additional training?
- Where are the users located (onsite, offsite, remote)?
- Will there be issues of localization and language support?

Answering these questions identifies who and where the users are, as well as some additional needs of the application that might not have been addressed.

Identifying Users

The design phases of the development process should always include users because this is the target group for the application interface. The application can be perfect in every respect, but if the users are unable to use the system, the solution does not work.

One of the aspects of the user base to keep in mind is the overall technical level of the group. Designing an interface for power users is a much different process than designing an interface for novice users.

Another task that should be completed when identifying the user base is the roles of the users within the business, as well as the application.

The first focus on users should be their interactions within the business, as well as interactions with other groups. Determine the user's specific role (payroll clerk, accountant, salesperson, manager) and the interactions with other users. For instance, a payroll clerk interacts with the payroll managers and members of the accounting department. It is handy to draw these interactions between groups. Figure 1.3 shows the payroll clerk's interaction diagram.

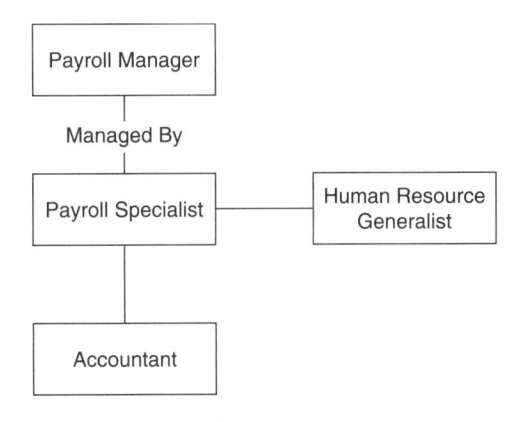

```
┌──────────────────┐
│ Payroll Manager  │
└──────────────────┘
         │
     Managed By
         │
┌──────────────────┐     ┌──────────────────┐
│Payroll Specialist├─────┤ Human Resource   │
└──────────────────┘     │   Generalist     │
         │               └──────────────────┘
         │
┌──────────────────┐
│   Accountant     │
└──────────────────┘
```

FIGURE 1.3
One type of interaction diagram.

34 CHAPTER 1 Analyzing Business Requirements

These interaction diagrams come in handy in later stages of development when the business processes are finalized and security is implemented.

After the interaction diagram is complete, the general business interactions should be diagramed. The following is an example of a business interaction diagram and description:

An accounts payable specialist enters an invoice. A senior A/P specialist must approve the payment before it can be processed. An internal auditor later reviews invoices for accuracy. This interaction diagram would look like Figure 1.4.

These diagrams become business objects and workflow later in the development process.

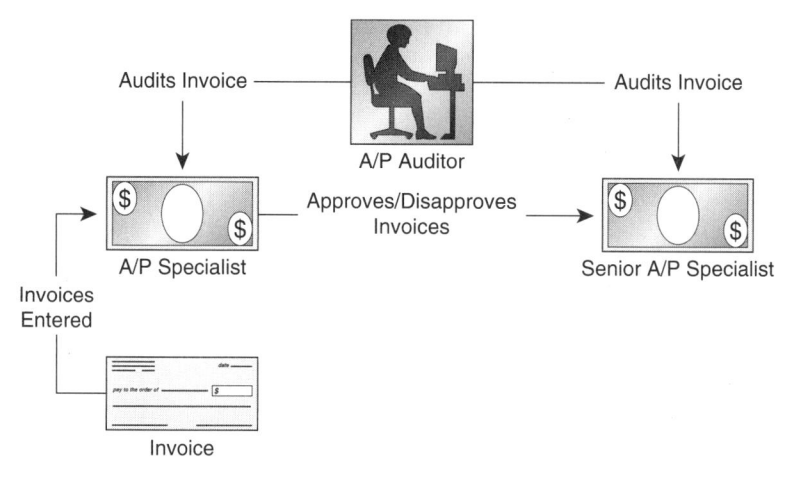

FIGURE 1.4
Another form of interaction diagram.

Training

When planning for training, several factors need to be addressed:

- Type of training required (onsite, offsite)
- Knowledge level of the users (novice, intermediate, power users)
- Areas of training (application developed, third-party applications, operating systems)
- Total number of users who require training
- Length of training

All of these factors need to be addressed because each of them has an impact on the design of the project and the budget. The project design can be affected because a complex system might require too much training and have such a high learning curve that the implementation of the project would not be cost or time effective. The budget is affected because the total cost of limited staff, training costs, and training time must be budged for or costs can skyrocket.

The type of training required for users is an important issue to identify. Onsite training is typically more cost effective than offsite training, but onsite training is usually not as thorough or complete as offsite training. Offsite training is given by professional instructors who are used to teaching and are well versed in their areas. The major problem with offsite training comes into play with the schedule and syllabus. Some less popular courses might only be offered once per month, whereas popular courses are offered every week. These offsite courses are not typically flexible with the material covered.

Table 1.1 provides an overview of the pros and cons of the different types of training.

TABLE 1.1

PROS AND CONS OF TRAINING TYPES

Training Type	Pro	Con
Onsite	The course can be tailored to the needs of the users.	Internal trainers in smaller organizations do not have the experience of full-time outside trainers.
	Courses can be scheduled around specific shifts or staffing times.	In-house material is not as thorough or complete as external training material.
	Costs are typically lower.	
Offsite	Instructors are well versed in their areas and typically are more experienced.	The course information being taught cannot easily be tailored.
	No training development time or cost is needed.	Overall costs are higher.
		Scheduling might be difficult.

Local and Remote Users

The geographic location of the user base of an application presents unique challenges to a development project. Issues of security, performance, and availability must be addressed before the development of a project begins.

The first group of remote users to a system can be linked via a WAN and are always online. These users might suffer from performance issues arising from the speed of the WAN connection. In this case, targeting performance would help the remote users effectively use the system. Ways to target these performance issues are as follows:

- Use database replication to maintain data in multiple locations. This would increase data retrieval and updates because the data does not need to be carried across the WAN for every inquiry.

- Move business objects to local servers. This reduces network traffic because the bulk of the application traffic would be on local LANs (local area networks) within the WAN.

The second group of remote users is made up of offline users, such as a traveling sales force. This group does not have constant access to the system and usually does not have fast access to a LAN. Performance is a huge issue because the application might be running on a 100-megabit network, but the remote users are limited to 56k modem connections.

- Create a Web-based application for remote users. This would allow almost all of the data processing and data transfer to occur on internal servers and networks.
- Create a VPN (Virtual Private Network) that enables users to access private networks from any network connection.
- Utilize a messaging server, such as Microsoft Message Queue Server, to allow offline updates within the application.

> **NOTE**
>
> **VPN (MSDN)**—A Virtual Private Network (VPN) connects the components and resources of one network over *another* network. VPNs accomplish this by enabling the user to tunnel through the Internet or another public network in a manner that lets the tunnel participants enjoy the same security and features formerly available only in private networks

> **NOTE**
>
> **RAS (MSDN)**—A Windows NT feature by which a single serial connection provides a remote workstation with host connectivity, NT file services, or Novell file and printing services (NWLink). Windows CE supports the standard Win32 RAS functions; however, it allows only one connection at a time. RAS functions can be implemented for direct serial connections or dial-up modem connections. The acronym stands for Remote Access Service.

Localization Issues

Localization is the process of developing your application so that it can be used in other languages or locales. There are several features that are or can be affected by localization:

- Graphical representations of objects
- Languages
- Character sets

First of all, it is important to review all graphical icons when localizing an application. An icon that might be harmless in one language might have a completely different meaning in another—it could even be offensive. You should go back to the users or an internal group set up to handle localization questions anytime an application crosses cultural or language barriers. Verify that all text translates properly and all symbols are valid.

Localization also adds a level of complexity with issues such as data and currency formatting, character representation (English to Arabic or Chinese, for instance), and currency conversions. An application that runs in the United States, England, and France might need to be set up to handle currency conversions so that each country is able to see data in a native format. Issues like these are difficult to deal with because past data can be affected by daily currency changes and even intraday currency changes can affect large financial transactions.

Be sensitive to currency conversion, especially when dealing with data warehouses and historical data. Someone in England could buy 100 widgets today due to a strong pound, whereas three years ago, they could have only bought 90 widgets. These changes could drastically affect past data, and the system should be set up to handle situations like these.

> **NOTE**
> **Localization (MSDN)**—The process of adapting a program for a specific international market, which includes translating the user interface, resizing dialog boxes, customizing features if necessary, and testing results to ensure that the program still functions properly

INTEGRATION WITH EXISTING APPLICATIONS

The need for legacy application integration is not uncommon when designing a new system. Typically, customers do not want to throw away the investment (sometimes very large) in a legacy system for a new system. There is usually a period when the legacy systems will remain until a conversion occurs over a period of time. It is important to be sensitive to these issues and plan the application accordingly.

These are some of the main reasons why legacy systems need to exist:

- Valuable business logic that has evolved over a long period of time might be difficult or risky to attempt to implement in a short timeframe.

- Large investments in existing systems dictate that these systems stay in place for a specified period.

- Large amounts of data might exist in existing systems and data migrations might be difficult to implement within a release timeframe.

- Existing hardware can be leveraged for additional storage or processing.

Legacy Applications and Hardware

It might sometimes be necessary to incorporate a legacy system or some legacy software within a given solution. For instance, you might have an older library that cannot be updated and must continue to be utilized. Because the library is from a third-party vendor and the source is not available, a wrapper might need to be written to incorporate the old code with new technology in the new system. Utilize tools such as the Component Object Model (COM) and Microsoft Transaction Server to integrate legacy code into new systems.

Many techniques exist for utilizing legacy systems. Some systems, such as mainframes, use middleware applications to act as a gateway between the application and the existing system. Sometimes code can be wrapped into new libraries that use and enhance existing libraries. Other, third-party applications are sometimes used to fill a specific void in integrating current systems.

Migration to a New System

The migration of a legacy application to a new system is a difficult process. A great deal of testing needs to be completed so that the new systems will mirror the operation of the legacy systems. Keep in mind that some legacy systems have been around for ten or more years, so you might find that it is difficult to reproduce that amount of systems work in a significantly smaller time period. Ideally, a legacy system should be migrated in stages. These stages will allow for timely releases and more thorough testing during the migration.

Going back to the initial planning and business analysis, you should have gauged the business's flexibility and openness to change. This plays a large role when dealing with legacy systems because the difference between creating a middleware layer and migrating code makes a difference in how the application is designed and what the timeline will be.

Creating and Using Middleware

Middleware describes a layer of software that allows access to two heterogeneous systems.

Middleware is typically used in a system where the clients are PC based and the data and business services reside on a mainframe. Connections to mainframes are difficult because native connections do not exist and third-party applications must be used. Two types of middleware allow PC-to-mainframe access: Microsoft SNA Server (or similar system) or screen scraping thorough 3270 emulation libraries.

Microsoft SNA Server allows PCs to access mainframe data directly. Items, such as DB/2 databases and VSAM files, can access just as well as any native data source. The downside to SNA Server is the limited customization ability and the increased maintenance costs due to an additional server and software requirement.

> **NOTE**
>
> **VSAM (Virtual Sequential Access Method)**—These are database files that reside on mainframe systems as physical files. Many legacy systems rely on VSAM files for data storage. Middleware applications, such as Microsoft SNA server, allow PC applications to access VSAM files as a regular database file.

Screen scraping is the process of taking existing mainframe application screens (known as green screens due to the look of old terminal monitors) and getting or placing data on the predefined screens. For instance, if there is a customer entry green screen with a screen address of row 30, column 5, and a width of 30, developers can pull that section of the screen into a textbox or a label on a form. If the developer would like to write the address change back to the mainframe, the data needs to be placed on the exact spot on the green screen and updated through a transaction code.

Screen scraping allows for easy development of PC solutions for the following reasons:

- The business logic and database layer do not need to be rewritten because the application is still using the mainframe applications and database.

- Screens may be mapped to individual calls and essentially wrapped in an object.

- Forms and dialogs can emulate the old mainframe screens, cutting down on the learning curve required for the application.

- No complex middleware is required because the application is merely copying and pasting the data from the mainframe

When dealing with the possibility of creating a custom middleware layer, explore all of the possibilities. There are obvious benefits to an SNA–based middleware solution, screen scraping, and custom middleware. Table 1.2 contains a list of some of the pros and cons.

TABLE 1.2

PROS AND CONS OF VARIOUS MIDDLEWARE SOLUTIONS

Interface Type	Pro	Con
SNA	High speed direct access.	Higher cost due to administrative and infrastructure overhead.
	Solid technology due to production testing and large customer base.	Minor limitations might affect the overall effectiveness of the solution.

continues

TABLE 1.2 CONTINUED

Interface Type	Pro	Con
Screen Scraping	Allows for the use of existing screens and existing mainframe transactions.	Changes in existing screens force a modification of existing applications.
	Very little programming involved to implement communications	Might be slower than direct access.
	Large third-party software base for terminal application APIs.	
	Implementation cost and development cost are low.	
Custom Middleware	Optimized for an existing application or line of business.	High development and implementation cost.
	Highly extensible.	Higher level of testing required because there is no off-the-shelf solution or existing interfaces to access.

Connectivity

Connectivity to legacy systems can be a problem during development because many legacy systems use connections that might not be consistent with current networking standards. For instance, attempting to connect to a RMS file on a UNIX or VMS machine might require a third-party application to act as an ODBC data source to the native files.

> **NOTE**
>
> **RMS (Record Management Services)**—A series of I/O routines that allow for record-level access of data files. Files that use this interface are referred to as RMS files. VMS systems have RMS routines built into the system level functions.

Another example would be accessing a mainframe system through 3270 emulation libraries. Each of these situations adds both a level of complexity and integration of third-party applications.

Connectivity issues can greatly impact bandwidth and performance. If the application is communicating through 3270 emulators to a mainframe for batch processing, the application might have a severe bottleneck. This connection might possibly force design changes on the application end to handle the communication wait times, as well as handling request timeouts.

Data Conversion and Character Translation

Connecting to existing data might not be the only legacy system issue that needs to be dealt with. There might be times when the data is not in a format that is easily readable on the target system (ASCII to EBCDIC, for instance). You might need to create an application layer that converts or translates data between a host and a client system. This is also an area for application performance and bandwidth issues. Character translation can be slow, so developers need to plan for these application delays and possible timeouts.

BUSINESS METHODOLOGIES AND LIMITATIONS

At times, the major issues with an existing system are not due to the system design but to the structure and practices of the business implementing the system. When identifying a solution, pay attention to the business practices around you.

Current Business Practices

When analyzing existing problems and defining solutions for those problems, an important question is whether the application is not functioning as it should or whether the current business practices go against the application design.

You might notice that the application is working correctly, but it was not necessarily designed to work the way the business is structured. These business practices are important to note because while the application logic might be correct, it might not be executing in the proper order or the application may need to "know" about the business practices.

Knowing how a business runs and identifying potential problem spots is important in fully understanding the business problem.

Business and Organizational Structure

The business organization and structure also helps dictate some of the application design and business logic. This information is important when implementing a security mechanism for your application.

Business diagrams (see Figure 1.5) help during the design process when you are looking at infrastructure design and data flow.

This type of diagram shows some of the application components and component interactions, which helps to drive the design and development of the application. This is also important in the design phase because this layout helps to define some of the milestones for development. For instance:

- First milestone: Integrate the sales force with the sales/inventory database.
- Second milestone: Integrate the distribution system with the sales system.
- Third milestone: Enable the system to automatically route orders from the sales and distribution systems to the proper warehouse and shipping department.

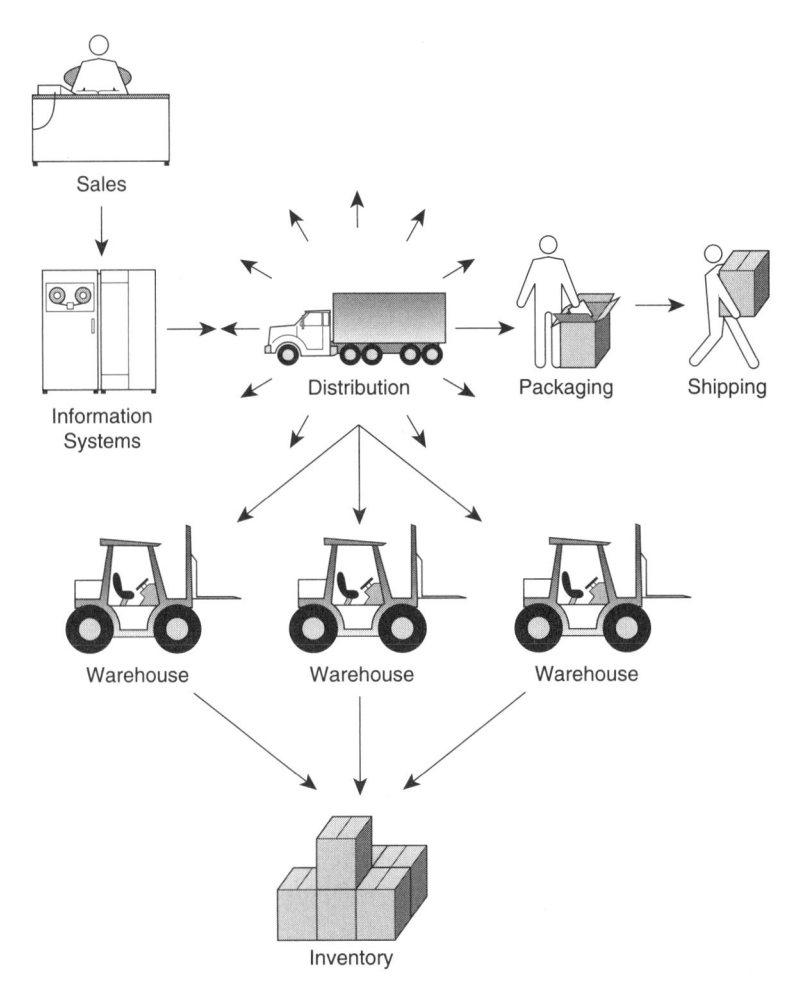

FIGURE 1.5
An example of a business flow diagram.

Organizational structure diagrams (or organizational charts) help to define users and roles within a business environment. This is useful during the security planing phase and during the business logic development. User–interaction diagrams come from these organizational charts and help to define workflows.

Customer's Needs

The business diagram identifies the key processes and users of a given system, but it does not identify what those users need to do their job. After the process is understood, the users must be brought into the planning phases.

We know from Figure 1.5 that the sales force must go through the systems to send information to the distribution department. We must now find out from the user how the data gets there now and how it should get there. A key part of this process is to identify areas that decrease productivity, are prone to errors, and adversely affect the ability of the users to do their jobs.

The main problem with an existing system is often due to the design on the end-user side. An application might be perfect from the business logic and data processing end, but the users might not be able to use the system. Identifying these problems early in the development processes will produce large returns in the long term and will boost productivity and satisfaction in the short term.

SECURITY

Security is an often overlooked aspect of solution development. Security takes on many faces when working through the vision/scope phase of development. Security can manifest itself through user and group security or through the limitation of object extensibility. Not only should the users be organized and granted specific access, but the interfaces built into business and data objects should be limited, too.

Security Models

Application and network security are important to any enterprise application. Without a proper security mechanism, users would be able to approve their own raises or change the corporate budget. Security should be designed both to limit capabilities and to manage information. Low-level clerks should not have access to sensitive payroll information, and payroll should not be able to modify invoices in the accounts payable department.

System

System-level security is an implementation of security that is outside any predefined network security levels. An example of system-level security would be with Microsoft SQL Server. Users and permissions can be set within SQL Server that do not correspond to network logins. System-level security must be programmed within the application itself in order to implement either a user model or a group model. This security scheme allows for an additional level of security but increases the administration overhead involved with the maintenance of the system.

Server/Machine

Server/machine security is the limitation of physical access to a machine. This is more common on mainframe and UNIX systems where network groups cannot easily be integrated into their own security models. Server security generally requires an additional login in order to gain access.

This is an additional layer of overhead from an administration side, but it adds an additional layer of security when combined with group- or user-level network security. By requiring an additional login, a system cannot be compromised by a user who leaves a machine unattended.

User

User-level access is the most flexible access model to implement, but it is also the most difficult to administer. User-level security enables administrators to tailor access to individual users. This type of access is not practical to implement in a large organization because there might be large numbers of resources that must be set on individual users; also, access might change as the user's role in the organization changes. User-level access should be implemented only if there is a specific security need for it because the overall TCO of the application will increase quickly.

Group

The group security model is the easiest level to implement. Group security is typically based on the functional roles of the users. Typically, an organization has a structure where groups of people can be easily identified as administrators, payroll, managers, and so on. Groups can be classified by physical location, such as corporate, remote, or Charlotte users.

Group security allows for the ease of administration for users who might need access to a range of resources that would be difficult to administer on a per-user basis. An accounting manager might need to access the same resources as managers, payroll, finance, and accounting. In a group security model, this user simply needs to be added to the four groups named above. In a user model, this user would need to be added to individual resources that cross four different groups. In a large organization, that could consist of hundreds of shares and printers.

When using Windows NT, you need to be aware that the NT security model strictly enforces "no access" privileges to users. If the payroll group has "no access" set, then our accounting manager will lose access. Specific "no access" privileges are different from not setting any security at all because "no access" is telling the operating system that this user should never have access to a resource.

File

File-level security is the lowest level of security. At this level, you are granting or denying access to individual files on a physical machine. This has the highest possible overhead due to the fact that file-level security must be set on each object unless you are allowing objects to inherit security information from a parent object, such as a folder. This security scheme should be used only on the most sensitive of information because the overhead is so high that implementation becomes impractical. A more practical approach to file-level security would be to share the folder that contains the files and set share-level permissions to the whole shared folder.

Database

Database security can be implemented within applications such as Microsoft SQL Server by utilizing both built-in security and custom database programming. You can utilize items such as views to limit the information that a user has access to by defining a subset of the data. Clerks would have access to employee data without information such as salary and authorization levels, whereas finance would be able to view the data without having access to benefit and dependant information.

You can utilize object-level security within SQL Server to limit access to direct data entry. Employees who have access to an employee table can modify any piece of data. By using mechanisms such as stored procedures, you can disallow direct access to the table but allow changes in the stored procedure that limit what data may be changed by a user.

Microsoft Transaction Server (MTS) can be utilized as an additional layer of protection for your data. MTS has its own security built-in, so you can utilize a combination of application, system, MTS, and SQL Server security to build multiple levels of security into your system.

Securing your data should be a primary concern on any application because the data is the most valuable piece of any system. Without accurate and secure data, any system could be considered unreliable and even useless.

Identifying Roles

When identifying security roles within a solution, you must evaluate the need for either user-level or group-level security. Roles of users should correspond to the logical security groups on the network. The system administrators belong to an administrators group, guests to a guest group account, and clients (accounting, finance) to their respective groups.

The easiest way to identify roles of users is to go by the job the user performs. Job functions typically translate into a logical group. For instance, the payroll deportment has clerks, specialists, and managers. On the payroll domain, you might have group account names CLERK, SPECIALIST, and MANAGER. Grouping users by logical job is the best way to generate groups within an organization and identifies users who cross business units.

Auditing

Auditing is the process of logging attempts to access resources or modifications to data. Auditing carries a high performance hit due to the overhead required for verifying and logging auditing information, but it provides valuable information concerning security problems or modifications to sensitive data.

Windows NT allows for the logging of resource level information (see Figure 1.6).

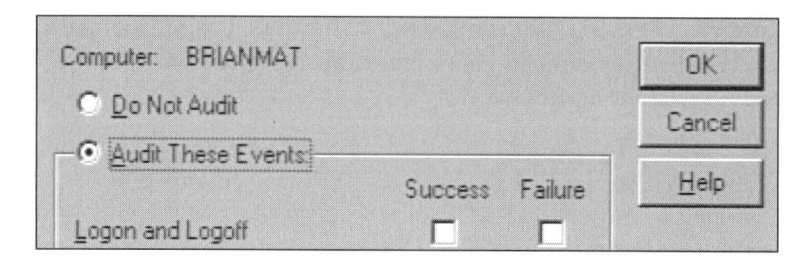

FIGURE 1.6
Microsoft Windows NT auditing dialog.

SQL Server allows for the auditing of login information (see Figure 1.7).

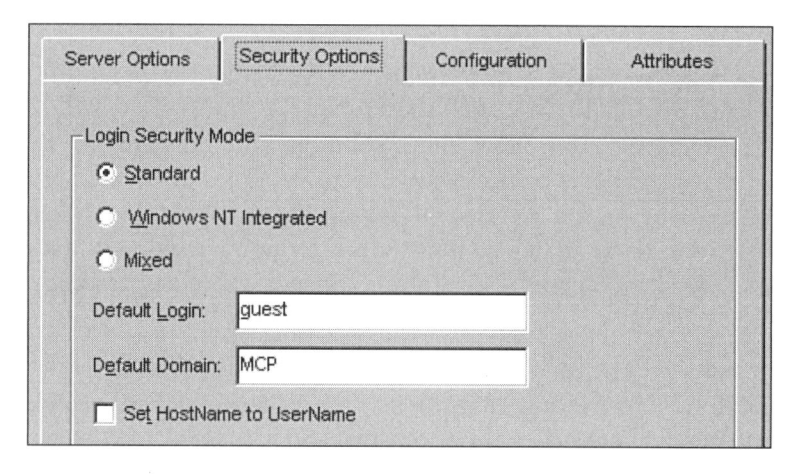

FIGURE 1.7
Microsoft SQL Server auditing setup.

SQL Server allows for data information to be audited through stored procedures and triggers. A database administrator can set up an update or delete triggers on the employees table to log changes made and keep a copy of the old data. This not only prevents malicious data changes, but provides a historical report of data changes. Auditing a table enables you to go back and look at prior data as it was at the time of the change.

Auditing is primarily used for data recovery purposes or the general logging of activity. Keep in mind that auditing carries additional overhead that might run very high. Do not get carried away with auditing information—especially in a database. There is also additional storage overhead required to maintain audit tables. If you plan on auditing data, be sure you have the additional server power and disk space to implement it properly.

Fault Tolerance

Fault tolerance is the capability to recover from system errors or hardware failures with no downtime. Fault tolerance can be implemented in hardware and software.

Hardware Fault Tolerance

Hardware fault tolerance is built into the Windows NT operating system. Windows NT can implement this fault tolerance through the following:

- Disk Duplexing and Mirroring
- Disk Striping
- RAID

Disk Duplexing and Mirroring

Mirroring disks is a fault tolerance system that uses two physical disks to maintain redundant data. The process of mirroring allows for the failure of one disk without affecting the second disk. Overall, performance is degraded because all data must be written twice.

Duplexing is a form of mirroring where the disks are on separate controllers. This method is a bit faster because the additional controller is used and is a bit safer because the failure of a disk and a controller is protected.

Mirroring (see Figure 1.8) is the easiest form of fault tolerance to implement because only two disks are required and Windows NT has built-in support for mirroring. Disk mirroring is considered to be RAID level 1.

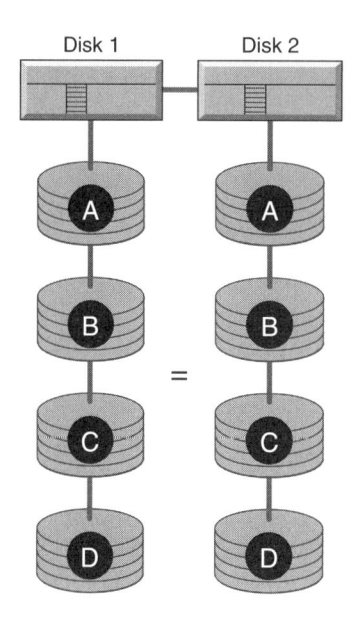

FIGURE 1.8
Fault tolerance: Disk mirroring.

Disk Striping

Disk striping is the process of maintaining parity information about the data to allow for the failure of one disk while still allowing for the regeneration of the physical data. The parity information is written to a different disk on each write. This parity information allows the disks to regenerate the missing information from the failed disk without requiring a backup to be restored.

Disk striping (see Figure 1.9) allows for larger volume sizes because the data is not being mirrored on each disk. For instance, if you have five 1GB hard drives and create a stripe set, the volume size would be 4GB because the parity information would take up a one disk overall.

RAID

There are several levels of RAID implementations. Windows NT supports several of the most common RAID levels (See Table 1.3).

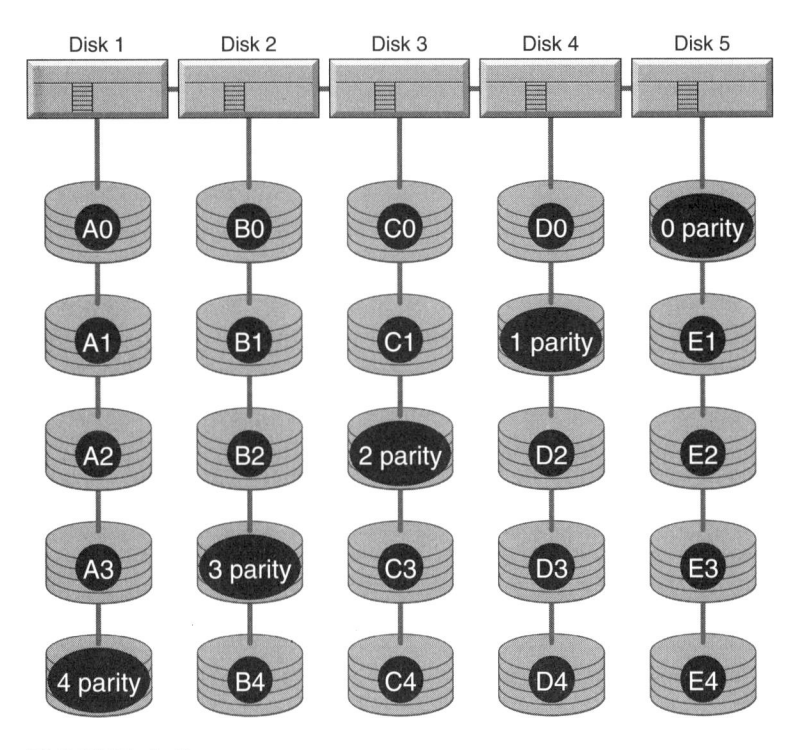

FIGURE 1.9
Using disk striping for fault tolerance.

TABLE 1.3

RAID LEVELS SUPPORTED BY WINDOWS NT

Level	Type	Notes
0	Striping	Does not contain fault tolerance.
1	Mirroring	Provides fault tolerance. Increased read performance but decreased write performance.
5	Striping with parity	Higher degree of fault tolerance than level 1. If a stripe member is missing, read performance is degraded. Uses a parity bit to maintain data integrity.
10	Mirroring with striping	Uses twice as many disks as level 5 because the entire stripe set is mirrored. This is the most fault-tolerant level and allows for the best read and write performance.

Software Fault Tolerance

Software fault tolerance would utilize items such as transactions (using Transaction Server or SQL Server transactions) or pool managers. *Trisections* allow for the posting of data or the execution of functions only when the data can be verified that there are no errors. In the event of an error, all information can be restored to its prior state without resorting to backups or being required to know the previous information.

> **NOTE**
>
> **RAID**—RAID stands for Redundant Array of Inexpensive Disks.

> **NOTE**
>
> **Transaction (MSDN)**—A series of processing steps that results in a specific function or activity being completed, ensuring that a set of actions is treated as a single unit of work.

PERFORMANCE

Performance is key to any application. Key issues, such as bandwidth, response time, peak usage, and offline capability, should all be addressed during the planning phases of development.

Bandwidth

Application bandwidth use is an important issue because the available bandwidth and application use might limit your ability to implement a solution. In an *n*-tier application where, for instance, Microsoft Transaction Server and Microsoft SQL Server are supporting a user base of 100 users, an exceptionally high amount of bandwidth might be required to run without service interruptions. On a 100megabit LAN, this might not be a problem, but where a WAN is in use with a 256Kbps connection, the application might not allow more than a handful of users to have access. Figure 1.10 shows how the decrease in bandwidth can limit data transfers.

Determine the amount of bandwidth required by the application and identify the possible areas within the application where bandwidth utilization can be reduced. For example, when accessing DCOM objects, pass parameters to the objects rather than object references. This reduces the marshalling bandwidth required by DCOM and increases the speed of your application. If using SQL Server, utilize server-side cursors (where data resides and is processed on the database server) and stored procedures. Optimizations like these reduce overall bandwidth, allow for a more responsive application due to the decreased network traffic, and allow more users to access the system.

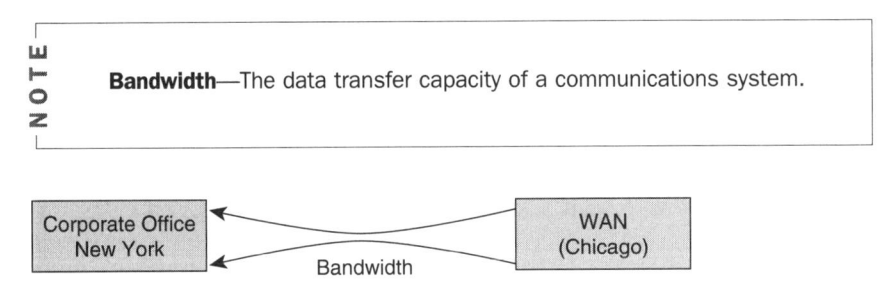

> **NOTE**
>
> **Bandwidth**—The data transfer capacity of a communications system.

FIGURE 1.10
Bandwidth limiting data connections.

A bottleneck in bandwidth limits the capability of an application to run on a wide area network with a slow communication connection. In Figure 1.10, the Chicago office might be connecting through a 256kb connection. This limits the amount of traffic that can go through the WAN and limits either the number of users a system can handle or the speed and functionality of the system.

Upgrading the Chicago connection to a T1 line allows for the full amount of network traffic to travel through the WAN without interruption (see Figure 1.11). All applications will run in Chicago as well as they will at the corporate offices in New York.

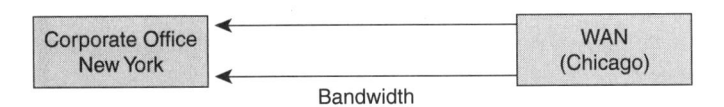

FIGURE 1.11
Eliminating the bottleneck.

Peak Usage

Plan for spikes in application usage properly. An application might be able to support 100 users without a problem, but there might be a short period every day when usage will spike and adversely affect the performance of your application.

For instance, your application supports two sales centers, one on the East coast and one on the West coast. The application might run well from 9:00 until 12:00, but when both centers are open between 12:00 and 5:00, the user base and network utilization has doubled. It is important to plan for growth and to develop the application so that the significant addition of users will affect neither the network nor the application.

Online/Offline Hours

Some applications require some offline time for special processing. You might need to run a nightly batch through a mainframe or weekly rollups for a data warehouse that requires that all users exit the systems and avoid making changes. It is important to analyze the impact that offline time will have and make the appropriate plans or design changes to incorporate offline processing or some mechanism to handle the systems disconnection.

Offline processing might require a messaging server, such as Microsoft Message Queue (MSMQ) Server, or a custom offline processing mechanism.

MSMQ is a system that allows applications to communicate over a heterogeneous network that might be temporarily offline. MSMQ acts much like an email server, in which the application messages are forwarded and stored until the processing application retrieves them. MSMQ allows for guaranteed delivery due to the built-in transaction mechanisms for storing the messages. Developers do not need to worry about messages being partially transmitted because MSMQ does not remove a message from the queue or add a message to a queue until receipt or delivery is verified.

MSMQ allows for a level of connectionless communication that is important during these offline hours. The application can continue to process information, such as orders, whether the system is online or offline. In prior discussions about local and remote users, MSMQ played an important role in system design. Connectionless systems are important for the following reasons:

- Offline availability
- Remote disconnected users
- Application fault tolerance

Response Time

Response time deals with two key aspects of the application: physical response time and perceived response time.

Physical Response Time

Physical response time is the time it takes to make a request to an application server and receive a response. On a large enterprise system, a few seconds of processing can easily translate into hours of lost productivity per day.

Some items cause long response times that lower the overall productivity of an application:

- Underpowered servers—A network server attempting to service 300 users should have adequate memory and processing power. Adding an additional processor or more memory can help to double the amount of processing that a system can handle.

- Poor application logic—Check the code behind common routines and determine whether the code can be optimized. A Microsoft Visual Basic function that uses variant data types is several times slower than a function that uses explicit data types.

- Limited network throughput—Increasing a network from 10 megabits to 100 megabits significantly increases the amount of data that can travel on the network and the speed that the data travels.

- Optimize data services—To limit network traffic, utilize stored procedures and try to avoid cursors. If you have to use a cursor, it should be server-side.

- Utilize additional layers—Use applications, such as Microsoft Transaction Sever, to keep data connections open and pool objects to decrease the time it takes to create objects and connect to databases.

Each of these items does not adversely affect the response time of an application and can increase the overall performance of the application. Saving a few seconds here and there saves both time and money due to increased end-user productivity in the application.

Perceived Response Time

An application that had been optimized for the shortest response time might still seem to be slow to the user. Feedback is important when the application is processing data or waiting on a response from the server. The use of status bars, progress bars, and other graphical status indicators tells the user that the application is still working. If the users feel that the application is no longer responding, they might terminate the application and cause data corruption, or they might lose work that was not saved. Always tell the user that the system is working and how much time is left. Even though the application is not running more quickly, users will think it is because they are not left wondering how much longer the application will be processing.

Transaction Processing

Utilizing transactions decreases overall response time, especially when accessing databases. Transactions allow for an "all-or-nothing" approach to writing data and allow for batch system updates. Utilizing a transaction for a record update writes all of the data at once rather than a field at a time. Less network traffic is generated because only one call is made to the database rather than several individual calls. Batch updates allow for groups of records to be updated at once. Like record updates, overall traffic is reduced because all of the operations are completed within the same connection rather than through a series of connections.

Utilizing a middle-tier application (such as Microsoft Transaction Server) that is both a transaction processor and a connection pooler increases overall response time. Database connections are pooled between users, and the time required to connect to a database server is not necessary due to the reuse of open database connections. Connections are shared as users open and close connections to the database server. This form of pooling is efficient and makes for a more stable and responsive system.

Maintainability

Maintainability is a key issue with application development. An application can be efficient and utilize some of the most advanced programming techniques, but if the system cannot be maintained, it is not an effective solution. A balance between ease of maintenance and application complexity must be maintained in order to lower the TCO of the application. If the maintenance of the application is too high due to the structure of the application, the following problems might occur:

- Bugs are harder to find and fix.
- New bugs are easier to generate.
- Finding advanced talent to maintain the system might be difficult.
- The application might not be flexible enough to allow for future changes.

Application Distribution and Upgrades

Applications can be distributed in many ways. Administrators may use software packages, such as Microsoft System Management Server, to automate the installation of upgrades. Applications, such as SMS, allow for the remote distribution of system files and application upgrades automatically. SMS can push files to some or all computers in the enterprise so that users do not need to be concerned when new applications are needed or files are updated. Other ways of distributing a file would be to place new setup files on the network or sending CD-ROMs to users. Each medium has its pros and cons, and it is important to know which method fits your project.

Writing applications in a modular fashion that conforms to COM standards eases deployment to users because only updated files are required on the client machines. This is especially helpful in situations where bandwidth is limited, and you only need to upgrade a 200kb file and do not want to force the users to set up the entire application (which might be several megabytes). Additionally, COM components that run on a middle tier can be upgraded without the users noticing. This can often be completed without rebooting a server or interrupting service for more than a few minutes.

The various pros and cons of these distribution methods are outlined in Table 1.4.

TABLE 1.4

PROS AND CONS OF APPLICATION DISTRIBUTION METHODS

Distribution Method	Pro	Con
CD-ROM or disk	Allows for mass distribution to users not accessing a central system.	Expensive to create and ship.
	Gives users a physical medium to access if a system has to be installed from scratch.	Forces the user to keep up with updates and versions. Might be easy to lose or misplace.
Network setup	Easy to update.	Must inform users of the new software.
		System might be offline.
SMS	Upgrades happen automatically without user intervention.	Requires SMS software and an administrator.
Automatic upgrading	No user intervention required.	You must create the code to install new components.
		System files must be on a network server that might be down.

Any application distribution on a common system presents the problem of mismatched versions. It is important to be sure that all users are on the same version of the application or major problems might occur. Data corruption might be a problem due to data or logic changes, application crashes might occur due to server or object changes, and support will be difficult because a user might be using an incorrect software version.

Support

Application support is a part of enterprise application development that often is overlooked. After a system is in place, users will have questions and bugs will arise. Proper planning takes this into account and plans on having a staff of individuals to handle questions and keep the system up and running. A support staff will be made up of a number of people (see Figure 1.12).

- Administration—The administration staff is on hand to handle systems issues, such as backups, software upgrades, and general maintenance. This group is in charge of network servers and mainframes. Generally, the administration support staff does not interact with the users directly and works behind the scenes.

- Helpdesk—Helpdesk (or desktop support as it is also known) handles end-user application questions and problems. This group is the link between the customers and the administration and development staff. Their job is to support the users by attempting to answer questions, logging bugs, and routing questions to other groups. An efficient helpdesk is critical to the long-term success of an application because a knowledgeable support staff is capable of filtering bugs and feature requests to development for further enhancements.

- Training—The training staff is responsible for training end users in application functionality and training new employees on all aspects of the system. The training group also handles training for application upgrades and enhancements. Typically, a training group is responsible for some end-user documentation and printed resources. Due to the costs involved with training, only large organizations usually have dedicated training groups to handle these issues.

- Maintenance—The maintenance staff is made up of developers who are on hand to work on application bugs and implement new features after the application is in production. This group works with all of the above groups to handle system issues, upgrades, and fixes. Most medium to large organizations have a dedicated maintenance staff that might be part of the helpdesk staff, depending on the size of the organization.

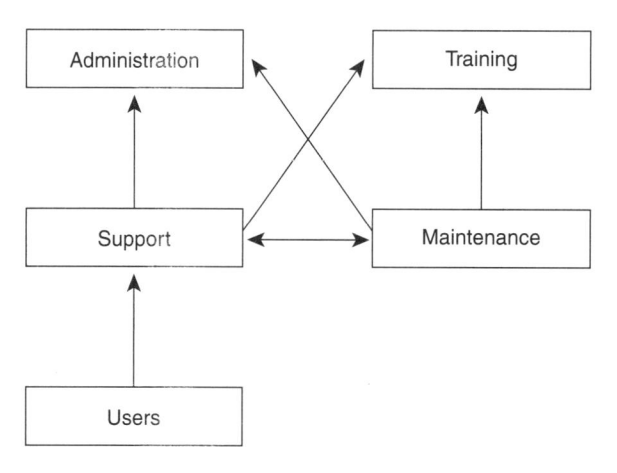

FIGURE 1.12
Support staff interaction.

Future Planning

Keeping the application modularized allows for future growth and expansion of the product. Planning for the future decreases the total cost of ownership over the life of the project and allows for easier maintenance.

Utilizing products such as Microsoft Internet Information Server (IIS), SQL Server, and Transaction Server allows for future enhancements by utilizing the features implemented in these products over their lifetime. Using mainstream third-party products lets you utilize the development efforts of the vendor where custom development requires larger development and test teams internally. Always look at the suite of products available and determine what path will allow the application to grow easily.

A true enterprise application never stops evolving. The development process continues as business or user needs change. Utilizing a multitier development model (covered in detail later) with the modularization of the application helps to keep the system going through incremental changes over the long term.

Availability

Applications do not always run, and servers are not always online. Upgrades must be performed, service packs must be installed, and hardware must be upgraded. How you plan the application and infrastructure has a major impact on how this is accomplished and how it impacts the business.

Geographic Scope

The physical location of machines and users has an impact on availability, especially when SQL Server is set up in a replication scenario. SQL Server might not replicate data until 1:00 a.m., so the operating sites will not have access to the updated data until well after that. This creates a time when data might be inconsistent and out of date. Replication scenarios require additional planning and additional training at the operating sites. There is no easy fix in a replication scenario other than waiting until the databases have been replicated. The key to setting this up with the least amount of user inconvenience is to pick the time of night when utilization is lowest. This avoids massive data updates during peak times that slow down the servers and adversely affect the users.

Operational Timelines

Not all enterprise solutions are considered equal. Some applications are designed to be run by a large number of users for only a portion of the day. Other applications are designed to be up 24 hours a day, 7 days a week. The operational time of the system is an important factor because a full-time application does not have a timeslot that can be used for maintenance and administration while the users are offline.

A Web application that takes orders on the Internet should always be online. In the information age, a Web site that is down is a lost customer. The application and infrastructure should be designed so that maintenance and administration can be performed as seamlessly as possible. One way to achieve this is to utilize mirrored servers that can go online as another server is taken offline. Maintenance is performed, and the main server is bought back online. The mirroring and online/offline processes should be built into the application so that even when the system is down, there is a backup access method.

When doesn't your application need to run? That is a question that impacts application design and maintenance plans. Remember that downtime indirectly costs money. Plan for it and make the process as seamless as possible.

Impact of Downtime

Enterprise systems are designed to run constantly with little or no interruption of service. Because these applications are critical to the operation of a business, the impact of unscheduled downtime should be analyzed and planned for. Some basic questions should be answered:

- What are the contingency plans for a system problem?
- Is there any redundancy built in to handle server down situations?
- How will downtime impact the users or other parts of the business?

Not knowing the answers to these questions opens the application up to major problems if anything should go wrong. The more critical a piece of the application is, the more work should be put into minimizing the possibility for downtime and allowing for a backup plan. A backup plan might consist of a pool manager that calls objects on available servers and switches to a backup server if necessary. Another example of planning for downtime would be to integrate Microsoft Message Queue Server to handle offline processing of data.

Downtime should also be translated into a dollar amount. This aids in the design process when implementing features. If a server goes down, what expense can be expected? For instance, if a database server goes down, all users are impacted. One hour of downtime costs the company $2,000 in lost productivity. Up to 10 hours per year of this type of downtime can be expected. By calculating a downtime cost, you can plan to lose $20,000 over the course of a year. Implementing a redundant system costs $5,000 in development. In this case, adding redundancy is not only good planning, it is highly cost effective.

SCALABILITY

As enterprise applications expand and grow, they need to be able to take advantage of more powerful hardware and software. If an application is not properly designed, hardware and software improvements will not be easily integrated to the application and major changes must be made to the application.

Scalable applications have a lower total cost of ownership and typically have a longer life due to the flexible nature of the design. Developing an n-tier application mode and taking advantage of generic procedure calls drastically increases the scalability of any enterprise application.

Planning for Growth

The major reason for making a system scalable is to properly plan for the growth of the application. A Microsoft Access-based system can be scaled to SQL Server with little problem if the application is designed properly. This planning enables you to take a small application and turn it into a true enterprise application in a short time.

Future growth might require that a system utilize other application layers, such as object servers. Once again, a Microsoft Transaction Server layer can be implanted to act as an object broker. If this is the case, an application that was designed for growth will not maintain state information for objects. Stateful objects consume resources and bandwidth that might be too limited for the application's use. If the application were designed for growth, then stateless objects would be developed to assist in future development.

A stateful object is an object that lives through the storage of properties. A server might contain an employee object that keeps the SSN, name, and department of an employee. This object is stateful because the server is keeping the information in its memory and cannot free resources to other applications looking to create an employee object.

A stateless object has no properties, only methods and events. A server may have an employee object that has methods called Add, Retrieve, Search, and Delete. These methods would take the necessary parameters to create a stateful employee object that would be sent back to the client.

Stateful objects should be on the clients and stateless objects on the clients or the servers.

Organizational Changes

How do changes in the core business or processes affect the application? If the application is scalable and extensible, changes won't cause a difficult transition. Planning for future design changes is difficult because changing business processes can affect logic across the entire application. By segmenting code and creating layers of objects, logic can be inserted and removed as necessary as the business changes.

When working on the initial application design, it is good practice to obtain more information about the future direction of the business. If a pattern arises in what appears to be the application's future, you might want to perform additional development work to address these possibilities.

For instance, the invoicing system does not handle partial shipments of orders. The decision makers in the organization would like to implement partial shipments and partial billing in the future so they can work with warehouses across the country to ship their products. In this instance, you might want to add logic that would make this implementation easier in the future without actually coding this logic into the application.

Expanding Data

As the business and the application grow, so does the data. Does the database server currently support growth? Is the database server scalable? As time passes, you might need the ability to create a data warehouse for previous data or to triple the number of users accessing the system. Enterprise databases, such as SQL Server, scale as the business grows. Databases, such as Microsoft Access, are not designed to handle this type of growth. An investment in scalable database systems up front will save both time and money in the future. Try to anticipate how the needs for data storage will increase and plan accordingly.

What Is Important to Know

- TCO and ROI are key elements of software design. Recovery calculations reveal the most cost-effective solutions.

- Users can be online or offline. Identify areas of the application where these users are impacted and plan accordingly.

- Identify key business processes from a high level using process and flow diagrams. Later, these will be used to identify the individual steps in the business logic.

- Use milestones as a basis for development in order to implement more stable applications and release code in a more efficient fashion.

- Adhering to component-based development using COM decreases TCO, increases maintainability and extensibility, and eases distribution.

- Use localization to create a common code base that can be used in other countries where dates, times, currencies, and languages differ.

OBJECTIVES

- Specify the relationships between entities
- Develop a conceptual data model using standard normalization techniques
- Identify the key components of a data model
- Identify appropriate levels of denormalization
- Choose the foreign key that will enforce relationships between entities and will ensure referential integrity
- Convert a logical data model to a physical data model

CHAPTER 2

Developing Data Models

Database design has two phases: *logical* and *physical*. The logical design step includes database objects, rules, and relationships that exist. The physical design phase takes the logical design and creates a series of tables and indexes that reflect the logical design.

During the logical design phase, the process of *normalization* occurs. Normalization is the process of designing the tables to avoid redundancy and increase efficiency for transaction-processing databases. Database tuning occurs during the physical design phase. Database tuning is the process of further normalizing or denormalizing a database for increased performance for the application.

Logical Design

A logical database design utilizes an entity-relationship (ER) diagram. ER diagrams are used to graphically display the data and relationships within a system. ER diagrams are a critical component of system design because the organization of your data into logical units is critical to system performance and future maintenance. Without a thorough ER model, database design becomes haphazard and disorganized, virtually guaranteeing problems during the later stages of development.

ER diagrams are typically created through software, such as ERWin or DataModeler. Tools such as these enable you to generate the database directly from the model, but software is not necessary. ER diagrams are merely a logical representation of your data. These can be stored in complex modeling software or hand drawn. There is no hard-and-fast rule to using tools to create an ER diagram. If you keep the key modeling concepts in mind during the design phase, the tools do not matter.

Several items make up ER diagrams: entities, attributes, and relationships. These items later translate into a physical database design and are used to generate tables and keys.

Entities, Attributes, and Relationships

Entities, attributes, and relationships are the key components to ER diagrams and relational database design. The items describe the data that you are working with and present a logical organization of this data.

The entities, attributes, and relationships that you create eventually translate to a physical data model. The physical model will be the actual database on your relational database server.

ER diagrams are an important piece of system documentation. A thorough ER diagram is invaluable during later stages of maintenance and enhancement. Because the key component of an enterprise system is the data it represents, a significant amount of time should be spent creating a complete and accurate logical data model.

Entities

Entities are the conceptual descriptions of your data and are typically nouns or noun phrases. Entities are people, places, things, or concepts that are key portions of the business. The primary entities are easy to find because they are the key focus points of the business or application.

Here are some examples of entities:

- Person: customer, vendor, employee
- Place: warehouse, building, location
- Thing: item, invoice
- Idea/concept: semester, order, course

When creating an ER diagram, look for key phrases that contain these easily identifiable nouns. The phrase "*customer* places an *order*" is an example of a phrase that outlines two key entities: orders and customers. During the planning and design phase of the development process, key interactions like this should be defined when describing the business cases. Go back to the initial documentation of the problem and the business functions, and you will be able to identify the key entities that need to be used.

Let's look at a typical order entry system. In a common order entry system, there is a need to track orders that are placed by customers. Employees enter the orders, and the inventory must be checked for availability and current stock levels before an order can be filled. If the product is in stock and there is a sufficient quantity for the order, that order can be filled. An order can consist of one or more items.

72 CHAPTER 2 Developing Data Models

By looking at the previous sample statement, you can see some of the entities and relationships for the system. In the following scenario, possible entities are in bold.

> In a common order entry system, there is a need to track **orders** that are placed by **customers**. **Employees** enter the **orders** and the **inventory** must be checked for availability and current stock levels before an **order** can be placed. If the **product** is in stock and the supply is sufficient to fill the **order,** that **order** is placed. An **order** can consist of one or more **items** or only one **item.**

Figure 2.1 shows an example of some of the entities that can be in an order entry system.

You might want to list all the key entities with a small phrase that describes the entity and what it represents. These phrases separate the entities from the larger business case and enable you to better organize your data and information. In a large enterprise application, there may be many entities, and improper organization of these objects will lead to an incomplete data model.

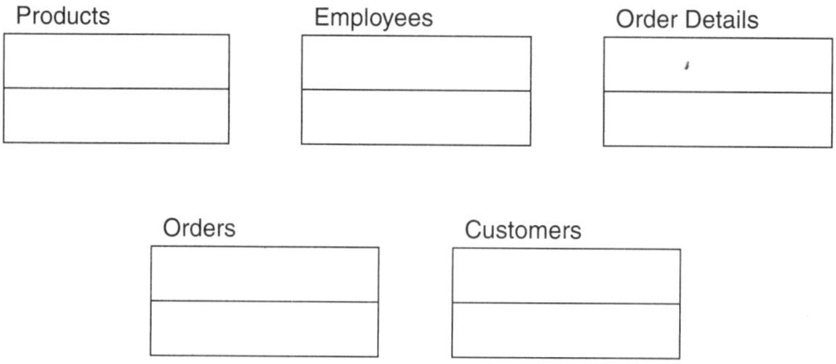

FIGURE 2.1
Entities for an order entry system.

The entity descriptions will come in handy later when you look at the relationships between entities. For example:

- Customer: a person who purchases items
- Student: a person who takes a specific class or series of classes
- Professor: a person who teaches one or more classes
- Vendor: an outside company that supplies the items we buy

You can see that all these entity descriptions also describe how these entities are related. At this point, we only know what the entities are and what *some* of the relationships are. This is by no means the complete relationship process. The designing of relationships is covered in more detail in later sections. Lack of thorough entity identification might cause you to redesign or make major modifications to the data model during the later stages of application design.

> **NOTE**
> **Entity**—An entity is a conceptual unit and is used to describe the data.

Attributes

Attributes provide additional information about their entities and are similar to properties of an entity. Attributes themselves will have their own individual properties after you start designing the physical database model, but the properties of the attributes are used primarily with the physical data model.

An example of attributes is a customer's name and address. The customer entity can still be used without these attributes, but they do not fully describe the entity, nor do they allow us to learn anything about the entities. You will usually be able to define attributes simply by looking at the business problem, but you might sometimes have to infer some information about entities. Defining attributes is one of the more difficult aspects of ER diagrams because not all the attribute information might be easily available. Further research into the entities or inference from the interactions between entities will assist you in defining all the attributes necessary to properly describe an entity.

Figure 2.2 shows examples of some of the attributes an entity can have.

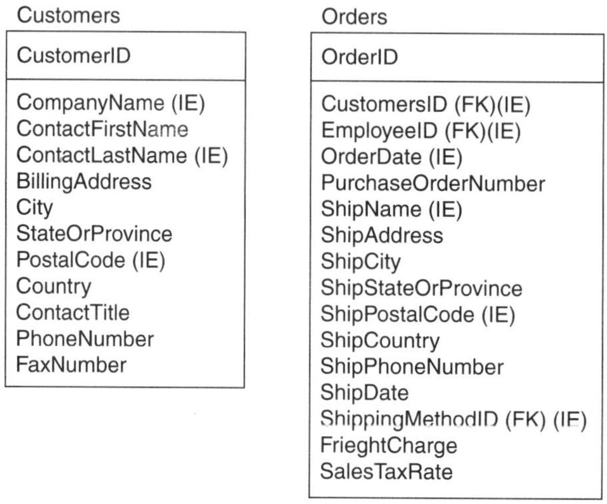

74 CHAPTER 2 Developing Data Models

```
Customers
─────────────────────
CustomerID
─────────────────────
CompanyName (IE)
ContactFirstName
ContactLastName (IE)
BillingAddress
City
StateOrProvince
PostalCode (IE)
Country
ContactTitle
PhoneNumber
FaxNumber
```

```
Orders
─────────────────────
OrderID
─────────────────────
CustomersID (FK)(IE)
EmployeeID (FK)(IE)
OrderDate (IE)
PurchaseOrderNumber
ShipName (IE)
ShipAddress
ShipCity
ShipStateOrProvince
ShipPostalCode (IE)
ShipCountry
ShipPhoneNumber
ShipDate
ShippingMethodID (FK) (IF)
FrieghtCharge
SalesTaxRate
```

FIGURE 2.2
Adding some attributes to the order entry entities.

In some situations, an attribute cannot be mapped directly to a database. Some attributes can actually be separate entities. Take, for instance, a contact tracking application that enables you to keep a listing of dependents for a contact. This data is modeled in such a way that an attribute "dependent" can be added, but "dependent" is actually a separate entity. If you just created the first model, it would look similar to the one shown in Figure 2.3.

This entity is correct, but "dependents" is really a separate entity because you can have more than one dependent, and each dependent should have its own attributes. Refining the diagram more brings us to a more complete model, as shown in Figure 2.4.

This is the complete entity list for the contact information. You might have multiple addresses for a contact, so that would be an additional entity. An attribute that can have its own attributes is a possible candidate for a related entity. Also, an attribute that can have more than one entry is also a candidate for a related entity. Sometimes, an additional entity can be created to make a data model more manageable. You will see this in more detail when one-to-one relationships are covered.

Logical Design 75

Contacts

ContactID
FirstName
LastName (IE)
Dear
Address
City
StateOrProvince
PostalCode (IE)
Region
Country
CompanyName (IE)
Title
WorkPhone
WorkExtension
MobilePhone
FaxNumber
EmailName (IE)
LastMeetingDate
ContactTypeID (FK) (IE)
ReferredBy
Notes
Dependents

FIGURE 2.3
An entity that needs to be refined.

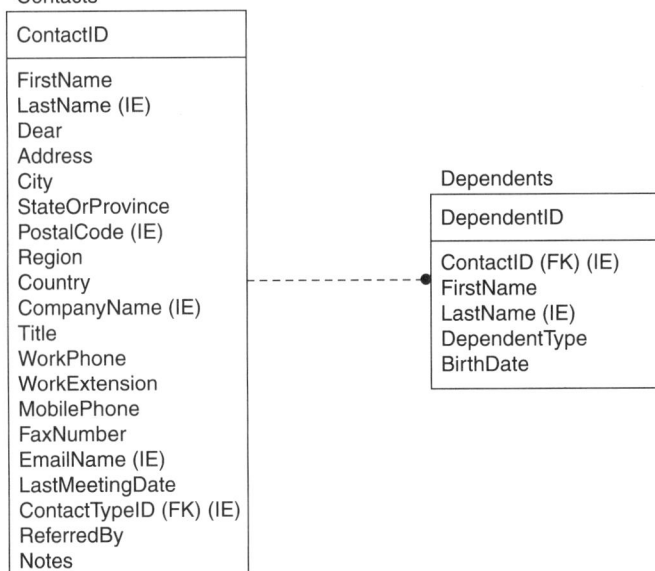

Contacts

ContactID
FirstName
LastName (IE)
Dear
Address
City
StateOrProvince
PostalCode (IE)
Region
Country
CompanyName (IE)
Title
WorkPhone
WorkExtension
MobilePhone
FaxNumber
EmailName (IE)
LastMeetingDate
ContactTypeID (FK) (IE)
ReferredBy
Notes

Dependents

DependentID
ContactID (FK) (IE)
FirstName
LastName (IE)
DependentType
BirthDate

FIGURE 2.4
The contacts entity after some modification.

It is not entirely necessary to define each of these subentities now, but when we get to the physical database design, we will need to generate the new entities because relational databases are not designed to handle these types of entity designs. Separate tables must be created to handle the data, so it might be more convenient to generate this information up front to avoid the need to re-create the ER model later.

> **NOTE**
>
> **Attribute**—Attributes describe the properties of an entity.

Relationships

Relationships are the logical associations between entities. These relationships enable you to link the entities together and form the other half of an entity relationship diagram.

When you get to the point that you need to generate the relationships between entities, go back to the entity descriptions you have put together. Most of your relationships will come from there. Any relationships that are not outlined in your entity descriptions should become more obvious after you look at the ER diagram. The following are some keys to completing your relationships:

- Are there any logical links missing from your entities? Most entities should be linked to another entity.

- Does it make sense to add additional links to entities? Entities can be linked to any number of additional entities.

- Are there any entities that do not exist? If a relationship between two entities creates a relationship but the relationship seems to be incomplete, you might be missing an additional entity that completes the data model.

Relationships require special indicators called *keys* that tell the entity that this is a piece of identifying information for the entity. Keys are used when you set up the different types of relationships that entities can have.

> **NOTE**
> **Key** (SQL Server Books Online)—A column or group of columns that uniquely identifies a row (PRIMARY KEY), defines the relationship between two tables (FOREIGN KEY), or is used to build an index.

> **NOTE**
> **Relationship**—A relationship is a logical association between entities

Keys

Keys are the portions of an entity that allow for relationships to be created. Relationships must have a primary key and a foreign key in order to be established and maintained. Keys are implemented though existing fields or though special counter fields.

Primary Keys

Primary keys are indicators for a unique field in a table. A primary key cannot have a duplicate entry in the table, or the uniqueness of the key is lost. Primary keys are frequently set to be numbers that automatically increment when a new row is added to a table.

> **NOTE**
> **Primary key (PK)** (SQL Server Books Online)—The column or combination of columns that uniquely identifies one row from any other row in a table. A primary key (PK) must be nonnull and must have a unique index. A primary key is commonly used for joins with foreign keys (matching nonprimary keys) in other tables.

The customer table, shown in Figure 2.5, has a special assigned datatype (in the customer_id attribute) that tells the database that all new customer entries should have a unique number assigned that is generated in a specific sequence.

Most relational databases have a special field that automatically increments a field value. In Microsoft Access, it is an autonumber field; in SQL Server, it is an identity column. Most other databases allow for this special datatype as well. An auto-incrementing field is an easy way to implement a primary key because the database handles all data integrity for the column. The major disadvantage to an auto-increment field is that the key does not describe the data. You gain an easy key implementation but lose the ability to easily find the data through the key. This is something to keep in mind when designing the logical data model and implementing indexes in the physical model.

You can use other fields as primary keys. A social security number can be used in an employee table for a primary key.

You can combine fields and create what are called *composite* keys. Composite keys are used when individual fields are not unique, but a combination of fields are unique.

> **NOTE**
>
> **Composite key** (SQL Server Books Online)—A key composed of two or more columns.

Customer ID	Company Name	Contact First Name	Contact Last Name
1	Let's Stop N Shop	Jaime	Torres
2	Old World Delicatessen	Rene	Phillips
3	Rattlesnake Canyon Grocery	Paula	Wilson

FIGURE 2.5
The customer table.

A company might have information for a specific product (a blue widget), and the inventory code for this widget is WDGT-BLUE. Blue widgets are stored at any of the company's warehouses. The inventory code is not by itself enough to uniquely identify the part, but a combination of the code and the warehouse code would be unique. This combination would enable you to track individual parts through multiple locations.

Composite keys can also be used in place of an automatically incrementing key in a child table (see Figure 2.6). As stated earlier, the main problem with autonumbers is that they do not describe the data. You are more likely to remember that a blue widget is WDGT-BLUE than you would to remember that the blue widgets are item number 34924 in the database.

Combining inherited data to create a composite key helps to describe the data and allow for more powerful searches.

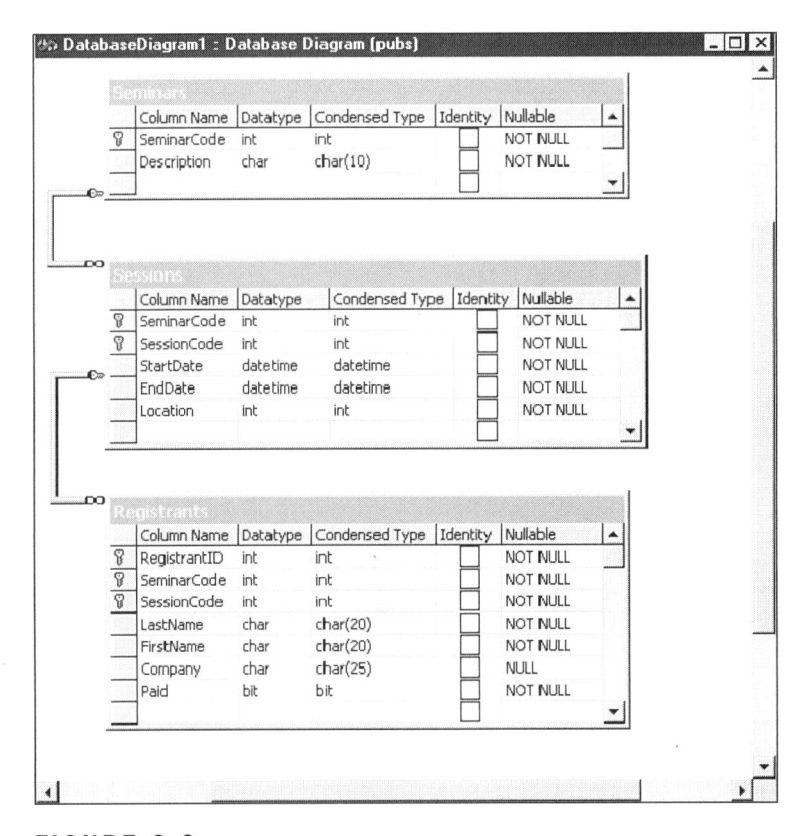

FIGURE 2.6
An example of cascading composite keys.

Inherited keys are implemented when you use a key from a parent as part of a composite key for a child. This has advantages through the capability to search for specific records without linking to a parent table (if the primary key is descriptive), but has its disadvantage through the implementation of the composite key. This is not the best approach; it is merely *another* approach to implementing relationships.

> **NOTE**
>
> **Parent**—The entity that maintains the primary relation between other entities. Parent entities are the "one" side of a one-to-many relationship. An orders entity would be a parent-to-order detail entities.
>
> **Child**—An entity that maintains data related to a parent table. Child entities are part of the "many" side of a one-to-many relationship.

Foreign Keys

A foreign key is a link on a child table to the primary key of the parent table. Foreign keys are suffixed with an (FK) entry in an ER diagram. Foreign keys are required in order to implement many of the relationships between tables.

> **NOTE**
>
> **Foreign key (FK)** (SQL Server Books Online)—The column or combination of columns whose values match the primary key (PK) or unique key in the same or another table. A foreign key (FK) does not have to be unique. A foreign key is often in a many-to-one relationship with a primary key. Foreign key values should be copies of the primary key values; no value in the foreign key, except NULL, should ever exist unless the same value exists in the primary key. A foreign key may be NULL; if any part of a composite foreign key is NULL, the entire foreign key must be NULL.

One-to-One

In a one-to-one relationship, only one association exists between two tables. In some cases, a one-to-one relationship can be created in order to decrease the size of a table and create a more structured data model. Other times, a one-to-one relationship can be unnecessary, and the data between the two tables can be combined.

Traditional relational database systems do not support one-to-one relationships natively. Code must be written in the form of business logic or triggers that implement the data validation for the relationship.

> **NOTE** **One-to-one relationship** (SQL Server Books Online)—A relationship between two tables in which a single row in the first table can be related only to one row in the second table, and a row in the second table can be related only to one row in the first table. This type of relationship is unusual.

One-to-one relationships come in handy when a given entity can have multiple representations. For the most part, these types of relationships are rare and must be implemented in specific ways.

One way to implement this type of relationship is to use the same primary key between both entities. Let's say that you are the government, and you allow only one vendor to supply one type of item. You would not be allowed to have Vendor A and Vendor B both supply blue widgets. We can implement a one-to-one relationship by using the primary key of the vendor and make a foreign key in the items. This foreign key would be a unique key that would not allow duplicates, essentially creating a second primary key. Most relational databases only allow for one primary key but will allow you to create other unique nonprimary keys.

Another way to implement a one-to-one relationship would be to implement a trigger that would not allow a second entry in the child table. This is not an ideal implementation because not all databases (especially desktop databases) can implement triggers. You could add this check into your program logic, but client/server systems should not attempt to validate this type of data.

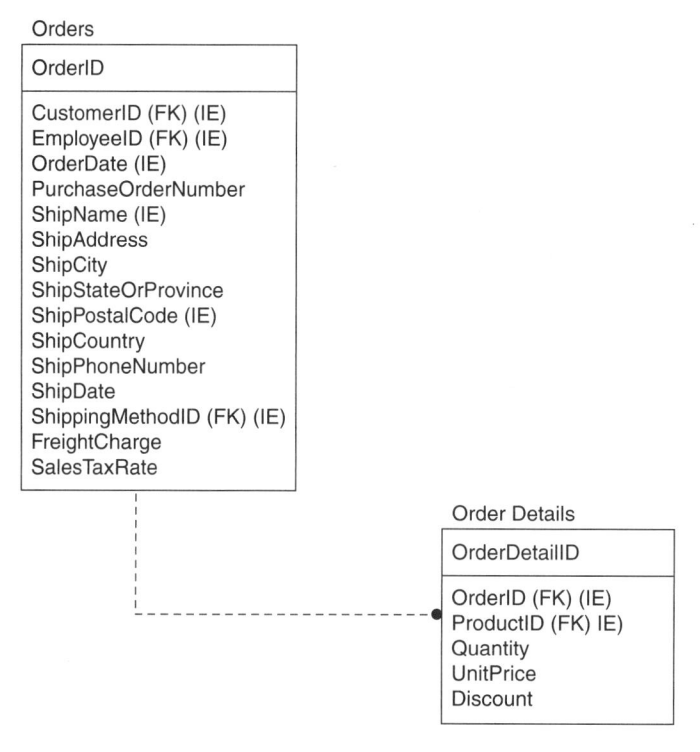

One-to-Many

One-to-many relationships are one of the most common relationships within relational databases. One-to-many relationships allow for a parent table with one entry to have a child table with many entries (see Figure 2.7). This allows for detail data to be stored within a separate table.

One-to-many relationships do not require any special design considerations. All that is required to implement a one-to-many relationship is a primary key in the parent table and a foreign key in the child table.

The advantage to a one-to-many relationship is that it allows for zero or more children. There is no lower boundary or upper boundary with respect to the number of related records. An unlimited number of children can be associated with a single parent. All relational databases support one-to-many relationships.

Orders

OrderID
CustomerID (FK) (IE)
EmployeeID (FK) (IE)
OrderDate (IE)
PurchaseOrderNumber
ShipName (IE)
ShipAddress
ShipCity
ShipStateOrProvince
ShipPostalCode (IE)
ShipCountry
ShipPhoneNumber
ShipDate
ShippingMethodID (FK) (IE)
FreightCharge
SalesTaxRate

Order Details

OrderDetailID
OrderID (FK) (IE)
ProductID (FK) IE)
Quantity
UnitPrice
Discount

FIGURE 2.7
A one-to-many relationship.

Logical Design   83

You can set up relationships so that the model will require zero-to-many or one-to-many. Specifying the minimum required in a relationship requires code in order to implement the relationship. Triggers and stored procedures must maintain the integrity of the data.

> **NOTE** **One-to-many relationship** (SQL Books Online)—A relationship between two tables in which a single row in the first table can be related to one or more rows in the second table, but a row in the second table can be related only to one row in the first table. A typical one-to-many relationship is between the publishers table and the titles table in the pubs sample database, in which each publisher can be related to several titles, but each title can be related to only one publisher.

Many-to-Many

Many-to-many relationships require a special table. Most databases are not capable of natively supporting a many-to-many relationship.

In order to implement a many-to-many relationship on most relational database systems, a third table is required. This table is referred to as the *join table* or *junction table*. The join table will serve as a link table between the tables on each end of the relationship. This link table actually implements two one-to-many relationships in place of the many-to-many relationship.

Many-to-many relationships come in handy when you are required to deal with complex interactions between entities. A simple example of a need for a many-to-many relationship would be in a doctor's office where a patient can see any of the doctors and the doctors have many patients. This would require a join table to link the patients with the doctors because there is an unknown number of relationships between the doctors and the patients.

84 CHAPTER 2 Developing Data Models

The join table is typically a table that contains foreign keys for both parent tables. There is no child table in a many-to-many relationship, so each table is referred to as the parent. The join table can also be used to store additional information about the data. In the DoctorPatient join table, you might have a field for the last visit date or next appointment date. This information would not be appropriate for either the patient or the doctor table.

> **NOTE**
>
> **Many-to-many relationship**—A relationship between two tables in which rows in each table have multiple matching rows in the related table. Many-to-many relationships are maintained by using a third table called a junction (also called a join) table.

For instance, there might be a many-to-many relationship between students and classes. Many students may take classes and many classes have students. Figure 2.8 shows how the ER diagram displays this.

Figure 2.9 shows how the database would be modeled with the addition of the link table.

Many-to-many relationships allow for the modeling of complex data and data that cannot easily be classified within a single one-to-many relationship.

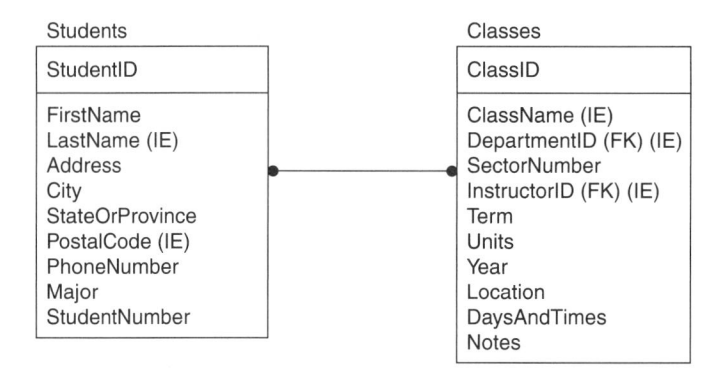

Students	Classes
StudentID	ClassID
FirstName LastName (IE) Address City StateOrProvince PostalCode (IE) PhoneNumber Major StudentNumber	ClassName (IE) DepartmentID (FK) (IE) SectorNumber InstructorID (FK) (IE) Term Units Year Location DaysAndTimes Notes

FIGURE 2.8
The ER implementation of a many-to-many join.

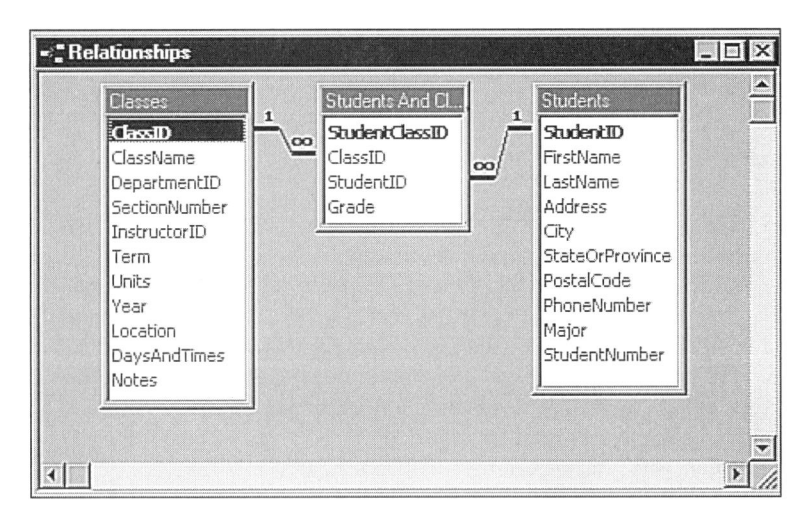

FIGURE 2.9
A physical many-to-many join.

Generating the Model

The best way to fully understand the key components to an ER diagram is to take a real-world example and translate the words into pictures. This is typically the series of steps that database developers would go through in order to generate a preliminary data model. After the first model is created, the developers and the users would refine the model to implement all of the business requirements and processes.

This scenario is a basic outline of an order entry system.

> ABC Corp. is looking to computerize their order entry operations. They currently maintain a list of customers that buy their products. They keep a listing of the vendors from which they purchase their products. Inventory is kept for all of the items they have in stock. Each item they have must tie back to one of their vendors, or they will lose the ability to audit their inventory. When a customer purchases an item, an order is placed and an invoice is generated. A customer cannot place an order unless the salesperson knows the name and address of the customer. The salesperson then makes sure that there are enough items to sell, or the order cannot be placed.

Now, look at the scenario again and notice that the key entities have been highlighted:

> ABC Corp. is looking to computerize their order entry operations. They currently maintain a list of **customers** that buy their **products**. They keep a listing of the **vendors** from which they purchase their **products**. Inventory is kept for all of the **items** they have in stock. Each **item** they have must tie back to one of their **vendors**, or they will lose the ability to audit their inventory. When a **customer** purchases an item, an **order** is placed and an invoice is generated. A **customer** cannot place an order unless the **salesperson** knows the name and address of the **customer**. The **salesperson** then makes sure that there are enough **items** to sell, or the order cannot be placed.

So, there are entities for customers, salespeople, vendors, orders, and items. These entities describe the data that we are planning to track. Notice that entities are typically nouns because they describe a person, place, or concept.

By using this information about your entities, you can draw a simple ER diagram, as shown in Figure 2.10.

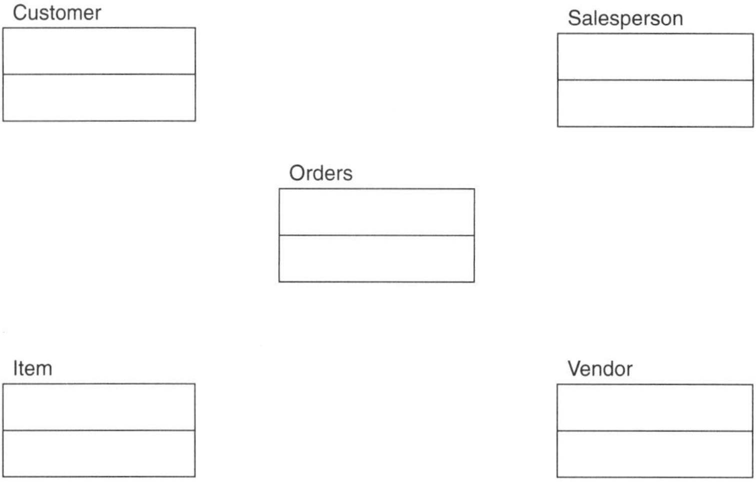

FIGURE 2.10
Step 1: Identify the entities.

Now you need to describe some of the attributes of the entities. For instance, you need to know some customer information, such as the name, address, and some unique identifier so you do not confuse one customer with another. See Figure 2.11.

You can now look at defining some relationships between the entities. Looking at the preceding scenario, you know that a customer places an order with a salesperson, vendors supply items, and orders contain items bought by a customer. This information helps to determine the relationships between entities. The relationships describe the interaction between the entities and, in the preceding scenario, yield the ER diagram shown in Figure 2.12.

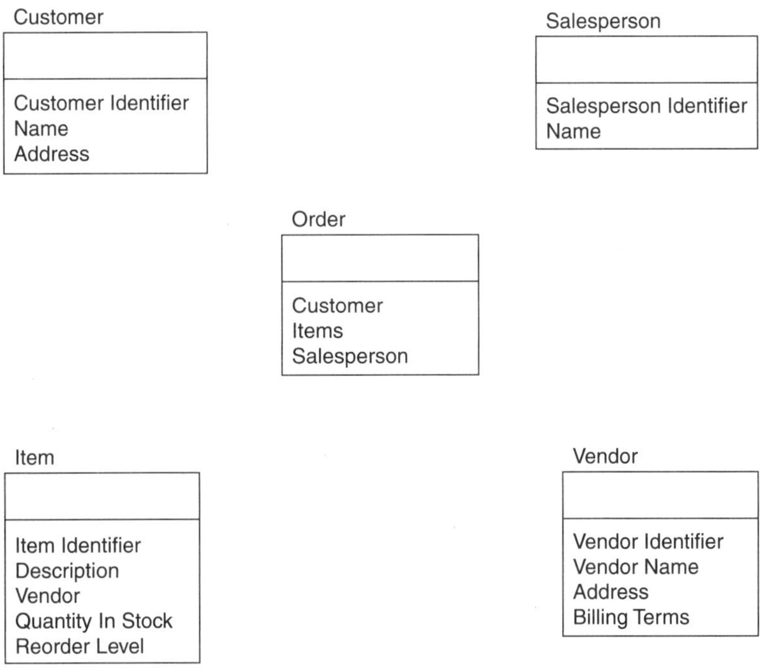

Customer

Customer Identifier
Name
Address

Salesperson

Salesperson Identifier
Name

Order

Customer
Items
Salesperson

Item

Item Identifier
Description
Vendor
Quantity In Stock
Reorder Level

Vendor

Vendor Identifier
Vendor Name
Address
Billing Terms

FIGURE 2.11
Step 2: Identify the attributes.

88 CHAPTER 2 Developing Data Models

Customer
- Customer Identifier
- Name
- Address

Customer places order

Salesperson
- Salesperson Identifier
- Name

Salesperson takes order

Order
- Customer
- Items
- Salesperson

Order contains items

Item
- Item Identifier
- Description
- Vendor
- Quantity In Stock
- Reorder Level

Vendor supplies items

Vendor
- Vendor Identifier
- Vendor Name
- Address
- Billing Terms

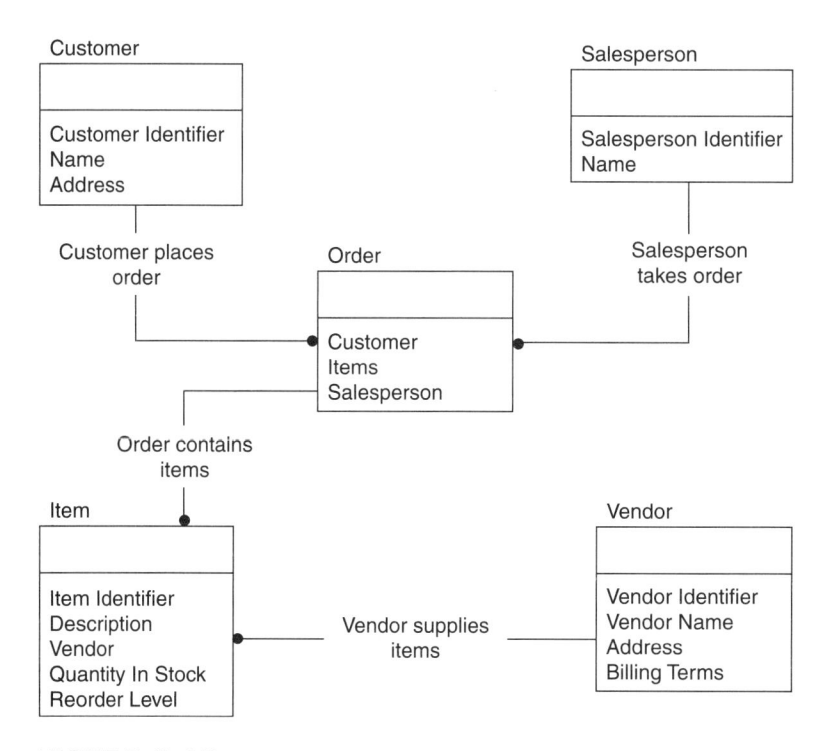

FIGURE 2.12
Step 3: Create the relationships.

There are some general tips to creating ER diagrams and organizing the data:

- Determine the entities by identifying the key nouns or concepts in a given scenario—customers, vendors.
- Describe in a phrase or sentence what the entity does—vendors supply items.
- Identify attributes by identifying the details of the entities—the salesperson must know the name and address of the customer.
- Identify the relationships of the entities by noting the interactions between them—a customer places an order with a salesperson.

Primary and Foreign Keys

Primary and foreign keys are used to implement relationships between entities within a data model.

A table can have only one primary key because this is the central identifier for the table. Primary keys are usually represented in an ER model with a (PK) prefix. Common primary keys are fields that automatically increment each time a record is added to the table. SQL Server uses an *identity* column and Access uses an *autonumber* field to implement fields that automatically increment on each add.

The main disadvantage with auto-incrementing fields is that they do not describe the data they are representing. A good database design uses some intelligent data to generate a primary key. For instance, a product might have a primary key that is a combination of the product group, type, and warehouse. This would enable users to create more effective queries because their key is more descriptive than just an arbitrary number.

Foreign keys are used in a child table to create the join back to a parent table. An order details table has a field to store the key to the parent order so the relationship between the orders table and the order details table can be made.

Many databases implement referential integrity through the keys. This allows the database to prevent users from creating orphaned records in the system.

> **NOTE**
>
> **Referential Integrity**—The process of maintaining the data between related tables so that data in a linked table must be related to a record in a parent table. Referential integrity prevents a parent key from being updated without updating all related child records.
>
> **Orphaned record**—A child record that does not relate to a parent record due to a parent record being changed or deleted. A record can also be orphaned if referential integrity is not implemented and the database system allows child records to be created without a valid parent record.

Normalization and Denormalization

The process of refining the data model and creating a high level of efficiency with a database is called *normalization*. Database designers can implement several levels of normalization. Each level builds on previous levels by reducing the amount of redundancy between tables. This typically increases performance and avoids problems with data consistency.

Redundant data wastes disk space due to the increase in table size. Data inconsistencies are also a large problem because the same data is being maintained in multiple locations. If the data is updated in only half of the locations where it is used, there will be no way to tell what the correct data is supposed to be, or you might lose the ability to link data between tables.

> **NOTE**
>
> **Normalization**—The process of refining the data model to eliminate duplicate or redundant data and increase the performance and efficiency of the database. A normalized database will decrease performance in a data warehouse due to the large number of joins required to create datasets.

In certain situations, you would want to *denormalize* the database. You might be implementing a data warehouse or refining the database to increase maintainability.

Each of these points is covered in more detail throughout this section.

> **NOTE**
>
> **Denormalization** (SQL Server Books Online)—The introduction of redundancy into a table in order to incorporate data from a related table. The related table can then be eliminated. Denormalization can improve efficiency and performance in a data warehouse schema but will reduce overall performance in an OLTP database.

First Normal Form

First normal form is the most basic level of database normalization.

The key to first normal form is to design the tables so that data is not stored in repeating columns. An unnormalized table would contain both the "one" side, as well as the "many" side of a relationship.

The table shown in Figure 2.13 is not in first normal form.

You can see that there is repeating data in the table shown in Figure 2.14. The table is not designed to handle more than two items before it runs out of storage space. You need to create a separate table to handle the order details to allow for an unlimited number of items. This eliminates the repeating data in the table and sets up the one-to-many relationship between the tables. Remember that a table that is not in the first normal form is both sides of the one-to-many relationship.

The order details table is now in the first normal form. The orders table shown in Figure 2.15 looks a bit smaller after applying the rules of the first normal form.

Here are the keys to creating tables in the first normal form:

- Eliminate repeating groups in individual tables.
- Create a separate table for each set of related data.
- Identify each set of related data with a primary key.

Second Normal Form

The first normal form is not a good database design, but it is a start. After you are able to remove some of the repeating columns from a table and generate a primary key, you can move toward the second normal form for your database.

Orders_denormalized : Table

Order ID	Employee ID	Order Date	Customer	Item1	Qty1	Price1	Item2	Qty2	Price2	OrderTotal
1	Buchanan, Steven	2/2/95	Let's Stop N Shop	Crystal Ball	2	$45.55	Tether ball	5	$9.65	$139.35
2	Buchanan, Steven	3/14/95	Let's Stop N Shop	Tether ball	1	$9.65	Football	1	$5.65	$15.30
3	Davolio, Nancy	4/18/95	Let's Stop N Shop	Tether ball	3	$9.65	6 Golf balls	1	$6.75	$35.70
4	Fuller, Andrew	5/21/95	Let's Stop N Shop	Football	2	$5.65				$11.30
5	Leverling, Janet	6/25/95	Let's Stop N Shop	Foosball	2	$17.85	6 Golf balls	1	$6.75	$42.45
6	Buchanan, Steven	2/1/95	Old World Delicatessen	Football	1	$5.65				$5.65
7	Buchanan, Steven	4/1/95	Old World Delicatessen	Soccer ball	2	$12.95	6 Golf balls	1	$6.75	$32.65
8	Davolio, Nancy	4/9/95	Old World Delicatessen	Soccer ball	1	$12.95	Basketball	2	$4.95	$22.85
9	Fuller, Andrew	5/11/95	Old World Delicatessen	6 Golf balls	1	$6.75	Crystal ball	1	$45.55	$52.30
10	Buchanan, Steven	6/12/95	Old World Delicatessen	Football	1	$5.65	Crystal ball	1	$45.55	$51.20
(AutoNumber)					0	$0.00		0	$0.00	$0.00

Record: 1 of 10

FIGURE 2.13
A table that is not in any normal form.

92 CHAPTER 2 Developing Data Models

OrderID	Item	Quantity	Price
1	Crystal ball	2	45.55
1	Tether ball	5	9.65
1	Basketball	2	4.95
1	Football	2	5.65
1	Foosball	4	17.85
2	Tether ball	1	9.65
2	Football	1	5.65
2	Soccer ball	1	12.95
2	Crystal ball	1	45.55
2	6 Golf balls	2	6.75
3	Tether ball	3	9.65
3	6 Golf balls	1	6.75
3	Crystal ball	2	45.55
3	Foosball	1	17.85
4	Football	2	5.65
5	Foosball	2	17.85
5	6 Golf balls	1	6.75
6	Football	1	5.65
7	Soccer ball	2	12.95
7	6 Golf balls	1	6.75
8	Soccer ball	1	12.95
8	Basketball	2	4.95
8	Baseball	1	8.75

FIGURE 2.14
Putting the order details into a first normal form table.

OrderID	Employee	OrderDate	Customer
1	5	2/2/95	Let's Stop N Shop
2	5	3/14/95	Let's Stop N Shop
3	1	4/18/95	Let's Stop N Shop
4	2	5/21/95	Let's Stop N Shop
5	3	6/25/95	Let's Stop N Shop
6	5	2/1/95	Old World Delicatessen
7	5	4/1/95	Old World Delicatessen
8	1	4/9/95	Old World Delicatessen
9	2	5/11/95	Old World Delicatessen
10	5	6/12/95	Old World Delicatessen

FIGURE 2.15
Putting the orders into a first normal form table.

When normalizing for the second form, you intend to create separate tables for repeating values and link to the tables with a foreign key. Once again, one-to-many relationships will be used to implement the second normal form.

Key candidate fields for normalization during this step would be items such as repeating description fields, names that are maintained in separate tables, and value data.

Frequently, value data is implemented through lookup tables that store a key value and a description. This enables you to update and maintain fields without introducing problems with data integrity for existing data. Because the tables are related through a primary/foreign key relationship, the description data can continually change while the key values do not.

In the order tables, you can further normalize by moving the item descriptions to an item table and relating the tables through an ID field on the item table. This reduces the redundant entries in the order details table and allows for easier maintenance of the items table. You can now change the description of the football to read "genuine leather football," and the order details table will be unchanged (see Figures 2.16 and 2.17).

This still leaves you with the orders table that still looks like the one shown in Figure 2.18.

You are maintaining data that you can further normalize when you move to the third normal form.

In order to normalize to the second normal form, you should do the following:

- Create separate tables for sets of values that apply to multiple records.
- Relate these tables with a foreign key.

94 **Chapter 2** Developing Data Models

OrderID	ItemID	Quantity	Price
9	1	1	6.75
7	1	1	6.75
2	1	2	6.75
5	1	1	6.75
3	1	1	6.75
8	2	1	8.75
1	3	2	4.95
8	3	2	4.95
3	4	2	45.55
9	4	1	45.55
2	4	1	45.55
10	4	1	45.55
1	4	2	45.55
1	5	4	17.85
3	5	1	17.85
5	5	2	17.85
6	6	1	5.65
2	6	1	5.65
1	6	2	5.65
10	6	1	5.65
4	6	2	5.65
7	7	2	12.95
2	7	1	12.95
8	7	1	12.95
3	8	3	9.65
2	8	1	9.65
1	8	5	9.65

FIGURE 2.16
Refining the order details to second normal form.

ItemID	Item
1	6 Golf balls
2	Baseball
3	Basketball
4	Crystal ball
5	Foosball
6	Football
7	Soccer ball
8	Tether ball

FIGURE 2.17
The items table is created through normalization.

OrderID	Employee	OrderDate	Customer
1	5	2/2/95	Let's Stop N Shop
2	5	3/14/95	Let's Stop N Shop
3	1	4/18/95	Let's Stop N Shop
4	2	5/21/95	Let's Stop N Shop
5	3	6/25/95	Let's Stop N Shop
6	5	2/1/95	Old World Delicatessen
7	5	4/1/95	Old World Delicatessen
8	1	4/9/95	Old World Delicatessen
9	2	5/11/95	Old World Delicatessen
10	5	6/12/95	Old World Delicatessen

FIGURE 2.18
Our first normal form orders table.

Third Normal Form

The third normal form is typically the last form that most database designers will normalize to. After the third normal form, the number of relationships between tables becomes very large, and performance begins to decrease on the database server.

The goal of the third normal form is to remove all data that does not depend on the primary key of a table. In your orders table, you maintain the employee who took the order and the customer who placed it. This data is not necessary in the orders table because the employee data and the customer data do not depend on the primary key. The important distinction to make here is that the employee and the customer are important to the order, but you would not want to maintain the data in the orders table because this data does not relate to an order.

To better understand this concept, let's look at an orders table with a few more customer fields (see Figure 2.19). This should help to clear up any confusion over the dependency on the primary key.

OrderID	Employee	OrderDate	Customer	Name	Address	City	State	Zip
1	5	2/2/95	Let's Stop N Shop	Let's Stop N Shop	87 Polk St.	San Francisco	CA	94117
2	5	3/14/95	Let's Stop N Shop	Let's Stop N Shop	87 Polk St.	San Francisco	CA	94117
3	1	4/18/95	Let's Stop N Shop	Let's Stop N Shop	87 Polk St.	San Francisco	CA	94117
4	2	5/21/95	Let's Stop N Shop	Let's Stop N Shop	87 Polk St.	San Francisco	CA	94117
5	3	6/25/95	Let's Stop N Shop	Let's Stop N Shop	87 Polk St.	San Francisco	CA	94117
6	5	2/1/95	Old World Delicates	Old World Delicates	2743 Bering St.	Anchorage	AK	99508
7	5	4/1/95	Old World Delicates	Old World Delicates	2743 Bering St.	Anchorage	AK	99508
8	1	4/9/95	Old World Delicates	Old World Delicates	2743 Bering St.	Anchorage	AK	99508
9	2	5/11/95	Old World Delicates	Old World Delicates	2743 Bering St.	Anchorage	AK	99508
10	5	6/12/95	Old World Delicates	Old World Delicates	2743 Bering St.	Anchorage	AK	99508

FIGURE 2.19
Our orders table with some additional data.

96 CHAPTER 2 Developing Data Models

By looking at this table, you can see some of the information that has been temporarily removed from the preceding examples. Here, the table contains not only the customer name, but also the customer address—clearly not information that is dependent on the primary key of the orders table.

You would normalize the database by creating a customer table and removing the customer-specific data. At the same time, you would remove the employee-specific data and create a relationship to an employee table.

You now have three tables: orders, employees, and customers. Each is linked through a primary/foreign key relationship (see Figures 2.20 through 2.22).

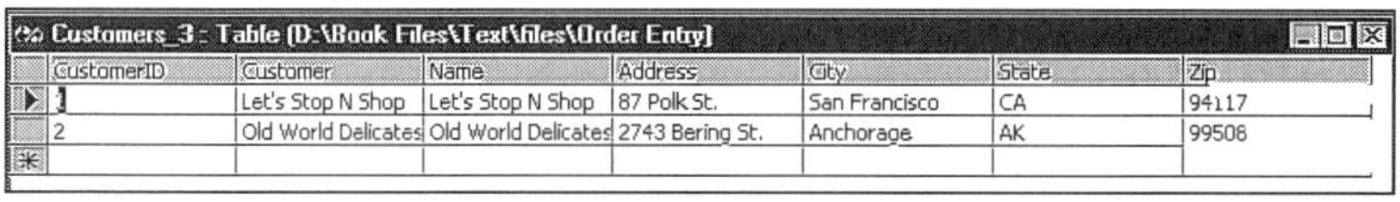

FIGURE 2.20
Creating a customers table through normalization.

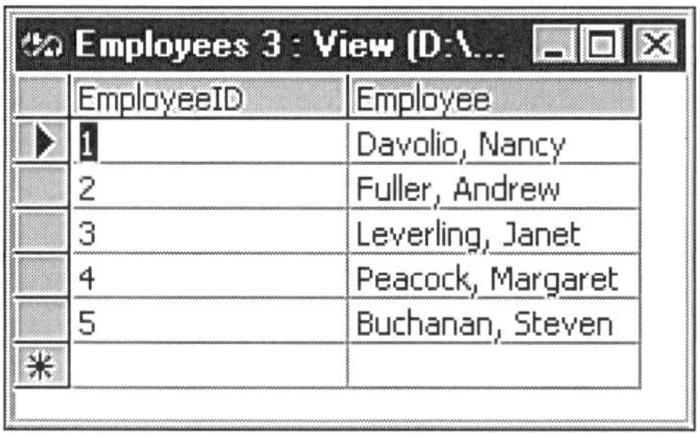

FIGURE 2.21
The employees table is created as well.

Logical Design

OrderID	Employee	OrderDate	CustomerID
1	5	2/2/95	1
2	5	3/14/95	1
3	1	4/18/95	1
4	2	5/21/95	1
5	3	6/25/95	1
6	5	2/1/95	2
7	5	4/1/95	2
8	1	4/9/95	2
9	2	5/11/95	2
10	5	6/12/95	2

FIGURE 2.22
Your orders table is finally normalized.

All nondependent information has been moved to secondary tables, and the database is in the third normal form. The full relationship diagram with all of the tables shows the cleaner table layout desired (see Figure 2.23).

To summarize the rule for normalization in the third form—eliminate fields that do not depend on the key.

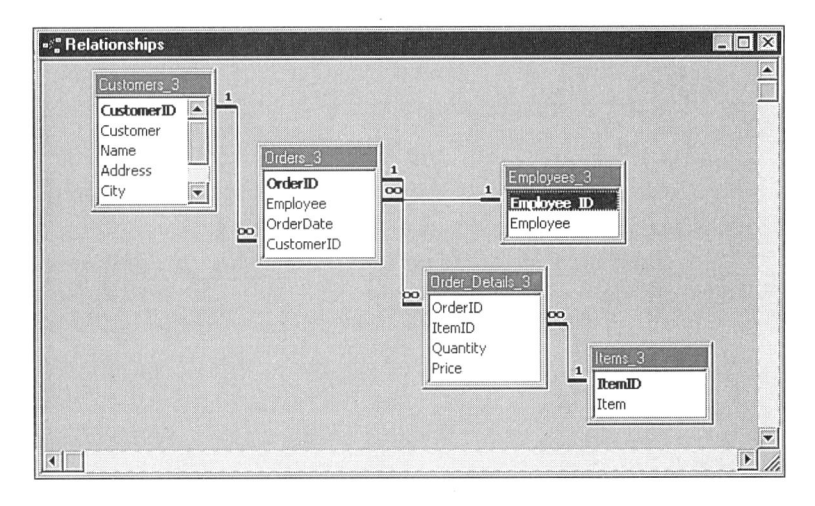

FIGURE 2.23
The physical data model after normalizing to the third normal form.

Denormalization

The process of denormalization is used when your data model exceeds the third normal form and maintenance becomes an issue. After a database is in fourth normal form or Boyce-Codd normal form, the database might become slower and harder to maintain because a large number of joins must be made in order to retrieve a full data set.

Another reason why denormalization would be used is when you are implementing a data warehouse. A data warehouse needs fast access, and multiple table joins that exceed four tables will start affecting the throughput of a database server. To retrieve data in an efficient manner, redundant data is maintained in multiple tables. The tables that the data is written to often don't use live data that is updated on a daily basis. A process called a rollup is used to generate the data warehouse information.

Finally, a database will be denormalized for general performance reasons. An example of denormalizing a table for performance reasons would be a case where you have a table that stores payroll data, and you frequently report the data with the employee name. The employee name might require multiple joins to retrieve the information. To increase performance and decrease the load on the server, you can denormalize the payroll table so that it contains the employee name. This happens often in database design because many joins use memory and processor time on the server. Denormalizing a third normal form database increases overall performance while still maintaining a relatively normalized database.

Normalization is a set of guidelines, but they are not hard and fast rules. If some tables are in second normal form and some are in third, you do not necessarily have a poorly designed database. Most production databases are not of third normal form and higher; they are typically a mix of second and third normal form.

Physical Design Considerations

When converting the logical model to the physical model, certain considerations should be taken into account:

- Many-to-many relationships will require a join table that usually does not exist in the ER diagram.

- One-to-one relationships will probably require triggers and stored procedures to maintain the integrity of the data. Relational databases that do not support triggers and stored procedures should use code to maintain the data integrity.

- Each entity will represent a table. If the entity contains data that is repeating, you might want to create secondary tables or lookup tables to maintain the data in a central location.

- Relationships that are of the one-to-two (or more) relationships will require stored procedures and triggers. SQL Server and Microsoft Access cannot implement these types of relationships. Code must be written to enforce these relationships between tables.

- Most entities in an ER diagram will be related to another entity. If there is an entity that is not related to any other, check the ER model to be sure that there is not a missing relationship or that the entity is necessary.

- When creating a one-to-many relationship, you need to be sure you have properly marked the one side and the many side. A one-to-many relationship is dependent on the proper identification of the parent and the child tables.

- Make sure all parent and child tables have the necessary keys established. A relationship between two tables cannot be created without a primary key/foreign key pair.

Most ER diagrams will be able to go from a logical model to a physical model with little or no problems. If the model does not easily translate to a physical model, now would be a good time to analyze the logical model and verify that it is diagrammed properly. A large amount of difficulty in conversion is the first sign of a weak logical model.

Be sure to note that not all relational database systems are alike. Desktop databases such as Microsoft Access will not support the full set of features and power that an enterprise database system, such as SQL Server, will. Later chapters cover the selection of a database system, but the logical design phase should get you to focus on the database architecture.

Attempting to implement complex functionality will require extra code within the application that might require additional testing and might be prone to errors. Upgrading from a desktop database to an enterprise database might reduce implementation, coding, and maintenance costs over the life of the project.

What Is Important to Know

The following bullets summarize the chapter and accentuate the key concepts to memorize for the exam:

- Logical data models consist of entities and relationships.
- Entities consist of attributes that describe the entity.
- When converting from a logical data model to a physical data model, entities become tables, attributes become fields, and relationships become joins.
- Use the third normal form for most physical database designs. Third normal form is the best mix of efficiency and maintainability for a database.
- A join between two tables requires a primary key in the parent table and a foreign key in the child table.
- Many-to-many joins require a third table called a join table. The fields of a join table contain the primary key of each table being joined.
- Data warehouses should be denormalized (first or second normal form) and OLTP databases should be normalized to the third normal form.
- Joins that require a minimum number of records (two or more-to-many) requires code within the data layer or at the database level. Traditional DBMS systems do not support these joins.
- Composite keys use more than one field to create a unique key.
- Referential integrity prevents records from becoming orphans by automatically cascading updates and deletes.

OBJECTIVES

▶ Construct a conceptual design that is based on a variety of scenarios and that includes context, work-flow process, task sequence, and physical environment models.

▶ Given a conceptual design, apply the principles of modular design to derive the components and services of the logical design.

▶ Evaluate whether access to a database should be encapsulated in an object.

▶ Design the properties, methods, and events of components.

▶ Given a business scenario, indentify which solution type is appropriate. Solution types are single-tier and *n*-tier.

▶ Incorporate business rules into object design.

▶ Assess the potential impact of the logical design on performance, maintainability, extensibility, scalability, availability, and security.

CHAPTER 3

Developing the Conceptual and Logical Design for an Application

Application Models

The design issue with the largest user impact is the application model to be used. The type of application being created has the greatest impact on users because the type effectively translates to the user interface to be used. The architecture will not have the impact that the user interface will, but it will have an impact on the implementation teams that maintain and administer the system.

Application Types

Several types of Windows interfaces can be utilized within projects. As with any design, each interface type has its advantages and disadvantages when dealing with implementation. The main interface types include SDI, MDI, console, service, and Web-based.

Each application has its advantages and disadvantages, and it is important to recognize these differences and apply the correct style to fit the problem. Certain application design types have inherent limitations. For instance, a Web application can expose a significant amount of code where a console application does not have an interface for normal users.

SDI

Single document interface (SDI) applications are Windows applications that utilize only one main window for manipulating data. Figure 3.1 displays an example of an SDI application. SDI applications are typically used where window management does not make a lot of sense or multiple open documents would not benefit the user.

SDI applications are the most common form of Windows application due to the relatively simple nature of implementing this type of system. Because only one document can be open at a given time, less focus must be made on handling multiple views and synchronization.

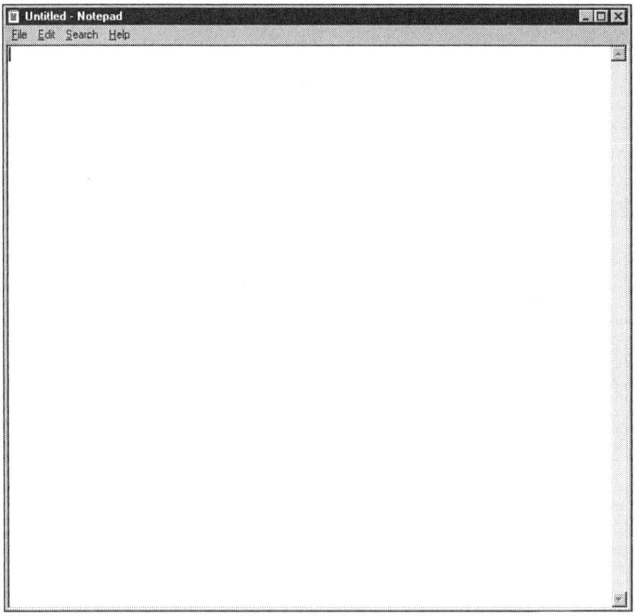

FIGURE 3.1
An SDI application.

MDI

Multiple document interface (MDI) applications allow multiple data windows to be active at a time. Microsoft Word and Excel (see Figure 3.2) demonstrate the MDI architecture by allowing the user to open and manipulate data on multiple files within an instance of the application.

Business processes are a large factor in the implementation of an MDI system Because more programming is involved in implementing this form of system, more development time must be spent focusing on synchronization, memory management, and menu navigation than with an SDI application.

MDI applications are primarily used in situations where you need to create multiple views for your data or where users are required to switch between several documents at a time. An example of this would be with a claims processor. The claims processor might have several claims open at a given time due to the nature of the business process, so it makes better sense to implement an MDI application than an SDI one.

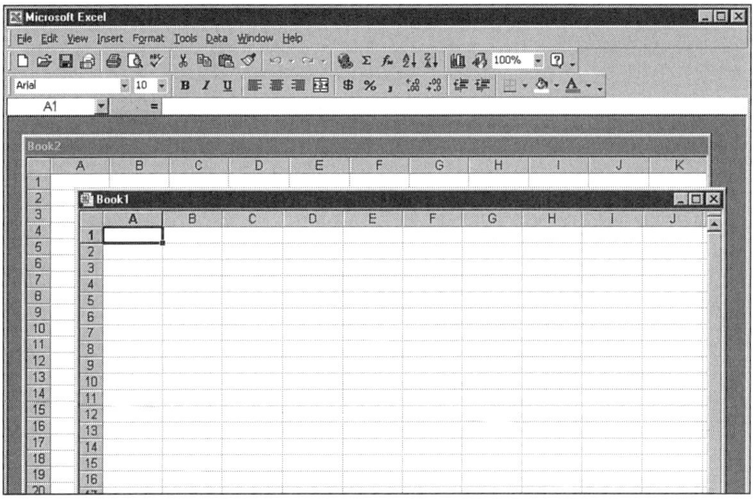

FIGURE 3.2
An example of an MDI application.

> **NOTE:** All Windows development languages from companies such as Microsoft, Inprise, and Symantec are able to implement MDI applications.

MDI applications carry additional overhead in process usage, memory usage, and development effort required. Even if a solution can fit an MDI application model, you should evaluate the application and the user base of the application. If you are dealing with basic users who are trained to perform a single action at a time, an MDI application might overwhelm them and decrease user performance and increase data inconsistencies.

Console

Console applications are applications that run at the MS-DOS command prompt and have no Windows interface. Console applications are more limited than SDI and MDI applications and are not user friendly. Console applications can be designed to expose more options for power users, and they allow for operating within scripts and batch files.

Console applications are usually created with an MDI or SDI application. The console application allows for faster execution and more flexible options for a power user. Console applications are written as supplementary applications to support a larger application. These applications are used infrequently or under such specific circumstances that an addition to the interface is not necessary or the creation of a new interface would require a lot of development work. For instance, the BCP command for SQL Server enables a user to bulk copy a text file into a database. This command is typically given infrequently and might need to be automated through a batch file.

> **NOTE** Applications such as Visual Basic, Visual FoxPro, and other rapid application development (RAD) tools do not allow for the creation of console applications. Visual C++ and other low-level C++ languages can be used to take advantage of console programming.

Console applications should be reserved for power users and administrators. There are few (if any) practical implementations of end user console applications, with the exception of legacy DOS-based interfaces (or the Windows NT command shell).

Service

A *service* is a Windows NT-specific form of application. Services are designed to run as part of the operating system by waiting in the background to intercept a service-specific call and act on it. Because the service is looking to intercept system calls, user intervention is not needed and users don't need to be logged into the Windows NT machine. An example of a service would be the Internet services (FTP, WWW, NNTP) in Internet Information Server (IIS). The service "listens" for calls and processes them accordingly.

Services are designed without a user interface. Note that IIS comes with a management console plug-in that enables an administrator to change the options of the WWW (World Wide Web) service, but the plug-in is an external application that is not part of the service.

Services only run on Windows NT, so there is a limited use for these applications. No corresponding Windows 95 or Windows 98 application acts as a service, with the possible exception of an application that runs out of the task bar. The key difference is that you cannot get a task bar application to impersonate a user (an administrator, for example), and you must log into Windows 95 or Windows 98 in order for the application to start.

> **NOTE** Services cannot be created from within Visual Basic 5.0 due to the implementation of the threading models of Visual Basic applications. Most services are written in some flavor of C++. If a given solution calls for a total Visual Basic solution, Windows NT Services should not be considered.

> **NOTE** **Service (MSDN)**—An executable object that is installed in a registry database maintained by the Service Control Manager. The executable file associated with a service can be started at boot time by a boot program or by the system, or it can be started on demand by the Service Control Manager. The two types of service are Win32 service and driver service.

Web-Based Applications

Web-based applications have gained tremendous popularity through the increasing use of the Internet and the lower cost of implementing corporate intranets. Web-based applications can be created in several ways:

- Client-side applications using Java, DHTML, ActiveX documents, and ActiveX controls
- Server side using Active Server Pages
- Server side using CGI libraries, such as PERL
- Database applications, such as Cold Fusion
- Client side using Internet-aware Windows applications

Currently, Web applications allow for a great deal of flexibility for development. Web applications are ideal for businesses that have a decentralized work force, such as a large sales organization. Implementing a complex dial-up interface along with the slower data transfer would be difficult to implement on a large scale. A Web application, on the other hand, allows the centralization of all data processing and enables faster display and response times. This type of application is easy to implement because each user can use any Internet connection to access the central system. There might be issues with Web browser capabilities, but the issues should be addressed in the planning phases, and an alternate method of access can be created.

Another key issue with implementing a Web solution is the inherent cross-platform integration available. A Web solution that does not utilize some specific technologies (ActiveX, for instance) can be used and accessed though a Macintosh system or a UNIX workstation. In a traditional application, a new application must be developed for each system that needs to have access to the central system. In this respect, Web-based solutions have by far the lowest TCO (total cost of ownership).

It is important to note that not all Web browsers are created equal. For example, Netscape Navigator cannot implement ActiveX documents, whereas Internet Explorer can (see Figure 3.3). In this situation, you might need to create an Active Server Page that allows for non-Microsoft browsers to access the system. You can also create a browser standard for the application and simply require that browser or a browser that can implement the same technology.

A key advantage of a Web application is the flexibility it gives to developers and users. Because HTML and ASP (Active Server Pages) are text, changes can be made without any recompiling or redistribution. Changes can be made in real time and can be updated on the server instantly. Web applications can take advantage of standard changes. As HTML is enhanced and ASP has new functionality added, Web applications can take advantage of the new functions and keywords seamlessly. These changes are made by large third-party vendors and do not force internal development teams to create these complex enhancements.

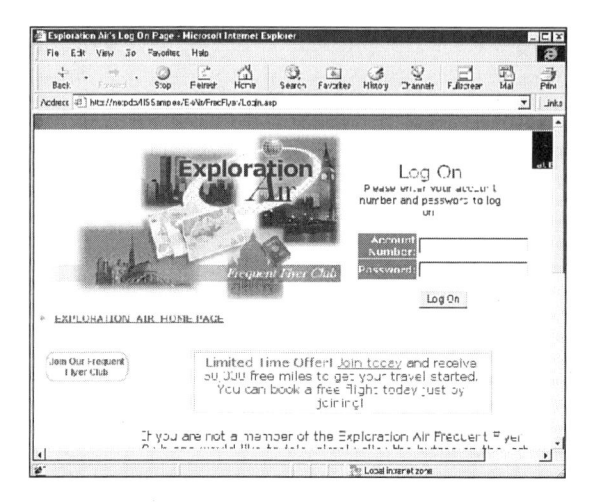

110 CHAPTER 3   Developing the Conceptual and Logical Design

FIGURE 3.3
A sample Web application.

Interface Pros and Cons

Each interface has its place. There is no application model that fits all problems. Each situation must be analyzed and the model should come from the user requirements. The pros and cons of various interface types are outlined in Table 3.1.

TABLE 3.1

THE PROS AND CONS OF VARIOUS INTERFACE TYPES

Interface Type	Pros	Cons
SDI	Easy to program	Limited flexibility when multiple files must be open at once
	Allows for a more structured user environment	Changes require a recompile and redistribution of applications

Interface Type	Pros	Cons
MDI	Allows for multiple files to be open at once	More difficult to program due to the window management functions
		Changes require a recompile and redistribution of applications
Console	Small and fast	Designed for advanced users
	No graphical overhead	
Service	Can be run with no user interaction	Very difficult to program
	Small and fast	Only runs on Windows NT
		May be dependent on security roles and network implementation
Web	Cross platform	Requires additional server to process applications
	Easy to modify and deploy	Rapidly changing standards require constant maintenance
	Increased capability as standards evolve	Exposes some source code through HTML
		Forces a greater focus on security issues

Client/Server Architecture

Client/Server is a term that describes the general design of an enterprise application. The type of client/server system developed depends on how the application handles individual services, such as user, business, and data services.

The application services (or tiers) are used to segment the main areas of the application. Traditional applications placed all the application services together. This caused applications to be larger and slower as the maintenance costs of these applications steadily increased. Recent changes in application design dictates that specific areas of the application should be separated out by area of functionality.

Segmenting the application allows the workload to be moved from the client computer onto more powerful application servers. By placing the main logic of the application on a central server, applications can be upgraded and maintained without affecting the users or possible problems with versioning.

User services describe the user interface and all graphical application design. User services do not handle the processing of any business logic or direct database access.

Business services are the "brains" of a client/server application. Business services handle all of the business-specific application logic. This portion of the application will handle items such as:

- Process flow
- Calculations for early payments or quantity discounts
- Internal financial calculations
- Data preprocessing functions

Data services handle the database access for the application. Items such as referential integrity, indexing, and transactions are handled within the data services. Data services can reside within objects like business services or can be handled internally by the database server. Occasionally, data services are implemented through an additional tier using applications, such as Microsoft Transaction Server or Microsoft Message Queue Server.

Table 3.2 provides an overview of the types of services being discussed here.

TABLE 3.2

OVERVIEW OF SERVICES

Service	Use	Specific Functions
User	Handles all the application graphical functions	Windows interface menus
Business	Processes internal business logic before being sent to the data service layer	Data validation; data processing; executing complex business functions
Data	Encapsulates database access and data integrity	Handles data integrity, relationships, and stored procedures; saves, adds, and updates transactions

Single Tier

Single-tier architecture is a client/server implementation where one machine handles all the processing and workload for the application. There is no segmentation between user services, business services, and data services. Single-tier applications typically are single-user applications, such as a small contact manager. There are some situations where a single-tier application is used as an enterprise application, but this instance is a special case that is covered in Figure 3.4.

Single Tier/File Server

Single-tier/file-server applications are primarily desktop applications where the data can reside on a local PC or be shared on a file server. The client application handles all the data processing and business logic. There is no processing being handled on the server. This model is inefficient because each workstation is processing all its data requests, and there is an increase in network traffic and a decrease in workstation performance.

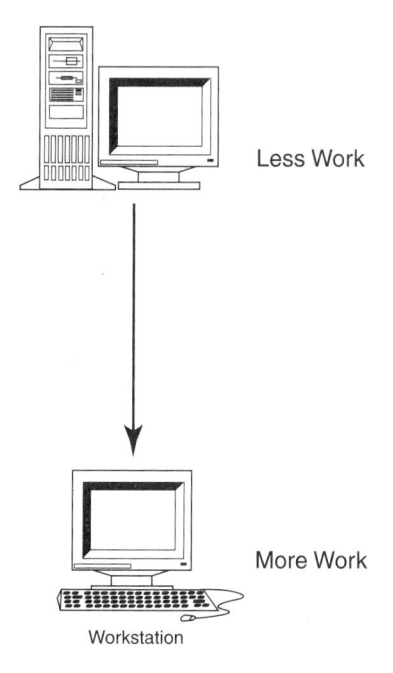

FIGURE 3.4
Single-tier system.

Single-tier systems are difficult to maintain because each PC must have the most recent application version; furthermore, distributing versions to individual machines is tricky and error prone because there is no central location that can be maintained for all users. If the data source is not shared in a multiuser environment, data must be replicated and multiple copies of the same data must be maintained.

Single-tier systems should only be used in desktop applications where one user is expected to use it. If more than one user is planned, a two-tier system (at the very least) should be implemented.

Thin Client/Terminal

Thin client/terminal applications are a special case in the enterprise. Microsoft Terminal Server gives users the ability to utilize less powerful machines to act as a Windows terminal (similar to UNIX Xwindows) and execute and process all applications on the server. Mainframe terminal applications also utilize the mainframe to process the application.

It is important to note that a terminal application is not completely a single-tier application. You can design a terminal application that accesses a true multitier application from the file server, but the implementation of the application is typically classified as a single-tier application.

Two Tier

Two-tier applications are the first step toward a client/server system. In a two-tier system, the data services are implemented though a database server, such as Microsoft SQL Server, Oracle, or DB/2. The data processing in this scenario is removed from the client application (see Figure 3.5).

More Work

Less Work

Workstation

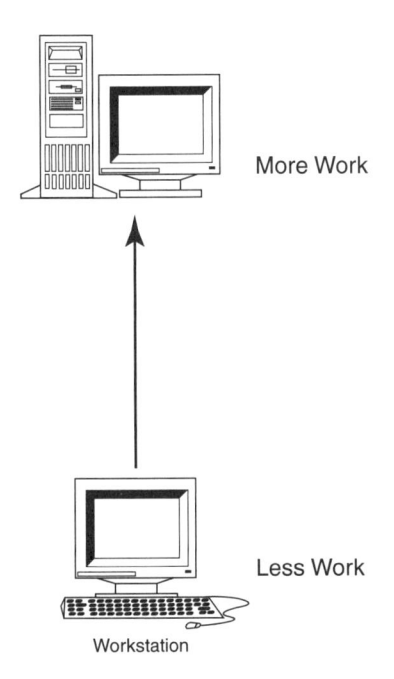

FIGURE 3.5
Two-tier application.

The major disadvantage of this type of system is the increased network traffic. Because the database server is handling all the data requests, the network might become overloaded. It is important that the current network architecture is designed to handle the increased traffic.

A second consideration when implementing a two-tier system is cost. Database servers have a higher cost than using a multiuser desktop database, such as Microsoft Access. The analysis of the business needs during the initial planning phase of development should determine what form of database should be used.

A two-tier system does not solve all the problems that true client/server systems are designed to fix. For instance, in a two-tier system, the business logic is generally in the application that is running on the client machine. If the business rules change, there is a major distribution issue that must be resolved in order for the application to function correctly. If 30 clients are running the new software and five are running the old software, there might be a major inconsistency with your data that will be hard to track. Also, the increased demands on the workstations might warrant new hardware to keep up with the demands of the application. This becomes costly in the long run for organizations without an endless budget.

The ideal situation would be to move the business logic from the individual machines and place them on a dedicated server so that the clients would not need to know about business logic changes. This is where a third tier is added.

Three Tier

Three-tier architecture is a true implementation of client/server systems. In a three-tier system, the user services, business services, and data services have been segmented into physical layers and can be distributed throughout the network (see Figure 3.6). As with two-tier systems, network traffic will be increased. Also, segmenting business objects to multiple servers will increase the demand on the servers. When planning a three-tier system, the network must be able to handle the increased workload, and the servers must be able to handle the increased demand.

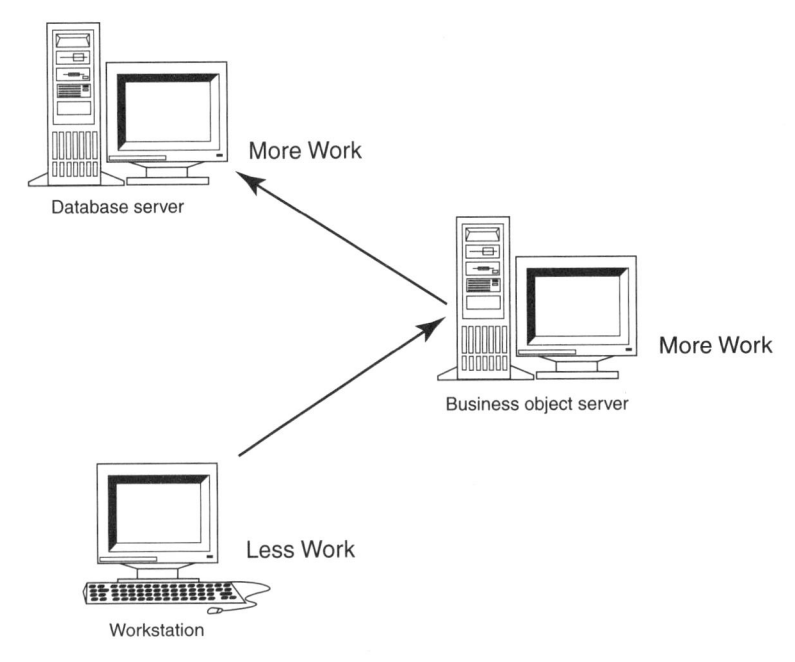

FIGURE 3.6
Three-tier application.

No easy method currently exists for distributing the workload on servers by utilizing an object broker. In the near future, Microsoft will implement some changes and introduce COM+, which will address some of the object distribution issues that hamper some enterprise client/server applications.

In a three-tier system, the workload is moved away from the desktop and distributed to the business and data layers. This allows larger and more powerful applications to run on smaller workstations. This helps to reduce the TCO of an application because the cost of technology decreases while the capabilities of the system increase (also giving a larger ROI).

n-Tier

n-tier applications are basically three-tier applications that add an additional service to aid in application processing. A message queue server or a transaction server would add the additional application layer that would call for an additional tier. Utilizing Web servers would also add an

118 CHAPTER 3 Developing the Conceptual and Logical Design

additional logical tier to the application. Figure 3.7 demonstrates the addition of a new logical tier.

New tools and technologies are being developed to assist developers in implementing items such as pool managers (MTS), messaging servers (MMQ), and transaction systems (MTS). These additional tools are reducing the amount of code that has been necessary in applications and building them into new layers of client/server development.

For instance, Microsoft Transaction Server and Microsoft Visual Basic 6.0 have been enhanced to work together to allow for built-in transaction processing in objects. In the past, there was no easy way to implement object-level transactions in systems. The capability to commit and roll back database transactions existed, but there was no easy mechanism for implementing nondatabase rollbacks. The new class enhancements to Visual Basic allow for transaction processing with as few as two lines of code, thus allowing for an almost automatic integration of a new client/server layer.

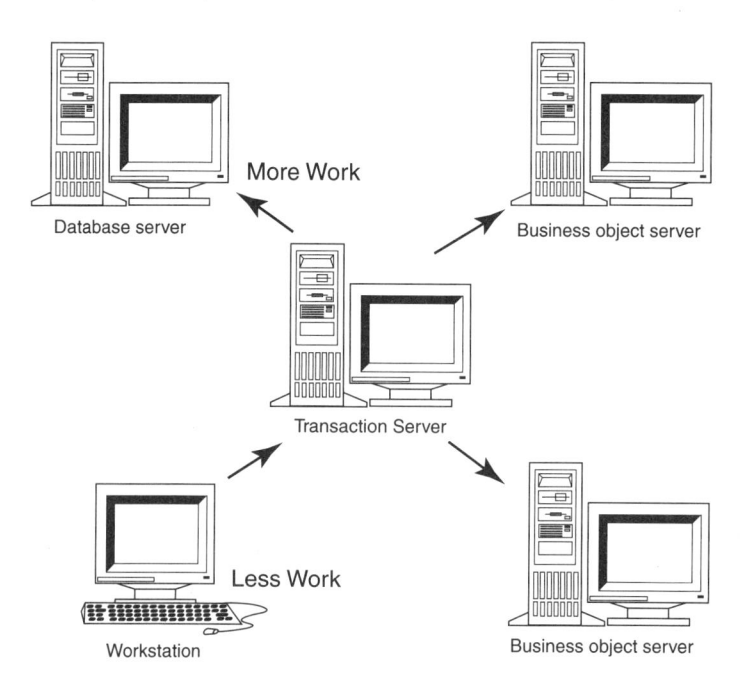

FIGURE 3.7
An *n*-tier application with an MTS layer.

n-tier applications are the most flexible and powerful systems that can be developed in the enterprise. Additional tiers allow developers to take advantage of more powerful middleware applications and application servers. Third-party systems can be leveraged to enhance existing applications with a minimal amount of coding changes.

An Introduction to COM

COM is the Microsoft Component Object Model that is used for the sharing of objects between applications. COM is the most common data-sharing format within Windows applications.

COM is a highly complex system that allows an application to create and access objects that are exposed by other applications. This enables developers to create reusable libraries of code that can be used by other developers that program in any COM-aware development environment.

The implementation of COM allows for these libraries to be updated independently of the application (with a few exceptions) because the applications make calls to generic *interfaces* that provide the information about the objects.

Within Visual Basic, VBA (which includes the Office application), and Visual C++, COM can be easily implemented to share these objects. Whenever you utilize an *n*-tier design, you must implement COM at a certain level to allow the multiple tiers to communicate. Typically, the remote instantiation uses distributed COM (or DCOM). If you do not utilize COM, you will not have access to some of Microsoft's middle-tier server applications, and you will be required to write your own application communication layers over the network.

At the present, COM has a large backing by several vendors that allow this technology to run on VMS and UNIX systems, thus increasing the use of COM-based solutions. The COM is Microsoft's fundamental object model for sharing common objects and libraries. COM encompasses several technologies, including ActiveX and OLE. Some key points about the features and functionality of COM:

- COM is platform independent.
- COM can be distributed.

COM allows both for software interoperability between third-party applications and for a common object interface so that the integration of other COM objects does not require a custom connection mechanism for each object. The COM architectures allow developers to plug in new libraries without modifying system calls or the communication layers.

COM is a complex technology about which volumes of books and whitepapers have been written. Fortunately, Microsoft has built several technologies and tools to simplify the implementation of COM. Visual Basic, VBA, and FoxPro have had the complex architecture of COM simplified through the internal class building mechanisms, and Visual C++ has had enhancements to MFC and the ATL to simplify implementing COM.

> **NOTE**
>
> **COM (from Microsoft.com)**—The Component Object Model (COM) is a software architecture that allows applications to be built from binary software components. COM is the underlying architecture that forms the foundation for higher-level software services, like those provided by OLE. OLE services span various aspects of commonly needed system functionality, including compound documents, custom controls, interapplication scripting, data transfer, and other software interactions.

Interfaces

The COM specification requires that exposed objects implement an interface.

An interface is the central connection point for all COM objects. An example of an interface would be the workbook interface of the Excel library. The workbook interface exposes all the properties, methods, and events of that particular portion of the Excel library.

The easy way to remember the interface is that it is to the right of the dot operator—for example, for Excel.Worksheet, Word.Basic, and Access.Application, the interfaces are Worksheet, Basic, and Application. These connection points are where applications access the properties, events, and methods of an object.

> **Interface (MSDN)**—A group of semantically related functions that provide access to a COM object. Each OLE interface defines a contract that allows objects to interact according to the Component Object Model (COM). Although OLE provides many interface implementations, most interfaces can also be implemented by developers designing OLE applications.

Properties

A property is a state collector of an object. State objects are typically the nouns or adjectives of an object. For instance, a car object would have color, make, and model properties to signify the current state of the object (see Figure 3.8).

Properties can be derived from the description of the object. When analyzing a problem, you will often have the object described to you. You simply need to be able to separate the correct descriptive information from the problem. Take the following example of an object described within a problem.

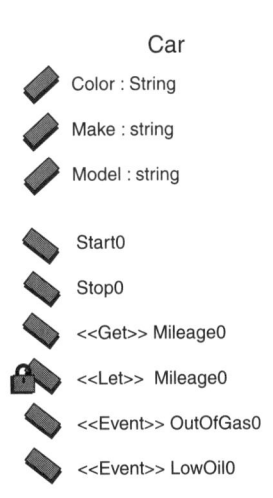

Car
- Color : String
- Make : string
- Model : string
- Start0
- Stop0
- <<Get>> Mileage0
- <<Let>> Mileage0
- <<Event>> OutOfGas0
- <<Event>> LowOil0

FIGURE 3.8
An example of an object list.

Each student takes a class that is composed of other students. The classes have an instructor, and each class is scheduled to be taught in a specific room. A class has a special identifier that is used as a short name. Each class must tie back to a specific department for funding purposes. Finally, a class has a limit on the number of students it can accept, and the person entering the registration should be notified if the class is full.

Given this description, you know the class object would look similar to the one shown in Figure 3.9 if diagrammed.

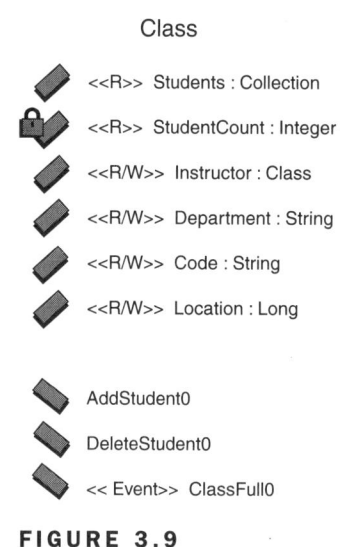

Class

- <<R>> Students : Collection
- <<R>> StudentCount : Integer
- <<R/W>> Instructor : Class
- <<R/W>> Department : String
- <<R/W>> Code : String
- <<R/W>> Location : Long

- AddStudent()
- DeleteStudent()
- << Event>> ClassFull()

FIGURE 3.9
An example of a class object.

You can see that we have some properties that are read-only (R) and read/write (R/W). An event will be raised if the class is full, and a property exists to tell you the current enrollment and size. You could add more information to the class as you see fit, but this should be a good demonstration in designing an object.

Properties can be the following types:

- Read-only
- Write-only
- Read/write

And they may be exposed in the following ways:

- Public
- Private
- Friend

Private properties may be declared as friend so that other interfaces that are within the same COM server can reference the property while keeping it private to all outside calling applications. This allows common libraries of code to access properties of other objects that appear to be private.

> **NOTE**
> **Property (MSDN)**—A named attribute of an object. Properties define object characteristics, such as size and name, or the state of an object, such as enabled or disabled.

Methods

Methods are actions of the object and are typically represented as verbs. The car object from the previous example has an onstart and onstop event along with its properties.

Methods are defined as procedures or functions within an object and, like properties, can be declared as public, private, or friend. Because methods can be functions or procedures, there may or may not be returned data, and the methods may or may not require parameters.

Methods (see Figure 3.10) are the primary interface to objects because they are the mechanism by which the object is told to "do something."

Because methods are the item that allows objects to perform user-specified actions, they are the key focal points of your objects. Properties merely store state information and rarely process any data that goes through the object (with the exception of data validation). This is why the methods of an object are so important. The methods act on the static property data to return data, call other objects, or read and write to databases.

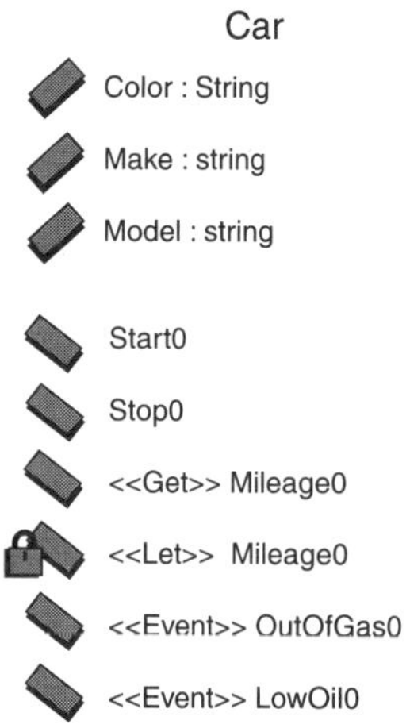

124 CHAPTER 3 Developing the Conceptual and Logical Design

Car
- Color : String
- Make : string
- Model : string
- Start0
- Stop0
- <<Get>> Mileage0
- <<Let>> Mileage0
- <<Event>> OutOfGas0
- <<Event>> LowOil0

FIGURE 3.10
An example of methods.

> **NOTE**
>
> **Method (MSDN)**—An action that an object is capable of performing. For example, list boxes have methods called AddItem, RemoveItem, and Clear, for maintaining list contents

Events

Events (see Figure 3.11) are a form of callback that allows an object to tell that application that something has happened. In the car object, there will be events for when the car runs out of gas or when the oil is low. These are items that the calling application should handle.

> **NOTE**
>
> **Event (MSDN)**—An action, recognized by an object, for which you can write code to respond. Events can be generated by a user action—such as clicking the mouse or pressing a key—by program code, or by the system, as with timers.

Car

- Color : String
- Make : string
- Model : string

- Start0
- Stop0
- <<Get>> Mileage0
- <<Let>> Mileage0
- <<Event>> OutOfGas0
- <<Event>> LowOil0

FIGURE 3.11
An example of events.

A key advantage of events is the capability to set up communication between multiple objects. Another method of implementing communication between objects is thorough callbacks. Both events and callbacks are asynchronous communications, but they are implemented and utilized in different fashions. You can look at events as an anonymous broadcast from one object to another, whereas a callback is a handshake between the objects.

In the example, the car object contains a LowOil event that fires if the oil falls below a predefined level. The event can be handled by a dashboard object that chooses to turn on a low oil light when the LowOil event is invoked by the object. This allows the dashboard object to continue normal processing without being required to continually check an OilLevel property. This also allows the car object to maintain a certain set of rules (called business rules) that allow it to handle these types of internal system checks.

When identifying the events of the object, ask yourself, "When ____ happens, I want to know about it." The identification of the specific actions that occur creates the events of your object. For instance, in an inventory application, you would know that:

- When you are low on inventory, you should be notified—an InventoryLow event would handle this.
- When a part goes on backorder, the application should be notified, and a PartBackordered event will be created.

Depending on the nature of your enterprise application, some events will be more critical than in other applications. There is no rule of thumb as far as which events are required; it all depends on how the object interacts with other objects in the system and how critical the information is. In a highly secure application, you might need to fire an event whenever someone logs on and off the system (for auditing), although this information is irrelevant on most systems.

Object Organization

Objects within an application can exist in specific layers that segment the application and allow for true client/server development. The layers that objects should be divided into are user, business, and data. These three layers make up three-tier client/server applications.

The creation of these layers and the details of these layers is covered in later sections of this chapter when the different layers of business logic are described.

User

User services are primarily the graphical front-end services of the application. User services are typically forms and not code libraries. A series of forms, dialogs, reports, and other graphical components make up user services. User services should be developed using a thin client design, thus moving most of the code out of the forms and into the specific classes. In an ideal system, the forms should be "codeless," meaning the only code in the forms would be for variable management, handling user actions, and updating any graphics routines. No code would process the data in any way; all data will be handled separately by the business and data services of the application.

> **NOTE**
>
> **User Services (MSDN)**—An abstraction used to represent the visual interface for presenting information and gathering data. User services also secure the business services needed to deliver the required business capabilities and integrate the user with the application to perform a business process.

Business

Business objects are the core components of a client/server system. Business objects contain all of the application-specific logic and validation required to properly implement a given system. Business objects contain all of the rules for a system. For example, an order in a sales system would require a valid customer, and there must be enough items in inventory before the order can be processed.

The business services layer acts on data that is received from the data services and is passed on to the user services. Business services can be considered the glue of a client/server system because all data must pass through this layer before being processed or displayed.

Business objects are typically the largest and most complex objects in an enterprise application. There often will be a detailed layer within the business services designed to handle the interdependent relationships between business objects. Great deals of design, development, and testing time must take place to properly implement the business objects.

There are several key design issues with business objects:

- Business objects should contain a minimal set of interfaces. This allows business objects to scale to other servers or integrate with transaction servers.

- Business objects should be the "brains" of the application and should process the majority of the application logic.

- Business objects act as a layer between the user objects and the data objects. This prevents the user objects from directly modifying the underlying data.

- Business objects should have specific functions. Avoid placing multiple objects into a single object. This improves speed and decreases the memory overhead of an object.

> **NOTE**
>
> **Business Object (MSDN)**—Representations of the nature and behavior of real-world concepts in terms that are meaningful to the business. For example, in an application, a customer, order, product, or invoice can be represented as a business object encapsulated for manipulation by users.

> **NOTE**
>
> **Business Rule (MSDN)**—The combination of validation edits, login verifications, database lookups, policies, and algorithmic transformations that constitute an enterprise's way of doing business. Also known as *business logic*.

Data

Data services are the back-end connections to a database that might take the form of additional classes, triggers, stored procedures, or methods within an object. The line between data services and business services might sometimes be gray; at other times, generic database classes can be created to form the distinct data layer.

The physical database is also part of the data objects because items, such as stored procedures and triggers, allow for additional data processing. Not all of the database code must be contained within the individual objects. When possible, try to leverage the power and flexibility of enterprise database servers to handle data integrity, retrieval, and querying.

The business objects and the data objects might begin to blend together sometimes. This is not entirely uncommon and is not necessarily bad design. On occasion, it is difficult to physically separate these two objects, and doing so increases maintenance costs and decreases performance.

Object Models

An *object model* is a visual representation of your objects and the relationships between those objects. Object models can be simple for small objects and code libraries, or they can be complex when used in the implementation of an enterprise client/server system.

Developing object models is a way to "draw" your application. These models enable you to show the interaction between objects, as well as sort objects by their layers (user, business, or data). The creation of an object model serves several purposes:

- Serves as a basis for the development of your application

- Enables you to spot weaknesses in the design of the system
- Creates system documentation
- Graphically displays the system so you can "see" how it is supposed to function

Object models can be developed in many ways and with many methodologies. The current methodology of choice is UML, the Unified Modeling Language. UML was designed by Grady Booch, Ivor Jacobson, and James Rumbaugh to create a modeling language that can truly represent both the objects that make up a system and the complex interactions between objects within a system. Other methodologies are used to represent object models, but UML combines the primary models (Booch, OMT, and Jacobson use cases).

Applications, such as Microsoft Visual Modeler (a scaled-down version of Rational Rose's Visual Modeler), enable developers to create complex object models. Figure 3.12 is an example of a UML model generated with Visual Modeler.

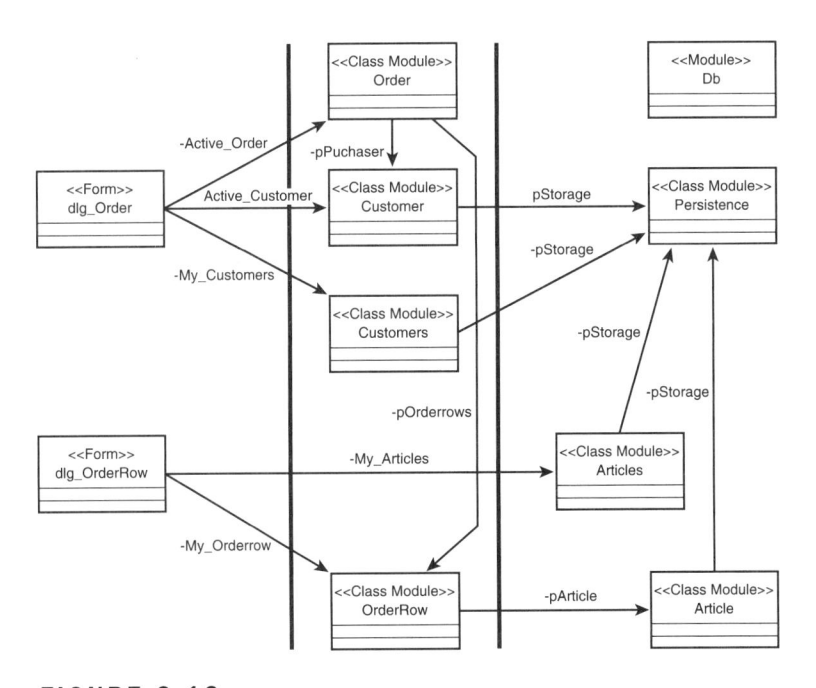

FIGURE 3.12
Visual Modeler Diagram (MSDN—The Visual Modeling of Software Architecture for the Enterprise—Grady Booch).

Modeling is a task that needs to be started and refined in the initial phases of development. As the development process moves on, the object model can be refined further or have additional objects created. When development is complete, the object model should still be a good representation of the initial object model. If the object model does not remotely resemble the original model, there were problems with the initial application design.

When creating the object model, pay close attention to the relationships of the object and the data flow between objects. The process flow within an application should be defined and documented before development begins.

> **NOTE**
>
> **Process Flow**—The interaction between objects and the logical linear path from the user services to the data services. The process flow defines how the objects must interact procedurally in an enterprise application.

ENCAPSULATING DATABASES

Many enterprise applications create an object layer that encapsulates the database into easy-to-use objects. This process helps to control developers and database access. Large applications must be efficient with data because one small error on a join can create a Cartesian product on two tables with tens of thousands of records. This would either bring down a database server or effectively slow it to a crawl. Encapsulating these data requests in an object enables you to better manage data requests and eliminate more general coding errors.

> **NOTE**
>
> **Cartesian Product**—When you join two database tables together and do not specify a link between the tables, a database combines both tables with all possible combinations of the two tables. Needless to say, this is highly inefficient and overloads the server and the network. When joining two tables together, be sure to specify a field in each table that is related.

Encapsulating the data into objects also adds extra security and decreases administration costs. If you create a single login on the SQL Server database and code that login directly into the object itself, you eliminate the need to create database logins for each user. On a large enterprise system, this reduces a great deal of administrative overhead and increases the overall total cost of ownership for the system.

The encapsulation of data brings a level of control into an organization. You can expose only the data that you would like to allow the users to see or only the queries and views that are appropriate for the users.

By not giving developers direct access to the data, you increase the data integrity, eliminate performance issues due to code bugs, and add an additional low-cost level of security to your application.

Table 3.3 compares and contrasts advantages and disadvantages of database encapsulation.

TABLE 3.3

ADVANTAGES AND DISADVANTAGES TO ENCAPSULATION OF DATABASES

Advantages	Disadvantages
Allows for tighter control over the database	Creates an additional layer of objects in the application
Defines the subset of data you want to be presented	May not be used with all controls and data access applications
Centralizes all data access to prevent coding errors	
Enhances the object-oriented design of the system and creates reusable database components	

Key Terms

- **COM (Component Object Model)**—An object-oriented model for building component-based software.
- **MDI**—multiple document interface.
- **Methods**—Functions or procedures within COM objects.
- **Object model**—A visual representation of an application's objects and interactions between those objects.
- **Properties**—Variables (or let/get/set functions) in COM objects.
- **UML (Unified Modeling Language)**—UML combines several popular OOD methods to produce a comprehensive object modeling language.
- **SDI**—single document interface.

WHAT IS IMPORTANT TO KNOW

- There are several types of software architectures: single-tier, two-tier, three-tier, and *n*-tier.

- *n*-tier systems are three-tier systems that utilize additional servers for the processing of business objects or add additional services, such as transaction processing, messaging, or other independent system services.

- There are three object layers used in client/server systems: user objects, business objects, and data objects.

- Placing business objects on centralized servers decreases maintenance costs because core business logic can be changed in one place for all users of the system.

- The key forms of application interfaces are single document interface (SDI), multiple document interface (MDI), explorer style, and Web-based interfaces.

- User objects call business objects that call data objects. The reverse should happen going back to the client. Going outside of this path defeats the purpose of using multiple tiers and complex business objects.

- Business objects and data objects should never contain any interfaces. Because these objects are probably run on separate unattended servers, an interface might halt executing while waiting for user input. All interfaces should remain in the user objects.

OBJECTIVES

- Given a solution, identify the navigation for the user interface
- Identify input validation procedures that should be integrated into the user interface
- Evaluate methods of providing online user assistance, such as status bars, ToolTips, and Help files
- Construct a prototype user interface that is based on business requirements, user interface guidelines, and the organization's standards
- Establish appropriate type of output

CHAPTER 4

Designing a User Interface and User Services

The user interface of an application is not the most critical business aspect of an application because the user interface presents only the data, right? Wrong. The business logic might be completely bug free, the technology might be top notch, and the database pristine, but if the users cannot figure out how to use the application, all of the developmental work did not solve the problem.

User Interface Basics

In order for an interface to be useful, it must have the following characteristics:

- The interface should be clean—do not clutter the screen with too many details.

- The interface should follow a style or layout that users are accustomed to. Utilize the designs of other applications, such as Microsoft Office, to build your user interface on. Not only have these types of commercial applications gone through a great deal of market testing, they are practically an interface standard.

- Navigation should be simple. Let the users decide whether they want to use the keyboard, mouse, or both.

- Help should be available when users get confused. Use several avenues for presenting help so that they can be more productive and decrease the support costs of the application.

- Users should get the appropriate feedback on what is required. Do not let users key in letters for a social security number field and don't allow numbers for a name. Let users know in a nice way what is required and refrain from abusive or demeaning error messages.

- Keep error messages clean and to a minimum. Users can understand "There was a problem printing; be sure the printer is turned on," but they have trouble with "Printer Error 33948. Unable to access device or network resource."

Using the Windows Common Control Library

Windows provides a library of common controls that provides many user interface enhancements. These controls are designed so that developers can easily adhere to the Windows interface standards with the least amount of effort.

Toolbars

Toolbars are an extension of the application's menus. A toolbar exposes a series of buttons that act as shortcuts to menu items. Each button can display text and/or graphical images that represent the operation that the button handles. An application such as Windows Explorer (see Figure 4.1) has some of the most frequently used items, as well as easy ways to change the application display properties.

Tabstrips

Tabstrips are designed to reduce the amount of data presented at one time by allowing developers to organize data into logical units that can be presented on separate pages. Each tab or page can contain almost all Windows controls. Figure 4.2 displays an example of a tabstrip on a property page.

This control helps developers reduce the physical size of a form and the inherent clutter involved with presenting too much data in one location. Tabstrips are frequently used in property pages where a single form needs to be used to present many options to users.

FIGURE 4.1
An example of a toolbar.

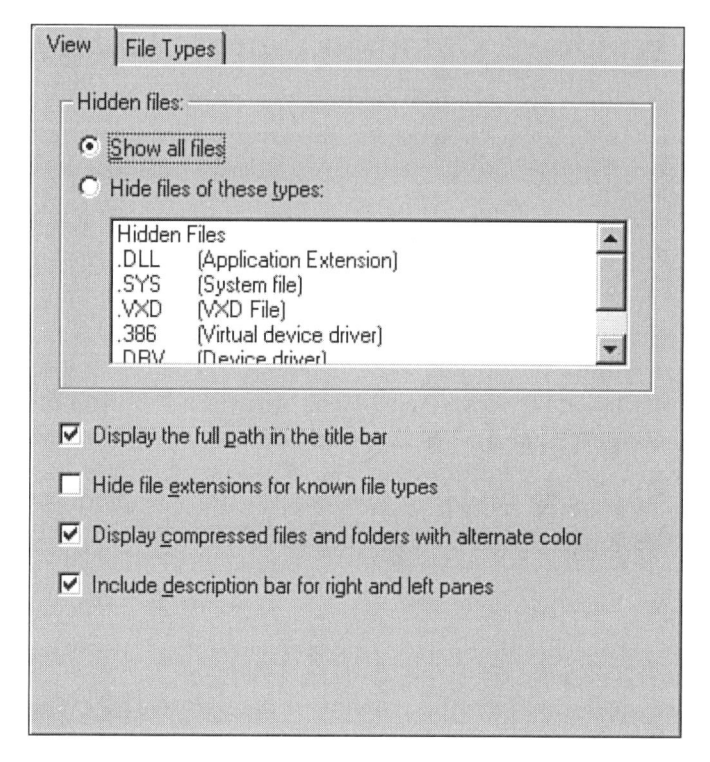

FIGURE 4.2
An example of tabstrips.

Treeview

The treeview control is a hierarchical control for representing a series of *nodes* that are related to parent items. A treeview control is ideal for displaying items such as the layout of a hard drive or other parent-child data items. Windows Explorer (see Figure 4.3) uses a treeview to display the layout of a computer's file system.

Listview

The listview control is typically paired with a treeview control to display detail information from the treeview. The listview has several display modes—large/small icons, list, and report. By using the report mode (see Figure 4.4), you can display details within individual columns on the screen. For instance, you can use the treeview to display customers and related orders while the listview window displays the line items of the order.

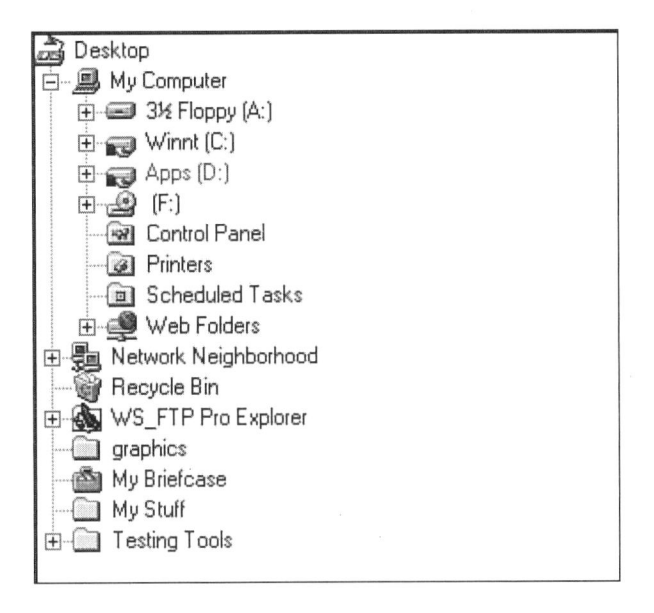

```
┌─────────────────────────────────────────┐
│ 📇 Desktop                              │
│ ⊟ 💻 My Computer                        │
│   ⊞ 💾 3½ Floppy (A:)                   │
│   ⊞ 🖴 Winnt (C:)                       │
│   ⊞ 🖴 Apps (D:)                        │
│   ⊞ 💿 (F:)                             │
│      📇 Control Panel                   │
│      🖨 Printers                        │
│      📅 Scheduled Tasks                 │
│   ⊞ 📂 Web Folders                      │
│ ⊞ 🖧 Network Neighborhood               │
│   🗑 Recycle Bin                        │
│ ⊞ 📡 WS_FTP Pro Explorer                │
│   📁 graphics                           │
│   💼 My Briefcase                       │
│   📁 My Stuff                           │
│ ⊞ 📁 Testing Tools                      │
└─────────────────────────────────────────┘
```

FIGURE 4.3
An example of a treeview.

Trackbar

A trackbar (or slider) control is used when a specific input range is required—0 to 100, low/medium/high, and so on. Windows interface guidelines recommend trackbars for this form of input over scroll bars. Scroll bars are used for navigation within a document and do not give accurate feedback on the value being set because there are no positional data indicators.

Trackbars set a definite range and can even be used in place of an array of radio buttons. The graphic in Figure 4.5 is from the virtual memory settings of Windows NT. The trackbar is setting the foreground application boost, and the options are none/medium/maximum. You could have used a series of radio buttons for the same input, but the trackbar takes up less space and represents a more familiar design for increasing data options.

140　CHAPTER 4　Designing a User Interface and User Services

Name	Type	Total Size	Free Space
3½ Floppy (A:)	3½ Inch Floppy Disk		
Winnt (C:)	Local Disk	1.95GB	748MB
Apps (D:)	Local Disk	5.89GB	2.86GB
(F:)	CD-ROM Disc		
Control Panel	System Folder		
Printers	System Folder		
Dial-Up Networking	System Folder		
Scheduled Tasks	System Folder		
Web Folders	System Folder		

FIGURE 4.4
An example of a listview.

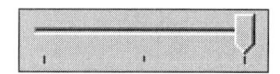

FIGURE 4.5
An example of a trackbar.

Progress bar

Progress bars (see Figure 4.6) are used to give feedback to users on time-consuming operations by relaying the status of an operation from 0% to 100%. The values of the progress bar can extend well beyond 100, but the visual representation displays as a filled region that represents the current completion percentage of the operation. You can use status bars in many instances:

- Startup forms that display an application's initialization progress
- Copy operations that might take time to complete
- Data transfer operations
- Moving through records in a database

Keeping a Clean Interface

Interface design is of primary importance when developing the user interface. Windows that are cluttered or contain too much information decrease the overall productivity of users and lead to support problems or general inefficiency.

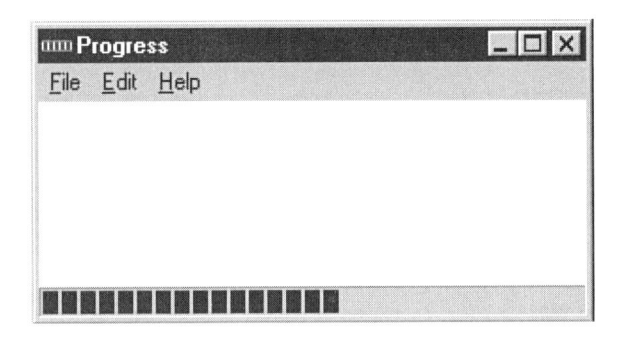

FIGURE 4.6
An example of a progress bar.

Try to limit the number of controls on a window. Use controls such as tab strips, tabbed dialogs, or wizards to unclutter windows and give the windows a better flow. Windows such as the one in Figure 4.7 can be better organized into efficient and organized applications.

You can see that Figure 4.8 is better organized and is a lot cleaner than the first form. This may be an extreme example, but some applications tend to put too much information on a single form.

Limit the numbers and types of colors a window uses. Too many colors create a confusing window and can cause eyestrain. Mismatching colors can cause eyestrain and headaches, which will lower productivity. Try to use basic grays and neutral colors because they are the current Windows standard for many applications. Limit color to areas of emphasis, such as required input fields, invalid data, or other visual cues. Keep in mind that a significant number of users are colorblind and cannot see many colors. That is one of the main reasons why developers should limit the numbers of colors used since two different colors might look to be the same color to a colorblind user. Instead of colors, use graphics as visual cues. Graphical arrows or stars beside required fields are better for all users.

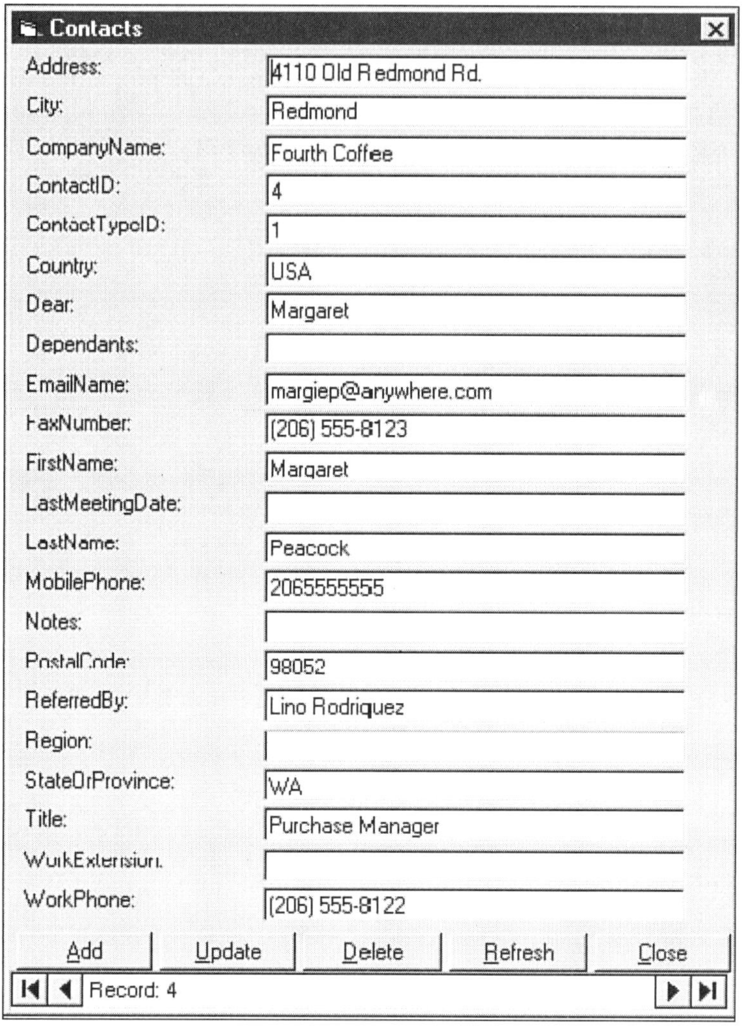

142 CHAPTER 4   Designing a User Interface and User Services

FIGURE 4.7
An example of a poor interface design.

Utilize bold or italic characters in place of colors for additional emphasis. This appeals to the majority of users and presents the data in a format the users can understand.

Avoid using controls and designs that are out of place for the users. Even though round windows look cool, they do not increase productivity and increase training costs because you are introducing the users to a new environment that they have never seen before. Keep the interface simple and follow the Windows design guidelines for maximum effectiveness.

For more information on the Windows style guidelines, refer to "Programming the Windows 95 User Interface" from the MSDN library.

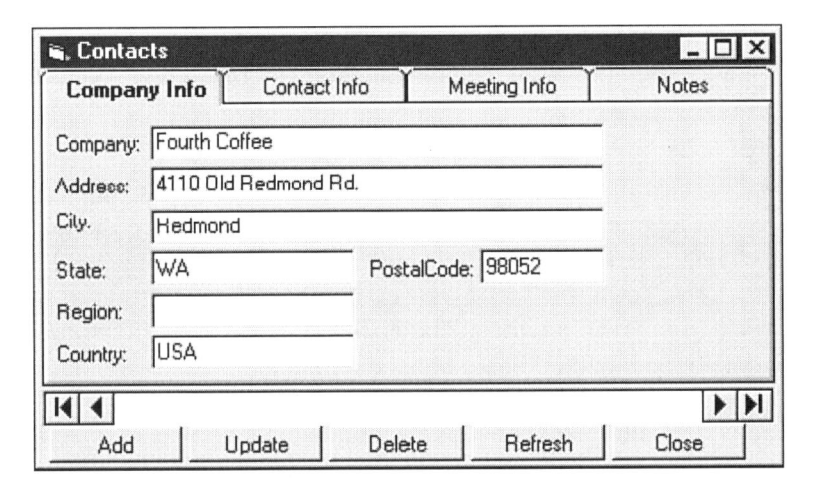

FIGURE 4.8
Cleaning up the interface.

That is not to say that you should not utilize "cool" effects if the situation warrants it. If you are creating a multimedia advertisement or promotional application, flash and style are paramount because you are looking to catch the eye of users. But, in a large enterprise environment, you want low learning curves and high productivity; both of which come with a standardized interface that does not deviate too far from the norm.

Navigation

Navigation within applications helps users to become more productive by giving them multiple ways to get to the fields and forms of the application. As the users become more experienced, they may choose to use hotkeys and accelerator keys to achieve common tasks. If you require users to click on each button and manually go to each field, they will not make effective use of the application, overall.

Accelerator keys are used to allow quick access to menu or toolbar commands. You can assign keystrokes such at Ctrl+P to print the file or Ctrl+S to save the file. This allows the user to navigate common menu items without forcing their hands to leave the keyboard. In intense data entry environments, a few seconds can translate to large amounts of unproductive time, and accelerator keys decrease this time. You can assign almost any key combinations to the menu items or toolbar buttons. The accelerator can be as simple as Ctrl+P or as complex as Ctrl+Alt+P; it all depends on how often the item is used and how well the users can remember these complex commands. Typically, accelerators that use more than two keys are reserved for functions that are not used often or are reserved for power users.

Additional navigation methods include auto-tabbing, auto-complete, and custom keystrokes. Auto-tabbing is the process of moving the user to the next field after the data has been entered. For example, after a user enters the ninth digit in the social security number, the cursor moves to the next field in the tabbing order. This enables the user to perform continual data entry on fields that are of fixed lengths: social security numbers, phone numbers, zip codes, dates, and so on. Auto-complete is where the system interprets the data the user is entering and completes the field by analyzing past entries. An example of this would be with Excel where typing the same values into columns automatically fills in like entries so that you do not need to complete the entire contents of the field before you proceed to the next field. This should be used with a bit of caution because auto-complete is not appropriate for every type of field. Finally, you can include some custom keystrokes to perform common actions. You can program the page up and page down keys to go to the next tab or previous tab in a tabbed form. This does not adhere to the Windows style guide, but it provides a valuable alternate navigation method.

Menus

Menus are a primary navigation option in any Windows application. Menus typically reside at the top of a form under the title bar, as shown in Figure 4.9.

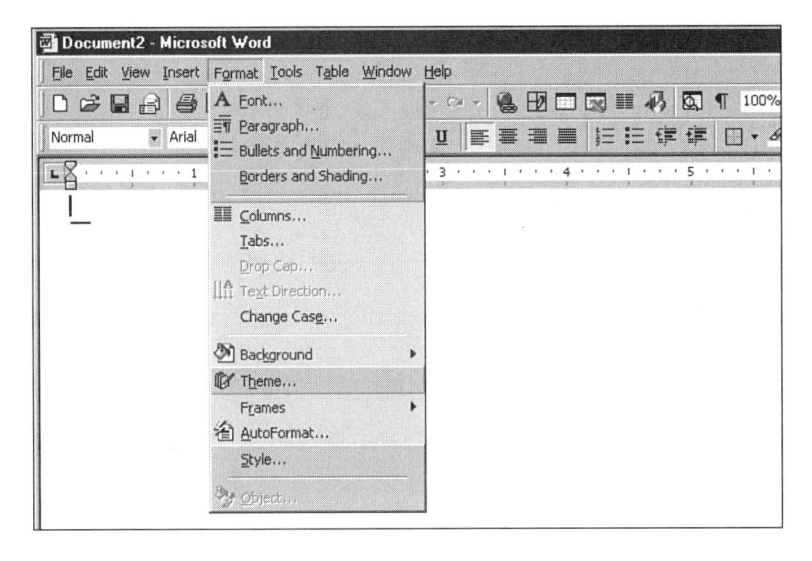

FIGURE 4.9
A sample menu from Microsoft Word.

There are several styles to adhere to when creating and using menus:

- Top-level menu items should drop down a menu.
- Menu names should represent the main categories of commands within an application.
- Menu order should follow the pattern File, Edit, View, user-defined menus, Window, Help.
- The window menu should be enabled for MDI applications only. SDI and Explorer-style applications do not benefit from the window menu options.

Menu shortcuts, such as Format, Style, can be accessed using the S key. When creating these shortcuts, the "&" character is used. The string &Style would enable the S hotkey when in the Format menu. Top-level menus, such as Format, must be accessed with the Alt key combination. This allows the fast access to the Style option to be Alt+O, S.

Shortcut keys can also be defined within menus to allow menu items to be executed outside of the menu. The File, Print command is an example of a menu item with a shortcut key (Ctrl+P). Shortcut keys should be used for frequently accessed commands that are not top-level menu items.

Menu items that are not available should be grayed out but not removed from the menu list. This lessens the confusion for users when menu choices "magically appear" in the menus. Disabled menus keep the structure intact while only allowing access to valid menu items.

You can present options to users though menus by allowing a menu choice to be checked or unchecked. Figure 4.10 displays an example of menu items that can be selected or unselected.

Checked menu items have the option of displaying an owner-drawn bitmap. This gives developers the option of displaying custom graphics for menu choices, like those in Word 2000 (see Figure 4.11).

More information about the Windows style guidelines for menus can be found in the MSDN library under Platform SDK, User Interface Services, Resources, Menus.

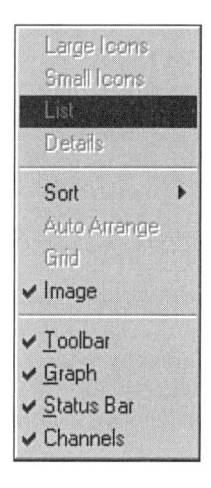

FIGURE 4.10
Checked menu items.

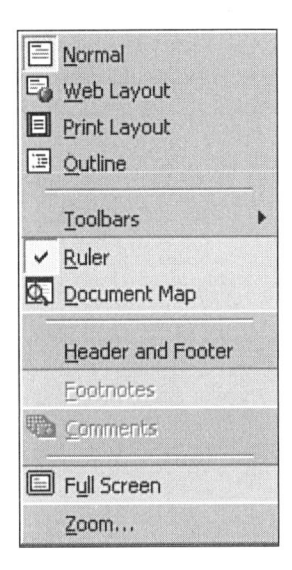

FIGURE 4.11
Checked menu items with owner-drawn bitmaps.

APPLICATION ASSISTANCE

Users need help with the applications you build. Remember it, live it, tape it to the monitor, but don't forget that the users need help. You might have a large group of power users in a group, but it takes only one user who wasn't sure, didn't understand, or couldn't figure it out to corrupt data and affect the integrity of the system.

Users are not stupid, but they are easily confused. What does that dialog mean? What am I supposed to put in this field? Employee turnover is an application killer in a corporate environment. If the user interface is very complex, then the time it takes to properly train users increases and productivity decreases. Simple methods may be employed to make applications easier to use.

Input Validation

Input validation is an easy assistance method to implement, but it takes a little extra time and effort. You might know that the part number field is formatted AAA-111A-1111, but the user might not have the alphanumeric syntax memorized. You might want to add additional code to the part number field that verifies the data when they finish data entry and

148 CHAPTER 4 Designing a User Interface and User Services

before you attempt to write the data to the database. This eliminates a possible data error or corrupt data. The form shown in Figure 4.12 gives an example of how the data can be verified and validated before the user can continue:

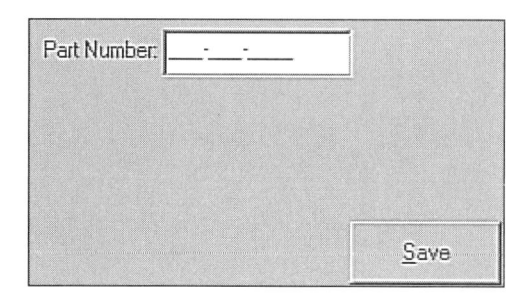

FIGURE 4.12
Formatting user input.

This input box displays to the user that this is the format for the part number. You can even set properties that tell the control what can go into the specific positions. In this example, Visual Basic was used with the masked edit control with a setting of ???-##?-####, which beeps back to the user if they try to enter numeric data in the character fields or vice versa. This is only one method of input validation, but it is effective because the user cannot enter incorrect data, and the form cannot transmit an incorrectly formatted part number. No errors occurred, and the user never had to take their hands off the keyboard. You can use additional items, such as status bars, to give additional information about the fields that you are in, but that comes later.

You can also validate data when you attempt to send a record to the database server. The valid range of data for one field is sometimes dependent on the data in another field. It is counterproductive to tell the user during data entry that they must go back and change the data now. You want the users to be able to go through the forms without changing fields several times. When you are saving the data, run a series of validation logic against the form, and inform the user at that point that they must fix the data in fields x, y, and z before they can save the record. For instance, the entry form shown in Figure 4.13 requires that parts in the 07 classification must have a reorder number of 1000 units or higher before you can save.

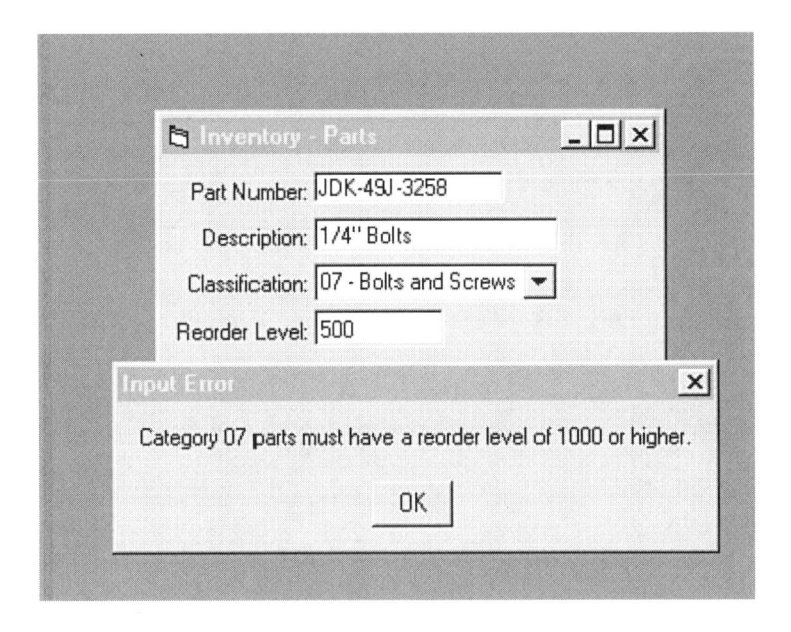

FIGURE 4.13
An entry form.

At this point, you can have the application put the user back into the reorder level field to correct the mistake. If the reorder field tried to validate the data prior to exiting, the user might have to continually navigate message boxes, increasing the time it takes to enter the data.

Generally, you trap at the field level when you need to verify that datatypes are correct. The easiest way to validate the data is to limit the data that the field will accept by discarding incorrect characters and beeping back to the user. Audio clues to data validation do not slow the users down, and they do not have to stop working to remove message boxes.

Trapping at the form level is used when there are interdependencies on the fields. If the value of X depends on Y, you would trap at the form level and inform the user when they try to move out of the form. Form-level validation is noninvasive and does not hamper data entry.

Visual Cues

Visual cues to users include adding graphics and colors to point out key fields, problems, or required information.

> **NOTE**
>
> Colors are commonly used to represent fields that are disabled, read-only, or required. There is a significant population that is colorblind and cannot see these visual cues. Keep in mind that you might need additional cues for users with special needs.

You can see an example of visual cues in Figure 4.14 (required fields are yellow).

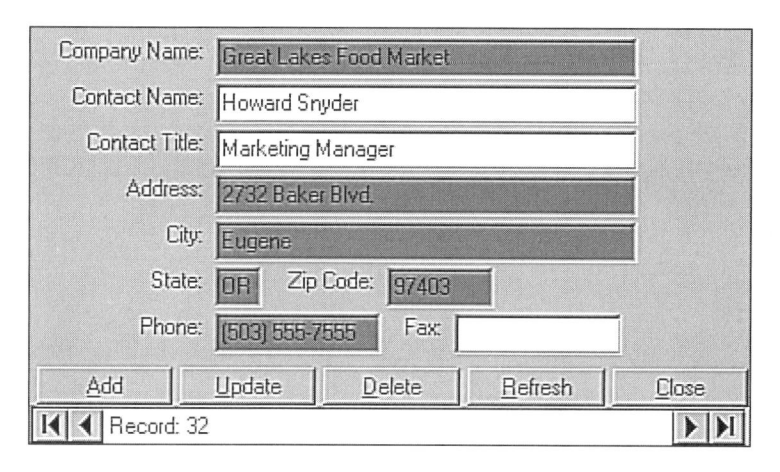

FIGURE 4.14
A typical data entry form with color-coded fields.

The visual cue given in Figure 4.11 tells us that the company name, address, and phone number are required fields, but the other fields are optional. If you want to program a form for people who are color impaired, another option would be to bold the text of the fields that are required (see Figure 4.15). Remember that someone who is colorblind sees what's shown in Figure 4.14.

Adding bold to the fonts helps the color impaired users to see what fields are required (see Figure 4.16).

Application Assistance   151

FIGURE 4.15
A normal form as seen though color-impaired eyes.

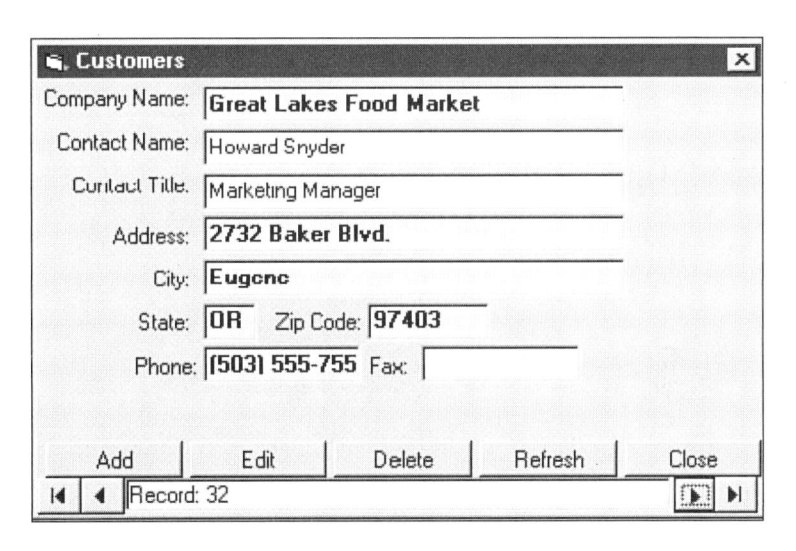

FIGURE 4.16
Adding visual cues for color-impaired users.

Formatting Input

You have already seen an example of formatting input with the data validation. Formatting can also be used to enable users to enter raw data and let the system handle the specifics of punctuation and symbols. A common example of this is with the formatting of phone numbers.

Users can easily enter 7045551212 and let the system format the number to (704) 555-1212. It takes a significant amount of time to have the user key in the special formatting and leads to data errors. The formatting is used to present the data, but the raw data goes to the database. This avoids having entries such as 7045551212, 704-555-1212, (704)5551212, and so on, in the database. This makes queries nearly impossible because you are required to check each possible combination of symbols and characters.

Storing raw data and formatting within the user interface gives you the ability to format the data according to localization issues or special circumstances. Data formatting affords you an extra level of application flexibility and increases your ability to effectively search database records for data.

USER FEEDBACK

User feedback can take the form of effective interface design rather than intrusive dialog boxes. Giving the user real-time feedback eliminates some of the need to search through help files or wait for the application to complain to the user. Windows comes with several standard interface options that enable developers to present this type of information to users.

Status Bars

Status bars are used to display several items of data to the user and are typically located on the bottom of the screen (see Figure 4.17). Microsoft Word displays information to the user such as the insert key mode, document size and current location along with other information.

You can use the multiple panes to display a large amount of status information. One of the common uses for a pane is for control assistance. When the user enters the address field, the status bay can have a message that says, "Enter the shipping address," so that the user can quickly see what the control is looking for. This provides some interactive help without moving the mouse to generate a ToolTip or launching the What's This help.

The status bar is a Windows common control and is guaranteed to be on any Windows machine. There are practically no disadvantages to using the status bar if only for general information, such as the date, time, and keyboard state. All of these items can be set without any coding at all.

FIGURE 4.17
An example of a status bar.

ToolTips

ToolTips are pop-up boxes that appear over controls when the mouse pointer is hovered over the controls (see Figure 4.18). ToolTips can be used to tell the user what the field needs, what a toolbutton's function is, or what the full data in a field is.

ToolTips carry little if any application overhead and can be used liberally throughout the application. ToolTips enable users to get help when they need it because the ToolTip is out of the way unless the mouse hovers over a control.

What's This Help

What's This help is a link between a ToolTip and full online help (see Figure 4.19). What's This enables users to take a mouse pointer and select a specific control to get more information on it.

What's This help can be used in conjunction with the full online help to give users key information about a component without forcing the users to search though help files to find basic information.

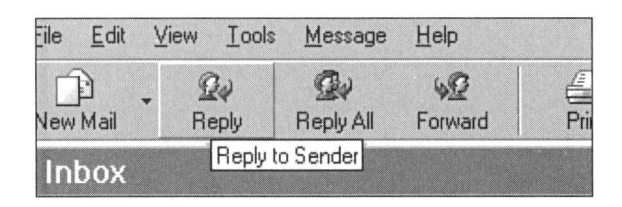

FIGURE 4.18
An example of a ToolTip.

> **Bold (Formatting toolbar)**
>
> Makes selected text and numbers **bold.** If the selection is already bold, clicking [B] removes bold formatting.

FIGURE 4.19
An example of a What's This help topic.

Wizards

Wizards are software components that step users though a complex process, such as setting up a preformatted Word document or creating a basic insurance claim. Wizards are handy for breaking down complex forms or forms that have logic that is based on input for other fields. The wizard enables you to validate data and make the appropriate changes during later stages before the user completes the process.

You can use these wizards as an option for new users. Experienced users might find a wizard to be a hindrance to performance, but new users welcome the step-by-step process (see Figure 4.20) until they become familiar with the environment. Wizards can also be used to control the application logic of a process since Windows applications can be complex and difficult to control from a control flow perspective.

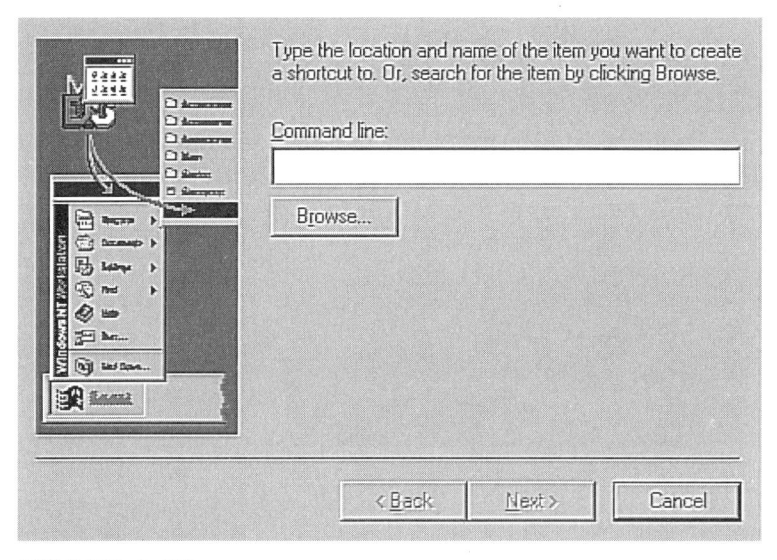

FIGURE 4.20
An example of a Wizard screen.

HELP FILES

Help files enable developers to provide a wealth of information about application topics, including usage guides, supplemental training material, or troubleshooting and technical support tips. It is impossible to provide this type of information while the user is running the application. So, ToolTips and What's This help are of minimal use when describing complex topics or operations. Microsoft provides two types of help interfaces, winhelp (standard help) and HTML help.

Standard

Standard help files are complex documents that use special formatting to generate a .hlp file. Standard help files cannot present complex data because the format was created before multimedia become popular for users and inexpensive to create.

Standard help files have the capability to link specific help ID numbers to specific forms and controls within an application. When you press F1 (the standard help hotkey), the application tells the helpfile to go directly to the topic in question or the table of contents if no topic exists.

Microsoft has stopped using standard Winhelp recently and has moved toward the new HTML help system.

HTML Help

HTML help is the next logical step in application help files because the Internet has become so popular and HTML has quickly become the standard cross platform presentation language.

HTML help is built with standard HTML files. Because HTML is used, advanced items such as dynamic HTML, full multimedia, Java, ActiveX, and the scripting languages can be utilized for more robust information delivery. HTML help provides a more flexible and graphically pleasing system than the previous Winhelp.

You can use either form of help engine in your application, but most developers are moving to the HTML help for ease of development and the capability to take the help files and generate a support Web site without duplicating the source of the help files.

ERRORS

Errors are the ugly side of applications. Error messages mean something went wrong, and when something goes wrong, developers need to know what, where, and how in order to fix them.

Presenting Errors

One of the biggest complaints about error messages from users is, "I don't understand what they mean." Developers can understand them just fine, but:

- You wrote the application so the error should make sense.
- You are not a user.

Because you are not a user, you might have some trouble seeing the application from their point of view. Imagine when you go to the mechanic for repairs, and you leave feeling confused because you don't understand a word of what your mechanic said. That is how your users feel. How can you alleviate some of the confusion and frustration when something goes wrong?

1. Create easy-to-understand error messages. Do not use vague numbers for errors; use English phrases rather than obscure programming terms. The error in Figure 4.21 is much easier for them to understand and much less intimidating than the one in Figure 4.22:

```
Could not write to the database, please try again.
                    [ OK ]
```

FIGURE 4.21
An easy-to-understand error dialog box.

Errors 157

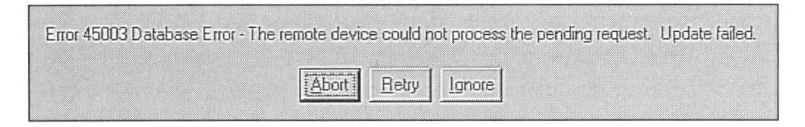

> Error 45003 Database Error - The remote device could not process the pending request. Update failed.
>
> [Abort] [Retry] [Ignore]

FIGURE 4.22
An error dialog box that is useful for developers but confusing to users.

2. Do not present messages to users that are confrontational or demeaning. Error messages such as the one in Figure 4.23 is a bit intimidating and confrontational. Try to tone down error messages so that you do not seem to be scolding the user or pointing out the fact that they do not know how to use the application.

> You cannot enter alpha data in a numeric field. Try again.
>
> [OK]

FIGURE 4.23
A confrontational error message.

3. A subtle message example is in Figure 4.24.

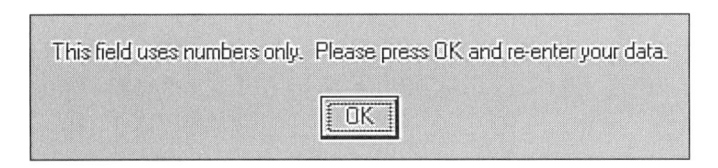

> This field uses numbers only. Please press OK and re-enter your data.
>
> [OK]

FIGURE 4.24
A nonconfrontational error message.

4. This is a bit less confrontational and easier for the user to handle. Always ask the user to do something; don't tell them to do it. This makes them feel in charge of the machine, rather than the machine appearing to be in charge of them.

5. Write information to files or database servers. Users do not care what the error number is, will not remember the error number, and will not remember how they received the error. Use special error handling and custom error objects to trap and log as much information to text files on the user's machine. This enables you to present friendly information to the user while providing development and technical support from a detailed log of what had occurred. Do not rely on the user to do the debugging.

6. Use better error handling. Users only see errors when there are problems. Try to update the application with bug fixes so that users will see fewer problems, and support will receive fewer calls. Nobody was ever burned at the stake for fixing bugs in an application. The fewer OK buttons a user needs to press, the more productive they will be.

Do's and Don'ts of Error Handling

Error handling is an important aspect of the user interface because both users and management view the effectiveness of an application by its perceived stableness. If you had a well-written application that had a nearly 100 percent uptime but informed users of every error that was trapped, then your application would look like its downtime is much higher. In a perfect world, the only errors you should show your users are errors the application is saying to them, "I don't know what this is; tell me what to try next."

The first tip is to trap errors appropriately. During testing, find the most common errors and plan for them. If the testers find an error, you can make it a sure bet that the users will find the same error, only much sooner than in testing. If you can trap it and anticipate it, try to find a way to make the application "smarter" by building specific error handling. General error handling should always be used within the application so that the user does not see every error that occurs. As most developers know, many errors can be ignored because they might be informative, or they do not directly affect the processing of the application. Good error handling traps these and never lets them get to the user.

Do:

- Write consistent error-handling routines.
- Give the user an English explanation of the problem.
- Handle errors gracefully. Abruptly exiting the application is far from graceful, as is forcing a reboot. Make the users' lives easier, not harder.
- Log all errors with details into a file for support or development to review later.
- Trap for errors in modules that you are calling. There is no guarantee that the object had adequate error handling, so be prepared.

Don't:

- Crash.
- Give the users obscure error numbers or memory addresses. They *will* forget.
- Let errors get to the users because "they should know what to do."
- Build so much error trapping that you lose sight of the purpose of the application. Remember the law of diminishing returns.

PROTOTYPING

Prototyping is where the development team puts together the user interface shell without any business logic or processing. This process enables developers and users to define the user interface without relying on the business logic or any code to be complete.

Prototyping allows for proof of concept applications where developers can demonstrate the ability to implement a new function or interface paradigm. Some projects use applications such as Visual Basic for prototyping the forms because it is so fast to create a user interface in Visual Basic that some first iteration prototypes can be completed in a matter of days, even for large enterprise applications.

Prototyping also allows for rapid buyoff from the users on how the general interface should look. As the development process moves forward, the interface changes according to business logic, specifications, or general interface cleanup, but the users will at least have a part in the general interface design.

Prototyping is a good practice because a general interface design gives developers another perspective on the application that they might not have just by looking at the code alone. A user interface lets them link the code with the interface and expose some of the inner workings between the business layers and the presentation layers.

KEY TERMS

- **accelerator key**—a key mapping that enables a user to send focus to a control or execute a command. Ctrl+P to print or Alt+S to save are accelerator keys.

- **HTML help**—a new Microsoft help system that uses HTML files to present interactive help systems.

- **prototyping**—the processes of designing a user interface shell with no code behind the application. Prototyping is used to display an interface concept before building the application.

- **Windows common controls**—a series of controls that are exposed by the Windows operating system that developers can use to present their application in a consistent and familiar format to users.

- **winhelp**—Microsoft's old help system. Winhelp was limited with multimedia support and functionality.

What Is Important to Know

- Implement the common Windows controls whenever possible to maintain a consistent interface design.

- When designing error routines, present the user with meaningful and informative messages. Try to avoid using complex error codes and messages. Utilize logging for detailed error information.

- Handle as many errors as possible within an application, but add routines that log information about untrapped errors.

- Microsoft's old help standard was the winhelp system, but that has been replaced with the HTMLhelp system. HTMLhelp can use regular HTML and DHTML to present interactive and full multimedia help files.

OBJECTIVES

- Identify technology standards such as EDI and POSIX
- Choose a data storage architecture
- Test the feasibility of a proposed technical architecture
- Develop an appropriate deployment strategy

CHAPTER 5

Defining the Technical Architecture for a Solution

The architecture design is a combination of the interface design and the tier-level design of the application. You may design a MDI (Multiple Document Interface) application using a three-tier design, and you may develop a single-tier Explorer application. Each type of application has unique requirements that help dictate the proper architecture design that is necessary.

Both the interface design and tier architecture have been discussed in detail in previous chapters (see Chapter 3, "Developing the Conceptual and Logical Design").

IDENTIFYING APPROPRIATE TECHNOLOGIES

In the course of application design, you might be required to implement certain technologies that are unfamiliar to you. Two of these technologies are POSIX and EDI.

Electronic data interchange (EDI) is used to transfer data between systems using a standard format structure. EDI is more of a concept than a concrete item. There is no "correct" way to implement EDI. EDI is common when migrating old data from legacy systems to new systems. EDI maps data from one system to another using this common format. EDI can also be used to package data from one system and to send it to a second system for processing. A financial application might package a series of transactions into a file and transmit them to a server at a financial institution for processing. This is another form of EDI.

Many systems on the market automate the EDI process, but there are times when the data might be in a proprietary format that the EDI system cannot access. If this is the case, you might be required to develop a custom EDI solution.

Portable operating system interface for UNIX (POSIX) is a set of application interface standards that provides a common set of interfaces to an operating system. POSIX-compliant applications can run cross-platform, provided that they strictly adhere to the POSIX standards. POSIX is a government requirement for approved operating systems. You can be sure that a POSIX application written under UNIX will run under Windows NT.

POSIX compliance exists at many levels. Windows NT is POSIX.1 compliant and passes government approval for POSIX compatibility. Table 5.1 outlines the POSIX standards.

TABLE 5.1
POSIX STANDARDS

	ISO Standard?	*Description*
POSIX.0	No	A guide to POSIX Open Systems Environment. This is not a standard in the same sense as POSIX.1 or POSIX.2. It is more of an introduction and overview of the other standards.
POSIX.1	Yes	Systems application programming interface (API) (C language).
POSIX.2	No	Shell and tools (IEEE-approved standard).
POSIX.3	No	Testing and verification.
POSIX.4	No	Real-time and threads.
POSIX.5	Yes	ADA language bindings to POSIX.1.
POSIX.6	No	System security.
POSIX.7	No	System administration.
POSIX.8	No	Networking
		A. Transparent file access
		B. Protocol-independent network interface
		C. Remote Procedure Calls (RPC)
		D. Open system interconnect protocol-dependent application interfaces
POSIX.9	Yes	FORTRAN language bindings to POSIX.1.
POSIX.10	No	Super-computing Application Environment Profile (AEP).
POSIX.11	No	Transaction Processing AEP.
POSIX.12	No	Graphical user interface.

DATA STORAGE AND DESIGN

Defining the needs of the database requires analysis of the technical and architectural aspects of the database systems. Issues such as transactions, storage, and scalability should be fully considered before making a final decision on the database system to be used.

Architecture

Many items need to be accounted for when defining the data architecture for a given solution:

- Volume and size of the data
- Number of transactions per minute
- Number of connections
- Number of users

One of the most important questions that needs to be addressed is the database size. Most databases have an internal storage limit. For instance, Access databases start to become unstable after 1GB and fail at 2GB. SQL Server, on the other hand, can store terabyte-size databases. This eliminates the idea of using Microsoft Access as a provider of GPS data and clarifies why SQL Server would be overkill for a single-user contact manager.

Even though a database might be small, it might have severe transaction requirements. An Internet application that uses a small database to temporarily store user information and order details might need to support hundreds or even thousands of transactions per minute. Although the size of the database is small, the demands are not. Analyze the capabilities of the database to be sure that it can support the maximum number of transactions you expect it to process.

Users and connections are the next big hurdles. The addition of Microsoft Transaction Server and the new capabilities of ODBC and OLE DB help to decrease the need for strict planning of users and connections. ODBC now supports connection pooling. Connection pooling keeps a database connection open for a specified period of time after a client has made a call to close a connection. It is feasible to use 100 connections in a minute while only actively using 30 database connections. If a connection is in the pool when a client requests a new connection, the ODBC manager will hand back to the client a connection that has not yet been closed. Users, on the other hand, can be a bigger problem. Databases have a limit on the number of users that can be in a system at a given time; the biggest issue, thought, is licensing. How many users can you afford to have in the system at a given time? Some systems use a per-user licensing fee that can push a given solution to the back for cost reasons.

Performance Considerations

When developing an enterprise application, you need to take into account performance on database servers, middle-tier servers, and the network infrastructure. A balance must be met in order to avoid having your database server come to a halt during peak hours and slowing the network to a crawl as well.

A key to balancing performance would be to utilize both stored procedures and views whenever possible. Views are queries that are compiled within SQL Server. The data is not stored, but the execution path of the query is stored and optimized. If you utilize common queries, a view increases server performance because it does not have to calculate the execution path for every SQL statement. This saves a great deal of time for every execution and decreases the demands on the server.

Stored procedures also decrease server demands because complex updates, transactions, and calculations can also be compiled into SQL Server, thus decreasing the need for SQL Server to preprocess the complex logic each time it is executed. Stored procedures typically return smaller result sets, include complex calculations, or update tables without forcing the application to directly open the table and transfer the data to the client.

Decreasing network traffic through good application design and utilizing the enterprise tools of SQL Server avoid major slowdowns due to excessive network traffic. Business objects that attempt to transfer thousands of records on each call will quickly overload a network segment and possibly crash and timeout applications and objects. In order to avoid possible bandwidth problems, take the following steps:

- Preprocess data on SQL Server to return smaller result sets.
- Limit the number of records you return in a single call. A result set that returns a thousand records is of little use to the user because most users cannot attempt to process that much data. Limiting returns to fifty records keeps the result set manageable.
- Do not allow users to create their own queries. Allow for some slight modification of existing queries, but a join in the wrong place can bring a database server to its knees (try a self join on a million-record table).

- Utilize static and persistent recordsets for data that does not change often (location codes, shipping zones, zip codes, and so on). Storing these values in memory reduces the need to query the database server and transfer a recordset on each lookup.

Allow middle-tier servers to process complex row-by-row calculations on small recordsets. Do not let the database server process every calculation, or you will not be able to keep the server running. You need to find a middle ground between underutilizing a database server and forcing it to do too much. You might be forced to run speed tests to see where the most efficient layer is. Middle-tier servers can be powerful machines, so use them accordingly.

Reporting

Reporting is an area of application development that is often overlooked due to the lack of proper planning or selection of reporting tools. Most databases are limited in reporting capabilities with the exception of tools such as Microsoft Access and Microsoft FoxPro. SQL Server has no built-in reporting other than the text output of a view or a stored procedure. A third-party application, such as Crystal Reports, will often be used. Be sure that the reporting package that you select can access the data you need to report. Many packages come in different flavors, depending on the database server you choose. Take this into consideration because an enterprise reporting package can cost up to ten times that of a desktop reporting package.

FEASIBILITY TESTING

Feasibility testing is the "Can we do this?" stage of development. Here you put all the design documents together and determine whether the project can move forward. Some typical questions that need to be answered in this phase would be:

- Can we do this with our existing resources?
- Does this fit our needs and solve our problems?
- Can we do this within a reasonable timeline?
- Will the current technology support the solution?

Meeting the Business Requirements

After reviewing the business cases and analyzing the problems, you need to determine which solution will be the most appropriate. You should use one of the following interface designs:

- Single-document interface (SDI)
- Multiple-document interface (MDI)
- Explorer style
- Web interfaces

You also need to determine what architecture you plan on using:

- Single-tier/file server
- Two-tier
- Three-tier
- *n*-tier using additional application servers and technologies

Determining the answers to these requirements will help you avoid costly design changes later. The feasibility testing phase should answer the question of whether a given implementation makes the most sense for the solution.

Meeting the Use Cases

Use cases are simply the business processes that were documented in earlier planning stages. Use cases are high-level application design specifications that must be met in order for the solution to produce the expected results. Review Chapter 1, "Analyzing Business Requirements," for more information on developing the business processes and use cases.

Falling Short of the Solution

There will be times during the development of enterprise applications when you will fall a bit short of the total solution. Budget cuts, changing requirements, and organizational issues might cause a solution to fall short of its intended mark.

Proper planning should include some scenarios in which a project falls behind schedule or a lack of resources hampers development efforts. You should have a series of contingency plans that can anticipate some possible changes in development that might affect the outcome of the planned solution.

The contingency plans should include some questions that address some possible roadblocks:

- What if the budget for new servers is not approved? Can we utilize other hardware resources?
- What if we find a limitation of the database server that will keep us from implementing the database? Can we use another vendor?
- Have we planned the milestones such that a shortfall in resources or funding will not keep us from delivering a working (albeit limited) version of the software?
- Can we replace staff in the event of a staffing issue? Is the product knowledge shared across the team, or is every member indispensable?

Considering these what-if scenarios exposes possible problems that could derail development efforts. If the budget falls short, could you deliver *something*? Planning on the front end eliminates some potentially deadly problems on the back end.

Analyze each key component of the application and list the potential impact of a problem with that specific component. Are there key components that can end a project if they do not work as planned? Are components so dependant on the inner workings of other computers that maintainability and extensibility are nonexistent?

DEPLOYMENT

Your deployment strategy should focus on several key factors: location, user base, and application design. Each of these factors affects how an application can be deployed initially and upgraded over time.

The largest deployment factor is location. If you have a large number of remote sites that connect through limited bandwidth, you might not be able to deploy the application from a central location. Your strategy might need to focus on deploying the installation and setup files to a server in each site office and deploying locally to the office. On the other hand, you might have a large amount of bandwidth available so that you can deploy from a central location without any problems or fear of running out of bandwidth for other applications and users.

The second major factor is the user base. An application that is being pushed to 50 users has a different focus and approach than an application that needs to be pushed to 10,000 desktops. When dealing with a large customer base, you might need to look at solutions such as SMS Server for application deployment. A small deployment can be done on a user-by-user basis or though a series of notifications via email.

Finally, after the application is in place, you need to change your focus to maintenance releases and upgrades. If you use middle-tier servers, you need to be able to deploy your system changes to all middle tiers. Failure to deploy properly can render servers unsynchronized and can yield different results for different users. Applications such as SMS decrease the burden of synchronization. Changes to the client applications might have to be pushed in full like the initial deployment, or you might need to upgrade individual components.

These are all the areas of focus for deployment. There are many ways to solve these problems. You can use SMS to push files to workstations and servers, you can use custom login scripts to verify application components, you can write a custom upgrade utility, or you can use one of many third-party tools to create setup files and deployment applications.

What Is Important to Know

The following bullets summarize the chapter and accentuate the key concepts to memorize for the exam:

- EDI allows for the transfer of data between independent and architecturally different systems.
- POSIX allows applications that implement only base UNIX functionality to run under Windows NT.
- When deploying solutions, be sure to identify key application components and any problems that might arise with distributing individual updates. Create a plan to push upgraded files to servers, local users, and remote users.
- Have plans in place for potential pitfalls such as budget shortfalls, staffing problems, and major market changes.
- Systems Management Server (SMS) can decrease the amount of time and effort involved with maintaining application and component versions in enterprise applications.
- The key data architecture considerations are architecture, performance, and reporting.
- Identify and estimate items such as the number of concurrent and total users, transactions per minute, and overall size of the data when planning the data architecture.

OBJECTIVES

Think of this as your personal study diary. Your documentation of how you beat this exam.

The following section of Objective Review Notes is provided so you can personalize this book to maximum effect. This is your workbook, study sheet, notes section, whatever you want to call it. YOU will ultimately decide exactly what information you'll need, but there's no reason this information should be written down somewhere else. As the author has learned from his teaching experiences, there's absolutely no substitute for taking copious notes and using them *throughout* the study process.

There's a separate section—two to a page—for each subobjective covered in the book. Each subobjective section falls under the main exam objective category, just as you'd expect to find it. It is strongly suggested that you review each subobjective and immediately make note of your knowledge level; then return to the Objective Review Notes section repeatedly and document your progress. Your ultimate goal should be to be able to review this section alone and know if you are ready for the exam.

OBJECTIVE REVIEW NOTES

Suggested use:

- Read the objective. Refer to the part of the book where it's covered. Then do as follows:

  - Do you already know this material? Then check "Got it" and make a note of the date.

  - Do you need some brushing up on the objective area? Check "Review it" and make a note of the date. While you're at it, write down the page numbers you just checked, since you'll need to return to that section soon enough.

  - Is this material something you're largely unfamiliar with? Check the "Help!" box and write down the date. Now you can get to work.

- You get the idea. Keep working through the material in this book and in the other study material you probably have. The more you get the material, the quicker you can update and upgrade each objective notes section from "Help!" To "Review it" to "Got it".

- Cross reference to the stuff YOU are using. Most people who take certification exams use more than one resource at a time. Write down the page numbers of where this material is covered in other books you're using. Or which software program and file this material is covered on. Or which video tape (and counter number) it's on. Or whatever you need that works for you.

Analyzing Business Requirements

▶ Objective: Analyze the scope of a project.

☐ Got it ☐ Review it ☐ Help!
Date: _____ Date: _____ Date: _____

Notes:
_____
_____
_____
_____
_____

Fast Track cross reference, see pages:
_____
_____

Other resources cross reference, see pages:
_____
_____
_____

▶ Objective: Analyze the extent of a business requirement.

☐ Got it ☐ Review it ☐ Help!
Date: _____ Date: _____ Date: _____

Notes:
_____
_____
_____
_____
_____

Fast Track cross reference, see pages:
_____
_____

Other resources cross reference, see pages:
_____
_____
_____

176 OBJECTIVE REVIEW NOTES

▶ Objective: Analyze security requirements.

☐ Got it ☐ Review it ☐ Help!
Date:____ Date:____ Date:____

Notes:
_____
_____
_____
_____

Fast Track cross reference, see pages:
_____
_____

Other resources cross reference, see pages:
_____
_____
_____

▶ Objective: Analyze performance requirements.

☐ Got it ☐ Review it ☐ Help!
Date:____ Date:____ Date:____

Notes:
_____
_____
_____
_____

Fast Track cross reference, see pages:
_____
_____

Other resources cross reference, see pages:
_____
_____
_____

► Objective: Analyze maintainability requirements.

☐ Got it   ☐ Review it   ☐ Help!
Date:_____   Date:_____   Date:_____

Notes:
_____
_____
_____

Fast Track cross reference, see pages:
_____
_____

Other resources cross reference, see pages:
_____
_____
_____

► Objective: Analyze extensibility requirements. Solutions must be able to handle the growth of functionality.

☐ Got it   ☐ Review it   ☐ Help!
Date:_____   Date:_____   Date:_____

Notes:
_____
_____
_____

Fast Track cross reference, see pages:
_____
_____

Other resources cross reference, see pages:
_____
_____
_____

OBJECTIVE REVIEW NOTES

Objective: Analyze availability requirements.

☐ Got it ☐ Review it ☐ Help!
Date:_____ Date:_____ Date:_____

Notes:
_____
_____
_____

Fast Track cross reference, see pages:
_____

Other resources cross reference, see pages:
_____
_____
_____

Objective: Analyze human factors requirements.

☐ Got it ☐ Review it ☐ Help!
Date:_____ Date:_____ Date:_____

Notes:
_____
_____
_____
_____

Fast Track cross reference, see pages:
_____

Other resources cross reference, see pages:
_____
_____
_____
_____

OBJECTIVE REVIEW NOTES 179

▶ Objective: Analyze the requirements for integrating a solution with existing applications.

- [ ] **Got it** Date:_____
- [ ] **Review it** Date:_____
- [ ] **Help!** Date:_____

Notes:
_____
_____
_____

Fast Track cross reference, see pages:
_____
_____

Other resources cross reference, see pages:
_____
_____
_____

▶ Objective: Analyze existing methodologies and limitations of a business.

- [ ] **Got it** Date:_____
- [ ] **Review it** Date:_____
- [ ] **Help!** Date:_____

Notes:
_____
_____
_____
_____

Fast Track cross reference, see pages:
_____
_____

Other resources cross reference, see pages:
_____
_____
_____
_____

OBJECTIVE REVIEW NOTES

► Objective: Analyze scalability requirements.

☐ Got it   ☐ Review it   ☐ Help!
Date:_____   Date:_____   Date:_____

Notes:
_____
_____
_____

Fast Track cross reference, see pages:
_____
_____

Other resources cross reference, see pages:
_____
_____
_____
_____

Developing Data Models

► Objective: Specify the relationships between entities

☐ Got it   ☐ Review it   ☐ Help!
Date:_____   Date:_____   Date:_____

Notes:
_____
_____
_____
_____

Fast Track cross reference, see pages:
_____
_____

Other resources cross reference, see pages:
_____
_____
_____

OBJECTIVE REVIEW NOTES

▶ Objective: Develop a conceptual data model using standard normalization techniques.

- ☐ **Got it**
  Date:_____
- ☐ **Review it**
  Date:_____
- ☐ **Help!**
  Date:_____

Notes:
_____
_____
_____

Fast Track cross reference, see pages:
_____
_____

Other resources cross reference, see pages:
_____
_____
_____

▶ Objective: Identify the key components of a data model.

- ☐ **Got it**
  Date:_____
- ☐ **Review it**
  Date:_____
- ☐ **Help!**
  Date:_____

Notes:
_____
_____
_____
_____

Fast Track cross reference, see pages:
_____
_____

Other resources cross reference, see pages:
_____
_____
_____

OBJECTIVE REVIEW NOTES

Objective: Identify appropriate levels of denormalization.

☐ Got it   ☐ Review it   ☐ Help!
Date:_____ Date:_____ Date:_____

Notes:
_____
_____
_____

Fast Track cross reference, see pages:
_____

Other resources cross reference, see pages:
_____
_____
_____

Objective: Choose the foreign key that will enforce relationships between entities and will ensure referential integrity.

☐ Got it   ☐ Review it   ☐ Help!
Date:_____ Date:_____ Date:_____

Notes:
_____
_____
_____

Fast Track cross reference, see pages:
_____

Other resources cross reference, see pages:
_____
_____
_____

OBJECTIVE REVIEW NOTES 183

▶ Objective: Convert a logical data model to a physical data model.

☐ Got it ☐ Review it ☐ Help!
*Date:*_____ *Date:*_____ *Date:*_____

Notes:

_____
_____
_____

Fast Track cross reference, see pages:

_____
_____

Other resources cross reference, see pages:

_____
_____
_____
_____

Developing the Conceptual and Logical Design for an Application

▶ Objective: Construct a conceptual design that is based on a variety of scenarios and that includes context, workflow process, task sequence, and physical environment models.

☐ Got it ☐ Review it ☐ Help!
*Date:*_____ *Date:*_____ *Date:*_____

Notes:

_____
_____
_____
_____

Fast Track cross reference, see pages:

_____
_____

Other resources cross reference, see pages:

_____
_____
_____

184 OBJECTIVE REVIEW NOTES

▶Objective: Given a conceptual design, apply the principles of modular design to derive the components and services of the logical design.

- ☐ **Got it**
  *Date:*_____
- ☐ **Review it**
  *Date:*_____
- ☐ **Help!**
  *Date:*_____

Notes:
_____
_____
_____

Fast Track cross reference, see pages:
_____

Other resources cross reference, see pages:
_____
_____
_____

▶Objective: Evaluate whether access to a database should be encapsulated in an object.

- ☐ **Got it**
  *Date:*_____
- ☐ **Review it**
  *Date:*_____
- ☐ **Help!**
  *Date:*_____

Notes:
_____
_____
_____
_____

Fast Track cross reference, see pages:
_____

Other resources cross reference, see pages:
_____
_____
_____

OBJECTIVE REVIEW NOTES 185

▶ Objective: Design the properties, methods, and events of components.

☐ **Got it** ☐ **Review it** ☐ **Help!**
  *Date:*_____ *Date:*_____ *Date:*_____

Notes:
_____
_____
_____
_____

Fast Track cross reference, see pages:
_____
_____

Other resources cross reference, see pages:
_____
_____
_____

▶ Objective: Given a business scenario, identify which solution type is appropriate. Solution types are single-tier and *n*-tier.

☐ **Got it** ☐ **Review it** ☐ **Help!**
  *Date:*_____ *Date:*_____ *Date:*_____

Notes:
_____
_____
_____
_____

Fast Track cross reference, see pages:
_____
_____

Other resources cross reference, see pages:
_____
_____
_____

OBJECTIVE REVIEW NOTES

▶ Objective: Incorporate business rules into object design.

☐ Got it ☐ Review it ☐ Help!
Date:____ Date:____ Date:____

Notes:
_____
_____
_____

Fast Track cross reference, see pages:
_____

Other resources cross reference, see pages:
_____
_____
_____

▶ Objective: Assess the potential impact of the logical design on performance, maintainability, extensibility, scalability, availability, and security.

☐ Got it ☐ Review it ☐ Help!
Date:____ Date:____ Date:____

Notes:
_____
_____
_____
_____

Fast Track cross reference, see pages:
_____

Other resources cross reference, see pages:
_____
_____
_____

Designing a User Interface and User Services

▶ Objective: Given a solution, identify the navigation for the user interface.

☐ Got it ☐ Review it ☐ Help!
Date:_____ Date:_____ Date:_____

Notes:
_____
_____
_____

Fast Track cross reference, see pages:
_____
_____

Other resources cross reference, see pages:
_____
_____
_____

▶ Objective: Identify input validation procedures that should be integrated into the user interface.

☐ Got it ☐ Review it ☐ Help!
Date:_____ Date:_____ Date:_____

Notes:
_____
_____
_____
_____

Fast Track cross reference, see pages:
_____
_____

Other resources cross reference, see pages:
_____
_____
_____

OBJECTIVE REVIEW NOTES

▶ Objective: Evaluate methods of providing online user assistance, such as status bars, ToolTips, and Help files.

☐ **Got it** ☐ **Review it** ☐ **Help!**
Date:_____ Date:_____ Date:_____

Notes:
_____
_____
_____
_____

Fast Track cross reference, see pages:
_____
_____

Other resources cross reference, see pages:
_____
_____
_____
_____

▶ Objective: Construct a prototype user interface that is based on business requirements, user interface guidelines, and the organization's standards.

☐ **Got it** ☐ **Review it** ☐ **Help!**
Date:_____ Date:_____ Date:_____

Notes:
_____
_____
_____
_____
_____

Fast Track cross reference, see pages:
_____
_____

Other resources cross reference, see pages:
_____
_____
_____
_____

OBJECTIVE REVIEW NOTES

▶ Objective: Establish appropriate type of output.

☐ Got it ☐ Review it ☐ Help!
Date:_____ Date:_____ Date:_____

Notes:
_____
_____
_____

Fast Track cross reference, see pages:
_____
_____

Other resources cross reference, see pages:
_____
_____
_____

Defining the Technical Architecture for a Solution

▶ Objective: Identify technology standards such as EDI and POSIX.

☐ Got it ☐ Review it ☐ Help!
Date:_____ Date:_____ Date:_____

Notes:
_____
_____
_____
_____

Fast Track cross reference, see pages:
_____
_____

Other resources cross reference, see pages:
_____
_____
_____

OBJECTIVE REVIEW NOTES

▶ Objective: Choose a data storage architecture.

- ☐ **Got it**
  Date:_____
- ☐ **Review it**
  Date:_____
- ☐ **Help!**
  Date:_____

Notes:
_____
_____
_____

Fast Track cross reference, see pages:
_____

Other resources cross reference, see pages:
_____
_____
_____

▶ Objective: Test the feasibility of a proposed technical architecture.

- ☐ **Got it**
  Date:_____
- ☐ **Review it**
  Date:_____
- ☐ **Help!**
  Date:_____

Notes:
_____
_____
_____
_____

Fast Track cross reference, see pages:
_____

Other resources cross reference, see pages:
_____
_____
_____

► Objective: Develop appropriate deployment strategy.

☐ **Got it**
Date:_____

☐ **Review it**
Date:_____

☐ **Help!**
Date:_____

Notes:
_____
_____
_____
_____

Fast Track cross reference, see pages:
_____
_____

Other resources cross reference, see pages:
_____
_____
_____
_____

PART II

INSIDE EXAM 70-100

Part II of this book is designed to round out your exam preparation by providing you with chapters that do the following:

- "Fast Facts Review" is a digest of all "What Is Important to Know" sections form all Part I chapters. Use this chapter to review just before you take the exam: It's all here, in an easily reviewable format.

- "Hotlist of Exam-Critical Concepts" is your resource for cross-checking your tech terms. Although you're probably up to speed on most of this material already, double-check yourself anytime you run across an item you're not 100% certain about; it could make a difference at exam time.

- "Sample Scenario and Sample Test Questions" provides a full-length practice exam that tests you on the actual material covered in Part I. If you mastered the material there, you should be able to pass with flying colors here.

- "Insider's Spin on Exam 70-100" grounds you in the particulars for preparing mentally for this examination and for Microsoft testing in general.

- "Did You Know" is the last-day-of-class bonus chapter: A brief touching-upon of perpheral information designed to be helpful and of interest to anyone using this technology to the point that they what to be certified in its mastery.

6   Fast Facts Review

7   Hotlist of Exam-Critical Concepts

8   Sample Scenario and Sample Test Questions

9   Insider's Spin on Exam 70-100

10 Did You Know?

OBJECTIVES

The exam is divided into five objective catagories:

- ▶ Analyzing Business Requirements
- ▶ Developing Data Models
- ▶ Developing the Conceptual and Logical Design for an Application
- ▶ Designing a User Interface and User Services
- ▶ Defining the Technical Architecture for a Solution

CHAPTER 6

Fast Facts Review

What to Study

This is a review of the key topics discussed in the preceding five chapters. After you are certain that you understand the principles discussed in those chapters, study these key points on the day of the exam prior to taking it.

Analyzing Business Requirements

The following items must be completed during the analysis phase of development:

- Establish the business cases
- Determine the cost and budget
- Identify and set priorities

Use the Microsoft Solution Framework (MSF) as your development methodology. MSF defines roles and responsibilities and a set of models for organization, design, and implementation.

Process Model—Defines a spiral and iterative development plan that is based on a series of milestones.

Application Model—Defines the services and physical layers of an application: user, business, and data. n-tier design is based on the application model of MSF.

More information on MSF can be found at http://www.microsoft.com/msf.

When defining the project scope, consider the following points:

- What are the existing applications and tools?
- What are the anticipated environmental and infrastructure changes?
- What is the expected lifetime of the project?
- What is the budget of the project?
- What are the time constraints for the project?

The expected lifetime of a solution impacts both the design and implementation of a project. A "quick fix" application might have a short lifetime and should be created with time as a major factor over scalability, extensibility, and maintainability. On the other hand, an enterprise application with a long life expectancy should focus development energy on maintainability, extensibility, and scalability at the expense of very short development times. The lifetime can also affect the approach and tools used with an application.

The single biggest deciding factor in the choice of tools and technology is the project budget. If you can't buy it, you can't build it.

The first step in the definition phase should be a statement of the problem. This statement should give a high-level description of the problem. It should be as small as a sentence, but no longer than a paragraph. It should not be a detailed description. Instead, it should be the target goal of the development process. All the little details come during later stages of design and development.

After the problem statement is created, a resolution statement should be created. The resolution statement gives the development focus and lists what you plan to do to solve the business problem. Combining the problem and resolution statements gives focus and goals to the project and puts all development efforts into perspective.

Thoroughly analyzing existing applications helps you determine which systems are out of date, which systems need replacing due to changing requirements, and which systems can be used and leveraged to decrease development time and cost. Leveraging existing systems decreases testing and development time by using code that has been tested and developed over a long period of time—sometimes for more than a decade. Not having to "reinvent the wheel" lets development teams focus on other development tasks.

When putting a project team together, try to balance skills while avoiding an excessive overlap in skills. A small team with three developers who have the same specialty is just as bad as a small team that has a number of generalists. Proper balance between specialists and generalists is important to building a productive team.

The cost of a project is not design and development time alone. This list of items greatly changes the total cost of a project:

- Hardware (servers, workstations, upgrades)
- Software (operating systems, database servers, third-party systems)
- Downtime
- Training
- Maintenance
- IT staff augmentation

Be sure to take these into account when planning a project. An application might be cheap to build, but the hardware upgrades and training costs might put the project out of reach for even a modest budget.

Planning for downtime is critical. Downtime is not at all free. Each hour that a system is down keeps orders from being placed and shipped, forces customers to go to other vendors for products, and keeps employees sitting on their hands until the system is back up. Remember that a system that is up 99 percent of the time is down for almost 88 hours a year.

Do not overload a first version of an application with unnecessary features. You should use the MSF milestone process that defines a series of versioned releases of an application. The first version should expose the core functionality of an application at the expense of user interface features. As milestones are reached, more user interface items are added as the number of fundamental core functions decreases. Don't worry about the application looking "pretty" the first time around. Instead, focus on the business logic and processing required to make the application work.

Milestone-based development allows a development team to produce a usable product faster than trying to implement all features at once. The same development time might be required to finish the project, but users will have more time to use, debug, and comment on the application. Overall, the development time between the two models might be the same, but the completeness and functionality will be more robust through milestone releases.

Create a feature list early in the development process. This feature list should list all the features required and requested in an application. This list should then be sorted by priority and necessity to develop milestones. This list should be reviewed with users, managers, and developers to reach a consensus and understanding of the milestone process. Getting buy-in from all parties is essential in application development and the success of a project.

Maintain a customer focus when developing applications. An application can fulfill all business needs, but if the users can't use the systems, the application has little practical use. Determine how the users work and interact, and try to model these interactions in an application. This keeps the application familiar and decreases training dramatically.

In order to create a customer-focused application, you should be able to answer a few questions:

- What do the users need to do, and what do they really do?
- Does the solution add value to their jobs or increase productivity?
- What is the technical level of the users?
- What user tasks can be streamlined or automated?

The core business problem might be manifested in areas that the users and management have overlooked. Review all processes and systems to determine whether the problem is actually much simpler than previously thought. Sometimes a system that seems to be noncritical and is often overlooked might be a contributing factor to the problem. A little extra work during the planning and design phases might reveal issues that can dramatically decrease the amount of development work necessary.

Total Cost of Ownership (TCO) and Return on Investment (ROI) are two key factors in the development process, because they deal directly with the bottom line. One of the main goals of an enterprise application is to return the money invested in the development of the application. An application with little or no ROI makes little sense at all. Your applications should focus on returning the cost of investment and, ideally, turning a profit in the not-too-distant future. A low TCO helps ROI by keeping maintenance, training, and administration costs to a minimum.

When calculating ROI, do not overlook any option and any approach. Most people have a tendency to look at the bottom line without looking at the return on the money invested. Be sure to show the overall numbers that demonstrate the most cost-effective solution. Do not discard any option for increasing ROI. The choices might be tough, like reducing headcount, but the bottom line is the budget. The solution might not be cheap in the beginning, and it might not be attractive.

Users inevitably need training on new applications. Many factors must be addressed to reduce the training costs that can seriously affect the project's budget:

- Type of training required (onsite, offsite)
- Knowledge level of the users (novice, intermediate, power users)
- Areas of training (application developed, third-party applications, operating systems)
- Total number of users requiring training
- Length of training

When identifying users, determine whether there is a need for remote user access. Remote users dramatically change the needs of the project, development efforts, and budget. Remote users have special needs, such as application performance over remote connections, the hardware and software needed for remote connections, and additional system uptime and transaction processing to avoid data loss over bad connections. The addition of remote users might change the application from a traditional Windows-based client/server system to a Web-based system.

If there are plans for application distribution in other counties, localization issues must be addressed. The development team must plan for text strings in the application to be localized in other languages, icon and graphics must be checked against local customs for possible offensive usage, and dates, times, and currencies must be handled in native formats. Needless to say, localization adds development and testing costs to the application, as well as additional planning. Be sure the budget can support this requirement, or you might find yourself short of cash at a critical point in development.

Remember that the majority of development projects fail completely or fail to deliver the desired results. Plan thoroughly and involve users in the development process and get buyoff from all parties whenever possible. The first release of the application is the wrong time to find out that you have been solving the wrong problem the wrong way.

When dealing with legacy applications, you have to analyze three approaches:

- Keeping the existing systems
- Leveraging the systems and slowly migrating off them
- Creating an entirely new system

A bank that is using IBM mainframes with all development in COBOL and CICS might not be too excited about scrapping the system entirely. On the other hand, a shop that uses legacy applications running on Novell servers might be inclined to migrate to a brand new system that utilizes newer technology.

Connectivity to legacy systems is always a development challenge. You need to determine the most cost-effective and stable solution for connecting to data. Third-party applications versus in-house systems need to be addressed. Each client is different, and each need is different. Do not discount any method of connectivity, because each has its merits.

There are several established security models:

- System
- Server/machine
- User
- Group
- File
- Database

System-level security is built into the application itself. This is not the most secure access, but combined with other security, it can be formidable in this age of hackers and intellectual thieves. Server/machine security limits a user's access to an entire machine. User- and group-level security are the most flexible forms of security but carry the highest administrative overhead. File-based security is actually more expensive from an administration standpoint, but is rarely used as a central security model. Finally, database-level security can provide the final lock on data and system access. Your data is the most important component within any application. Business logic can be re-created and user interfaces can be redesigned, but data cannot be regenerated. A highly secure system utilizes system-level security for initial access, user- and group-security on business objects, and an additional level of security for database access.

Focusing on maintainability reduces TCO over the long term. An application should be easily modified and should be flexible enough to allow for new features and functionality. An application that is not maintainable is destined to be rewritten or left "as-is" throughout its lifetime. Using component-based development increases maintainability. Segmenting an application into logical components allows parts of the application to be enhanced transparently within the system. Components that hold critical functions (such as database access) can be scaled and replaced without forcing any changes to other areas of the application. Components allow large systems to be maintained as if each part were a system in and of itself.

Enterprise systems should be fully scalable to allow for internal growth and expansion. Scalable systems can accept more users and more data, and they can take advantage of new technologies. Databases should be flexible, and Web applications should be designed to use new servers and standards.

DEVELOPING DATA MODELS

There are two phases of developing data models: logical design and physical design.

The logical design phase defines the key components of the model: entities, attributes, and relationships. Entities are the nouns that describe the data being collected (orders, customers, items, employees). Attributes are the properties of the entities (name, address, telephone number). Relationships are used to establish the link between entities and the type of link. You can have one-to-one, one-to-many, and many-to-many relationships.

Each entity should have a key. A key is an attribute or series of attributes that uniquely identifies the data in an entity.

When converting a logical model to a physical model, entities become tables, attributes become columns, and relationships become joins.

Most RDBMS systems cannot handle many-to-many joins and require a third table called a join table. The join table contains the keys from each of the other tables. This is how the many-to-many relationship is resolved. It might be necessary to have a third column in the join table for a primary unique key if the other two tables might have redundant joins.

Primary keys are unique keys for the data in a table. A foreign key is used to link one table to another. An order detail table will have an order primary key to allow the detail lines to relate back to an order.

The process of normalization is where a single table is broken into multiple tables to avoid redundancy. There are three main levels of normal forms, but many more exist. Typically, a table is not normalized beyond the third normal form due to the lack of maintainability and performance.

Denormalization is the reverse of normalization and is typically used when creating data warehouses. Denormalized databases enhance performance when searching for data, but make maintaining the integrity of the data difficult, error prone, and time consuming since the data is duplicated in many areas.

Developing the Conceptual and Logical Design for an Application

There are several standardized application models within Windows that developers can take advantage of:

- Single document interface (SDI)
- Multiple document interface (MDI)
- Console applications
- Services
- Explorer-style applications
- Web-based applications

SDI applications allow only one document to be open at a time, whereas MDI applications are designed to have many documents open simultaneously.

Console applications run from the command shell and contain no user interface. Console applications are typically support applications for debugging, batch file execution, and power users that do not want the overhead of a graphical system. Microsoft SQL Server contains an application called BCP (bulk copy program) that is a console application that is used to import large amounts of data into SQL Server. This application is handy to DBAs, because it can handle a large number of options that would be difficult to present within a dialog and allows for the automation of importing and exporting data.

Services run under Windows NT and are used to monitor system events and interact directly with the system. Services contain no user interfaces and do not require a user to log into the system. Microsoft Exchange Server runs as a service and "listens" to all mail server traffic that is sent to the server. Services are designed for low-level functions, such as printing for a print server, or for running enterprise systems, such as IIS, SQL Server, and Exchange.

Web-based applications are designed to run over the Internet or an intranet using the HTTP protocol. The processing of data and information happens on the server, and clients are used as thin clients for data presentation.

Explorer-style applications have a treeview window on the left and a listview window on the right with a toolbar on top and a status bar on the bottom.

Applications can have multiple tiers for application design.

Single-tier applications use the client for user interface services, processing, business objects, and data processing. Typically, single-tier applications are single-user applications, file-server applications, or thin-client applications.

Two-tier applications use a database server for data processing (such as SQL Server), but all user services and business logic remain on the client workstation.

Three-tier and *n*-tier applications use a middle layer for processing business objects and business logic and a database server for data processing. Client workstations only implement user services for data presentation. Multiple layers for collaboration, transaction processing, and message queuing can be used from the middle layers. *n*-tier design is the most flexible because key business objects can be updated in one location for all clients, and there is no fear of mismatched business processing.

The Component Object Model (COM) allows two objects to communicate. COM is platform independent, language independent, location transparent, and vendor neutral.

COM objects expose interfaces (objects) that describe the functionality of each object. An interface can have properties, methods, and events. Each object can expose one or more interfaces and can contain any number of properties, methods, and events. A COM object can expose one or more interfaces. Methods are functions or procedures within objects. Events are fired when a specified action occurs (the click event of a button) and is a form of a callback.

Properties maintain state for objects. In a distributed application where Microsoft Transaction Server is used, properties need to be avoided. Stateful objects require more network bandwidth and reduce the Transaction Server's capability to pool objects, thus increasing the amount of resources needed to serve objects. Use parameters of methods to pass information rather than through properties. Nondistributed objects see minimal performance decreases using properties within the same physical machine.

Three layers of objects make up an *n*-tier system: user, business, and data. The user objects provide user interface functionality in the application. The user objects communicate with the business objects but rarely communicate directly with the data objects. The business objects process all business logic and core application functionality. The business objects communicate with the data objects. The data objects serve data from the data store (typically a database) and provide it to the business objects for processing or pass it through to the user objects for display.

Object models are used to diagram objects and the interactions between objects. Object models serve several purposes:

- They serve as a basis for the development of your application.
- They allow you to spot any weaknesses in the design of the system.
- They create system documentation.
- They graphically display the system so that you can "see" how it is supposed to function.

A common graphical object modeling representation is the Unified Modeling Language (UML). A popular tool for modeling UML diagrams is the Visual Modeler that ships with Visual Studio.

DESIGNING A USER INTERFACE FOR A SOLUTION

A useful user interface has the following characteristics:

- The interface should be clean—do not clutter the screen with too many details.
- The interface should follow a style or layout that users are accustomed to. Utilize the designs of other applications, such as Microsoft Office, to build your user interface on. Not only have these types of commercial applications gone through a great deal of market testing, but they also are almost an interface standard.
- Navigation should be simple. Let the user decide whether he wants to use the keyboard, mouse, or both.

- Help should be available when users get confused. Use several avenues for presenting help so that the users will be more productive and, therefore, decrease the support costs of the application.

- Users should get the appropriate feedback on what is required. Do not let users key in letters for a social security number field and don't allow numbers for a name. Let users know in a nice way what is required and refrain from abusive or demeaning error messages.

- Keep error messages clean and to a minimum. The user can understand "There was a problem printing—be sure the printer is turned on," but he would have trouble with "Printer Error 33948—Unable to access device or network resource."

User interfaces should follow standard Windows-style guidelines for colors, controls, spacing, and control usage. All of these are part of the Win32 SDK within the Microsoft Developer Network.

Limit the number of controls visible at one time. An interface with too many items looks busy and confusing and might distract even the most seasoned users of the application. Use tabbed dialog boxes to organize data and present fewer data items per window.

Use caution when using colors for emphasis or coding items. Many users are colorblind and cannot see the different hues. Use bold characters, icons, or other graphical representations. Color can be used in addition to the graphical cues without alienating any users.

Use hot keys and accelerator keys for quick navigation and execution of commands. A well-designed application allows a power user to use the majority of the application's functionality without having to remove his fingers from the keyboard. Users who do not need to make the shift from keyboard to mouse and back are much more productive within the use of the application.

Other navigation items that can boost productivity are auto-tabbing and auto-complete. Auto-tabbing automatically sends the user to the next field in a form without forcing him to press the Tab key or select the control with the mouse. Auto-complete fills in a text box, combo box, or any other control after the first several keystrokes. The application looks at a list of frequently entered data and automatically completes the data entry based on past entries. This reduces typing of redundant information and is helpful in list boxes and combo boxes where the data items might otherwise take a significant amount of time to find in the lists.

There are two forms of help files—WinHelp and HTMLHelp. WinHelp is the original help system from Microsoft. WinHelp uses rich text format (RTF) documents to generate help files. The functionality of WinHelp was limited by the capability of RTF to integrate multimedia into files. HTMLHelp uses HTML files that can incorporate Java, ActiveX, and Dynamic HTML to present full multimedia data. HTMLHelp is easier than WinHelp to author because HTMLHelp uses standard HTML bookmarks and links to navigate files.

You can use controls such as Tool Tips and What's This Help to provide quick reference information on fields and controls. Status bars can present additional feedback to users, such as help, keyboard state, and application state. Status bars can be customized to present several critical pieces of information.

When presenting errors to users, try to follow these suggestions to minimize confusion and boost productivity:

- Create easily understood error messages. Do not use vague numbers for errors; give them English phrases rather than obscure programming terms.
- Do not present messages to users that are confrontational or demeaning.

- Write information to files or database servers. Users do not care what the error number is, will not remember the error number, and will not remember how they received the error. Use special error handling and global objects to trap errors and log as much information to text files on the user's machine. This presents friendly information to the user while providing for development and technical support a detailed log of what had occurred. Do not rely on the user to do all the debugging for you.

- Use better error handling. Users see errors only when there are problems. Try to update the application with bug fixes so that users will see fewer problems and tech support will receive fewer calls.

Here are the Do and Don't lists of error handling:

Do:

- Write consistent error-handling routines.
- Give the user an English explanation of the problem.
- Handle errors gracefully. Abruptly exiting the application is far from graceful, as is forcing a reboot. Make the user's life easier, not harder.
- Log all errors with details into a file for support or development to review later.
- Trap for errors in modules that you are calling. There is no guarantee that the object had adequate error handling, so be prepared.

Don't:

- Crash.
- Give the users obscure error numbers or memory addresses. They *will* forget.
- Let errors get to the users because "they should know what to do."
- Build so much error trapping that you lose sight of the purpose of the application. Remember the law of diminishing returns.

Prototyping is the processes of generating a rough user interface with no processing or logic behind the forms. This is used to test interface designs, build proof-of-concept applications, and rough out initial designs with users.

DEFINING THE TECHNICAL ARCHITECTURE FOR A SOLUTION

Electronic data interchange (EDI) is a method of transferring data across different systems and/or architectures. Many third-party tools can accomplish this, but many developers tend to write custom EDI applications. EDI is used often when migrating data from a legacy system to a new system.

Consider the following when choosing a data architecture for a system:

- Volume and size of the data
- Number of transactions per minute
- Number of connections
- Number of users

Balance performance on database systems between the client and the server. Keep in mind that when a client is required to process data, all the data must be sent over the network. If a table has 100,000 records and these are to be sorted, grouped, and calculated, all 100,000 records must be transmitted to the client workstations. If the actual result set is 100 records, there is a lot of wasted bandwidth and redundant client processing. On the other hand, do not overload the server with large numbers of requests to process 50 and 100 record queries. These can be easily processed on the client, and the network bandwidth will be minimal in comparison with the increased resources required on the server.

Here are some keys to increasing overall performance with databases:

- Preprocess data on SQL Server to return smaller result sets.

- Limit the number of records you return in a single call. A result set that returns a thousand records will be of little use to the user, because most users cannot even attempt to process that much data. Limiting returns to 50 records keeps the result set manageable.

- Do not allow users to create their own queries. Allow for some slight modification of existing queries, but a join in the wrong place can bring a database server to its knees (try a self join on a million-record table).

- Utilize static and persistent recordsets for data that does not often change (location codes, shipping zones, zip codes, and the like). Storing these values in memory reduces the need to query the database server and transfers a recordset on each lookup.

Offload some processing to middle-tier servers from the main database. Some often-required data can be stored within middle tiers, and the data can be sent back to the client without round trips to the database server each time. Static data is prime for this form of delegation. Some dynamic data can be delegated in this fashion, but caution must be exercised to avoid data that might be out of sync with the server.

Feasibility testing should answer the following questions:

- Can we do this with our existing resources?
- Does this fit our needs and solve our problems?
- Can we do this in a reasonable time?
- Will the current technology support the solution?

Deployment of enterprise solutions is typically a headache for large organizations. Utilize tools such as System Management Server (SMS) to push files to client desktops. Also use middle-tier servers for key business logic processing. This will allow you to update key files on one machine without regard to the size of the user base. The change is transparent to users and can immediately affect the entire organization. Avoid staged distribution of business logic, because this can lead to data inconsistencies and possible data loss due to changing and mismatched logic.

Build in contingency plans in the event that you fall short of the solution. Budgets are not set in stone, and resources may come and go. Make sure that there are backup plans in the event of a budget shortfall or major staffing problem. Identify features that can be cut or functionality that is not required. Always focus on the problem at hand and try to deliver a solution that addresses the problem. Additional features and functionality can come later, but do not lose sight of what you are trying to accomplish.

This chapter covers some Microsoft tools and technologies you might have had some exposure to. This is not intended to be a complete coverage of each tool; it is more of an overview of how they work, where they are used, and what their key points might be.

Following the products section, a definition section briefly defines some key development and technology terms you will encounter.

Finally, this chapter finishes up with some quick comparisons of the key tools and technologies.

CHAPTER 7

Hotlist of Exam-Critical Concepts

Products, Tools, and Technologies

In order to implement a solution, you should have a basic grasp of the available tools and technologies and how they can be leveraged.

Development Tools

Microsoft supplies many development tools that provide some unique functionality and limitations for different types of development efforts. This section looks at each technology and points out the advantages and disadvantages of each.

Visual Basic

Visual Basic is a RAD tool based on the BASIC programming language. Visual Basic (VB) is one of Microsoft's most popular development languages. VB has a very strong following in the development, corporate, and third-party communities. Many third-party applications are written to allow Visual Basic to extend its power and rapid development capabilities to further strengthen its position in the enterprise application world.

Visual Basic is fast from both a development and a system execution standpoint. Although VB is not quite as fast as a Visual C++ application, there are enough hooks into the Windows API or Visual C++ code libraries to allow Visual Basic to be a player in large enterprise applications and mission-critical applications.

Visual Basic does not allow for the development of console applications, device drivers, Windows NT services, and non-COM DLL libraries.

Visual Basic has one of the lowest learning curves of all the Microsoft development tools. This allows corporations to create Visual Basic applications with the current development knowledge from other development tools. The BASIC language is not as complex as C++ and assembler. Because many developers have worked on more complex languages, Visual Basic is easy to learn and use.

Visual Basic should be used in situations where development time is at a premium, developers are learning a new language, or a company wants to leverage a widely accepted language with a low TCO.

Visual Basic should not be used where device drivers are required, cross-platform compatibility is necessary, or where applications will need direct access to hardware and low-level system resources.

Here are some keys to Visual Basic:

- RAD tool
- Flexibility
- Low learning curve
- High industry and third-party support

Visual Basic should be used for

- Projects with a rapid time-to-market.
- Client/server systems that should support many users and be very extensible.
- Projects that need a low TCO.
- Projects that require COM components, such as DLLs, EXEs, and OCXs.

Visual Basic should not be used for

- Device drivers and low-level hardware access (such as game programming).
- NT services.
- Applications that need to be portable or cross-platform.

Visual C++

Visual C++ is Microsoft's semi-RAD C++ tool that leverages the Microsoft Foundation Classes (MFC) to allow for code reuse and rapid development of complex system functions.

MFC is a complex library of code written by Microsoft to allow access to vital functions such as multithreading, hardware access, and window creation and management. MFC is not designed for users who have little experience with the intricate details of the Windows operating system; thus, Visual C++ has a high learning curve.

Visual C++ shines when creating low-level system tools, such as device drivers or any application that requires special access to system functions that other high-level languages do not. Visual C++ can utilize items such as pointers, multiple inheritance, and multithreading that many other development tools cannot.

Visual C++, like Visual Basic, is a widely accepted development tool in enterprise applications. Many organizations utilize a hybrid development process where Visual Basic is used for interface design and nonintensive logic. Visual C++ is used for complex calculations, processor-intensive routines, and advanced coding that runs many times faster than Visual Basic code.

Visual C++ is used when development time is not the most critical development aspect, items such as device drivers and system tools are being written, and where speed is of absolute importance. Visual C++ requires an experienced development team in order to implement a given solution. Visual C++ can also be used where cross-platform development is needed, because Visual C++ and the MFC have been ported to other operating systems.

Visual C++ should not be used where a RAD tool is required, the staff is inexperienced, or TCO is of major importance, since Visual C++ applications have a higher TCO due to the complexity of the applications.

Here are some keys to Visual C++:

- Is semi-RAD (not as RAD as Visual Basic and Visual InterDev)
- Applications are fast and relatively small
- Requires an experienced staff due to the complexity of MFC
- Allows for full OOP/OOD (including multiple inheritance)

Visual C++ should be used for

- Cross-platform compatibility.
- Speed.
- Real-time and mission-critical applications.
- Device drivers, NT services, and console applications.
- Creating libraries of processor-intensive code and APIs.
- Creating COM components such as DLLs, EXEs, and OCXs.

Visual C++ is not suited for

- Applications that have a short time-to-market.
- An inexperienced development staff.
- Applications that need a lower TCO.

Visual FoxPro

Visual FoxPro is another Microsoft client/server development platform that has a much smaller following than Visual Basic and Visual C++. Visual FoxPro is built from the Xbase language and has many similarities to Visual Basic programming.

Visual FoxPro is tied tightly to a database system that is built from the high-performance Rushmore technology with a dBASE-style database. Database performance is very good with Visual FoxPro and is a better multi-user environment than Microsoft Access.

Visual FoxPro has a major advantage over the other tools in the sense that it is a RAD tool and is cross-platform (Windows, Macintosh, and UNIX). This makes the tool ideal for shops that need RAD tools that are easy to learn and utilize built-in database access methods for high-performance database applications.

Because Visual FoxPro does not have the following and backing that Visual Basic and Visual C++ have, many organizations are reluctant to utilize the technology, even if it is the better tool for the job. There is not as much third-party support of Visual FoxPro as there is for Visual Basic. Visual FoxPro is an interpreted language like Visual Basic, so it suffers some of the same problems Visual Basic does.

Visual FoxPro is ideal for database applications on small- to medium-sized businesses. Because Visual FoxPro does not support stored procedures and triggers, it is not an enterprise-level database system, but it can scale to SQL Server and provide true client/server systems.

Visual FoxPro should not be designed for code libraries or nondatabase applications. Because it is tied to its database environment, Visual FoxPro should also not be used for real-time applications due to the interpreted nature of the language.

Here are some keys to Visual FoxPro:

- RAD tool
- Tight database integration
- Devout following of existing customers

FoxPro should be used for

- Database and client/server applications.
- Projects that need to be portable or cross-platform.

FoxPro should not be used for

- Real-time applications.
- Device drivers and low-level applications (such as game programming).
- Creating COM DLLs.
- Utilizing full OOP, including inheritance.

Visual InterDev

Visual InterDev is primarily a Web RAD tool that allows developers to create complex client-side and server-side code to perform data processing and database access.

Visual InterDev can utilize COM components on the client side as well as the server side, making it a very extensible application-development platform. Visual InterDev can utilize HTML, dynamic HTML (DHTML), and active server pages (ASP) to deliver rich Web-based content.

Hotlist of Exam-Critical Concepts 221

Visual InterDev does not create compiled applications, so there is a level of exposure at the code level. Also, because Visual InterDev is a Web-based platform, it might be prone to attack from hackers and might not have the tight security that a compiled client/server application might.

Visual InterDev is useful when developing intranet/Internet applications or Web-based systems that must be flexible, extensible, and scalable.

Databases such as SQL Server, Access, and any ODBC-compliant data source can be utilized from within Visual InterDev. Additional layers, such as Microsoft Message Queue Server and Microsoft Transaction Server, can be utilized within the environment to create robust enterprise applications.

Enterprise applications that run across a WAN might benefit from Visual InterDev due to the Web utilization. Web applications are more flexible on remote connections because most of the processing can be completed on the server before the user even sees the data. Remote connections (even slow ones) will benefit from the integration within Internet Information Server.

Visual InterDev should not be used for mission-critical applications because the level of control and the lack of strong typed variables (Visual InterDev uses only variants) will definitely affect mission-critical applications in a negative way. Typical enterprise applications are key uses for Visual InterDev because the slower processing and lack of application control can be worked around and planned for in the design phase.

> **NOTE** Tools such as Visual Basic, Visual C++, and Visual FoxPro utilize strong typed variables for increasing speed and readability. Strong typed variables declare variables as a certain type (string, number, COM component, and so on). Variant data types are "unknown" data types that can contain any true data type. Variants are slow due to size and the need to determine the type of data stored for every variable access. InterDev uses only variant variables and cannot use strong typing. Moving critical functions into COM components increases execution time because the application is utilizing strong typing and compiled code.

Here are some keys to Visual InterDev:

- It is a RAD tool.
- The learning curve is low.

- The development environment is established on industry standard languages, interfaces, and protocols.
- Applications are very flexible.

Visual Interdev should be used for

- Rapid application development.
- Cross-platform compatibility.
- Projects where a mix of experienced and inexperienced developers are available.
- Integrating heterogeneous networks and systems.

Visual InterDev is not suited for

- Real-time applications.
- Applications that need to be fast and small.
- Stand-alone applications.
- Creating any COM components.

Visual J++

Visual J++ is Microsoft's implementation of the Java programming language. Visual J++ extends the basic Java environment to provide interfaces into the Windows environment so native Java Windows applications can be created and COM objects can be built. Java applets that use the Windows functions are not cross-platform and work only in the Windows environment. It is possible to code pure Java for cross-platform compatibility. Visual J++ gives the developer the choice.

For the most part, Java is a bit too new to be a primary enterprise development tool. Java is primarily used to create smaller libraries that are used through the Internet, but it is possible to create COM libraries within Java.

Java is using some C++ concepts and has some of the same problems with complexity that Visual C++ has. Java is completely object-oriented and requires a background in object-oriented programming in order to implement Java.

Java is a good tool for creating predefined code packages or objects for use over an intranet or the Internet. The bytecode is interpreted by a virtual machine to allow for cross-platform compatibility. Java is not designed to be used in real-time and mission-critical applications. Java can't create device drivers or access low-level system functions; you need to use Visual C++ to complete that task.

Java should not be used for the sole development of enterprise applications and should be limited to code packages. Integrating Java with InterDev is a good combination for speed and cross-platform compatibility.

Here are some keys to Visual J++:

- Semi-RAD tool
- Portable code, small footprint, cross-platform

Visual J++ should be used for

- Applications that want to leverage the power and flexibility of Java programming.
- Real-time applications.
- Cross-platform compatibility.
- Converting legacy C++ code.

Visual J++ should not be used for

- Enterprise systems.

Visual SourceSafe

Visual SourceSafe (VSS) is a version control system produced by Microsoft. VSS allows developers to maintain the history of changes and the incremental differences between specific versions of files or applications.

It also maintains information about specific versions of files that make up a labeled application.

VSS can be used in a single-user environment, as well as a large team environment. There is essentially no limit to the number of concurrent users that VSS can support.

If your team needs to maintain history for files, avoid overwriting changes, and keep application versions intact, VSS is the proper tool to use.

Database Servers

One of the key components to a client/server system is the database server that is selected. Business requirements dictate the server required, but you need to be clear about the advantages and disadvantages of the available technologies. This section covers the Microsoft database technologies in more detail.

SQL Server

SQL Server is Microsoft's enterprise database server that competes with Oracle, Sybase, and DB2. SQL Server is scalable and can handle very large databases and a large pool of users.

SQL Server runs under Windows NT only, with the exception of SQL Server 7.0, which can run under Windows 95. SQL Server can support triggers, stored procedures, custom data types, and distributed databases that are all key components of enterprise servers.

Replication is another key aspect of SQL Server. Replication allows SQL Server to publish data to other database servers (subscribers) so that remote locations can have local access to data without traveling across the WAN for all data access inquiries.

Security within SQL Server is centralized and can be integrated with Windows NT security to give a secure data connection. SQL Server is capable of further encrypting objects within the databases to prevent unauthorized browsing of stored procedures and views.

SQL Server should be used in the following situations:

- Scalability is important.
- Many users need access to data.
- Databases will be distributed.

- Security is a major concern.
- Databases need to store massive amounts of data or require complex queries.

SQL Server should not be used for

- Local databases.
- Small applications (fewer than 10 users).
- Mobile applications.

Access

Access is the database system provided with Microsoft Office and is primarily an end-user database system. Access is not a server database; it is a file-oriented database system. There is no access to stored procedures or views, and there is very limited built-in security.

Access can be upsized to SQL Server with tools that are provided by Microsoft. This allows developers to create and modify database schemas without using complex data modeling tools that are required to modify SQL Server tables.

Replication is available in Access, but it is not as robust as it is with SQL Server. Access replication is designed primarily for databases that are separated but must provide data updates that are to be synchronized at different times. Concurrency is not handled in a complex fashion, so it is easy for users to overwrite major changes to the data.

Access is a good database for a small environment where 10 or fewer developers need a database but do not need the complex features provided by an enterprise database server.

Access should be used for

- Small applications that are designed for 10 or fewer concurrent users.
- Unsecured database applications.
- Applications that do not utilize complex features of enterprise systems.
- Databases that store large amounts of data or that process complex queries.

Access should not be used for

- Mission-critical database applications.
- Applications that require scalability.
- Heavy transaction loads.
- Support for a large number of users.

Data Connection Services

You must know several database technologies for this exam. Some older technologies, such as ODBC, are being replaced by newer technologies, such as ADO. Each is important to know and understand.

ODBC

Open database connectivity (ODBC) is the core technology behind data access. ODBC allows vendors to write drivers for a database so that any Windows application can access one database in the same way it would access a completely different database.

ODBC is complex to utilize from a development standpoint because the API is not COM-compliant, and some calls might be difficult to make in languages such as Visual Basic and Visual FoxPro.

ODBC is utilized by ADO, RDS, RDO, and the other data-access tools developed by Microsoft.

The following components make up ODBC:

- ODBC API
- ODBC driver manager
- ODBC database drivers
- ODBC cursor library
- ODBC administrator

By using ODBC, applications can switch between databases without changing any code. Applications call the ODBC driver manager to load a specific database driver for a given data source. If a user changes the data source from Access to SQL Server, the application continues to function normally, but with a different database back end.

Developers will sometimes need to code directly to the ODBC API, because ADO is very efficient and much easier to implement.

ADO

Active data objects (ADO) is the newest database access technology from Microsoft and is part of the Universal Data Access initiative (UDA). ADO combines the best of DAO, ODBC, and RDO to provide a comprehensive and highly flexible database access technology.

ADO allows developers to access data stores that are not standard RDBMS systems, as well as standard RDBMS systems. ADO allows developers to access proprietary file formats, such as Microsoft Exchange Server, as they would any other database server. An ODBC-compliant driver is required for some ADO database access to older providers. New ADO providers can utilize OLD DB interfaces over older ODBC drivers.

ADO is also faster, easier to use, and uses less memory than the traditional database access methods.

One major advantage of using ADO for data access is the implementation of asynchronous events. You can both connect to a datasource and retrieve data from the datasource in asynchronous mode. This allows developers to run complex queries and store procedures while allowing the application to process other data in the interim.

Finally, the key items that ADO provides that the other data access methods do not are creatable and persistent recordsets. Creatable recordsets allow developers to create recordsets that do not go to a data source, but reside within memory on the current system. These recordsets can be used in place of arrays where searching and sorting require special coding. These recordsets can be bound to data-aware controls, and the data would look and act to the developer as if it came from a relational database. Persistent recordsets allow developers to save recordset data to a file on the disk and retrieve and use the data later like a regular recordset. This is very useful with a set of data that might be utilized by a remote workforce (a subset of the customer data, for example). This leads to a perfect solution where a developer can create a data set in memory, save to a disk, and add the records in the database after the user is connected to the network.

DAO

The data access object library (DAO) is used primarily to connect to Microsoft Access databases. DAO is now considered an older technology that is somewhat proprietary because it does not allow developers to use other data sources in the same fashion as ADO or RDO would.

DAO can use JET to connect to Access databases and manipulate the specific Access objects that other desktop databases might or might not expose. DAO can also use ODBCDirect to connect to remote data sources. ODBCDirect calls are actually sent through RDO to connect to remote data sources.

For the most part, DAO is slow and inefficient. It requires numerous libraries that must be loaded regardless of the datasource. The additional overhead, lack of flexibility, and Access-centric nature of the data access do not work very well in a large enterprise application. ADO is much more efficient with both desktop and remote datasources.

RDO

The remote data objects library (RDO) allows applications to call database functions in the same ways that DAO developers access Microsoft Access datasources. Many DAO applications can be converted to RDO with very few changes.

DAO applications that use ODBCDirect are actually routed through RDO to perform the data access. Cases might arise where DAO applications can use ODBCDirect with fewer changes to the code than when converting to RDO.

RDO must use a client/server database such as SQL Server or Oracle, because RDO does not have a query processor. RDO relies on the database server to process all queries and only return the result set, which is why DAO must be used on Access databases.

If an application is currently using DAO and is being upsized to a relation database server, RDO is an easy migration path. ADO can also be used for a data migration, but it is not as closely related to DAO as RDO is.

ADO has many advantages over RDO. Given the option, ADO should be used.

OLE DB

OLE DB is the foundation of the universal data access model. OLE DB is more powerful and flexible than ODBC and is COM-compliant.

By using OLE DB, an application can connect to nondatabase stores of data as it would to a relational datasource. OLE DB also allows for the retrieval of recordsets from completely different datasources.

Keep in mind that OLE DB can be programmed, but the majority of enterprise data access will be completed through the more established ADO interfaces. OLE DB is very flexible and is the primary basis for new database technologies due to its capability to connect heterogeneous datasources into a single datasource.

Networking and Infrastructure

The building blocks of any system are the operating systems and networks you will be building around. You might have more hardware flexibility on one environment while sacrificing security. You might also be using a network that is limited in available bandwidth, so you need to know the capabilities and limitations of your environment.

Windows 3.11

Windows 3.11 was the first real networked version of Windows. As with Windows 3.1, Windows 3.11 was 16-bit only and ran on top of a DOS shell. Microsoft migrated its user base to Windows 95 to allow for better performance, 32-bit architecture, and a dedicated operating system.

Because Windows 3.11 is very old and runs off of the now unsupported 16-bit platform, all steps should be taken to migrate users to a new operating system, such as the Windows 95/98 platform or the Windows NT Workstation platform.

Windows 95/98

Windows 95/98 was the first 32-bit operating system that was designed to be targeted to end users and corporate workstations. Windows 95/98 allows for some key advances:

- 32-bit application support
- Plug-and-play compatibility
- Backward compatibility with legacy hardware and software
- Preemptive multitasking

Because Windows 95/98 is very flexible, the major trade-off is stability. Windows 95/98 allows for direct access to hardware and major system functions. Operating systems such as Windows NT do not allow for this type of access and are much more stable at the cost of application and hardware support.

Windows 95/98 is inexpensive, does not require expensive hardware, and is easy for the typical end user to learn and use.

Windows 95/98 should not be used if security is a concern, because there is no built-in security services.

Windows NT

Microsoft Windows NT comes in two flavors: Workstation and Server. Windows NT Workstation is geared toward the desktop as a replacement to the Windows 95/98 platforms. Windows NT Server is designed for network servers that require a large number of connections and the need to run enterprise software. They are similar in background, but they have some key differences.

Workstation

Windows NT Workstation is a step up from Windows 95/98, but is not quite as powerful and flexible as Windows NT Server. Windows NT Workstation provides workstation-level security, better threading, a more robust kernel, and a more stable environment for mission-critical applications or development workstations.

If security, a very stable environment, or multiprocessor support is needed, users should be migrated to Windows NT Workstation.

If plug-and-play, advanced power management, legacy application support, or cost is a concern, Windows NT Workstation might not be the best operating system choice.

Server

Windows NT Server can be used as a file server for a large network or a domain controller for networks.

A domain controller allows for central administration of a network, network-wide security implementation, and network-wide resource sharing.

Networks that require security or have more than 10 users should implement a Windows NT domain. If security is not a concern, a network is very small, or the staff does not have high-level networking knowledge, a Windows NT network might not be suitable.

As a rule of thumb, NT Server should be used in enterprise networks because SQL Server, Exchange Server, IIS, and other key enterprise applications are designed to run only on Windows NT Server.

AS/400

AS/400 computers are IBM mainframe systems. These systems are designed to be scalable and allow for very large numbers of users and concurrent connections. Typically, these systems are capable of running very complex applications and calculations.

AS/400s are expensive to run and act as a terminal server to dumb terminals. AS/400 applications are limited on the user interface that can be used and are not as user friendly as Windows-based applications.

Windows applications cannot directly connect to AS/400 machines. Middleware must be created to marshal the data between the PCs and the mainframe. Many mainframe applications run in a batch cycle. A batch cycle is where the transactions are stored in system files and processed in one large group, or batch. This does not allow for real-time systems but does allow for very large transactions processing.

Mainframes and AS/400 machines have been in place for many years and might be running legacy code that is 10 to 20 years old. Connections through middleware to AS/400 transactions and data files allow developers to leverage well-established code and standard formats while integrating real-time Windows applications into the enterprise.

Networking

Networks come in many sizes and types. You need to be aware of the key limitations of each before embarking in the development process. Bandwidth is a valuable resource and should be a key part in the development planning processes. Running out of bandwidth on a network renders an enterprise application unusable.

LAN

A local area network is a series of computers that are physically linked within a given location, such as an office or building. LANs allow groups of users to share files and resources while implementing security and centralizing administration of the network.

WAN

A wide area network is a series of remote LANs that are linked though a high-speed connection that allows all the smaller LANs to act as one large LAN. WANs are expensive to implement because special hardware (typically routers) and a dedicated connection between the physical locations are required. WANs allow large organizations to communicate and be linked.

Network Speeds

Networks have speed caps (known as bandwidth) that allow only a certain amount of data to be transferred at a time. Many LANs use 10 megabit or 100 megabit network cards; these cards transfer 10 to 100 megabits of data per second. Networks that utilize 10Mbit cards can be easily upgraded to 100 megabit cards to increase the bandwidth of a network by 10.

WANs utilize direct connections that can range from modem speeds (33.6k/sec) to high-speed T1 connections. Most WANs that are connected through T1 connections appear to function like other nodes on the LAN. If the connection is slower, such as a 256k dedicated line, network performance might be affected, and the enterprise system might need to be distributed to remote sites for local data processing. Keep in mind that upgrading existing connections in a WAN might be enough to solve performance and multiuser issues.

RAS/VPN

Remote access services (RAS) and virtual private networking (VPN) are methods of remote system access. These two services allow users to connect to networks from remote locations, such as with a dial-up server or through network access via the Internet.

RAS is the most basic of the remote connection methods. RAS uses two modems to establish a dial-up connection from a workstation to a server. Except for the speed, all services should function the same as when the workstation is connected to the LAN directly. The main problem with RAS is the one-to-one connection between the workstation and the server. If an organization has 100 remote users, 100 dial-in connections might be needed. This is unreasonable for most organizations because of the expensive hardware and costly line-usage charges. VPN is a more financially feasible access method.

Virtual private networking allows users to connect to a LAN through a standard Internet connection. This approach has several advantages for remote access. First of all, because any ISP can be used to gain access to the Internet, a company does not have to be concerned with long-distance charges associated with RAS connections. Secondly, a company can utilize a direct Internet connection to take the place of multiple phone switches and phone banks that a large RAS pool would require. A single server can be used to service all remote users rather than a pool of servers. Finally, a remote user does not need direct access to a phone line, because any Internet connection can service a VPN connection. This allows users to use a client's direct Internet connection to establish communications with the corporate LAN.

If a few users need remote access and the organization does not have a dedicated Internet connection, RAS servers might be the best solution. However, if the company has a direct Internet connection, a VPN makes financial sense regardless of the number of users who need remote access.

Internet

The Internet is more popular than ever. Many companies are moving from traditional client/server solutions to Web-based solutions. Microsoft provides tools for integrating Web servers into the enterprise.

Internet Information Server

Microsoft Internet Information Server (IIS) is a complete Web server that supports the following protocols:

- HTTP
- FTP
- NNTP (routing only)
- SMTP (routing only)
- Gopher

Internet Information Server runs under Windows NT Server and Workstation and Windows 95/98. The version of IIS that runs on Windows NT Workstation and Windows 95/98 does not have the full feature set that the Server version does, and these versions have connection and security limitations. The Windows NT Workstation and Windows 95/98 IIS server is referred to as the Personal Web Server (PWS).

IIS is capable of hosting active server pages (ASP) that allow the server to process scripts and code prior to the client receiving the completed HTML page. ASP pages can access server objects and COM objects as well as databases through ADO.

Mainframe Computing

Companies that have been around for many years might have a big investment in mainframe computers. Before Windows NT became an enterprise server environment, IBM was big in the enterprise database and transaction processing arena. Many companies are looking to maintain their investment in mainframes, whereas others are slowly weaning themselves from the high cost of mainframe ownership. Understanding the mainframe world will help you implement solutions effectively and leverage the investments that customers have made, thus reducing the implementation and development costs that come with enterprise development.

Microsoft SNA Server

Microsoft SNA Server allows PCs to connect and utilize data on mainframes by using several connection mechanisms. Typically, applications use the 3270 emulator libraries or the LU 6.2 protocols to connect to VSAM or DB2 data residing on mainframes.

SNA Server allows Windows applications to connect to native datasources through OLE DB. Recent additions to SNA Server allow CICS and COBOL code to be used as COM objects that Windows applications can call directly. This greatly enhances the ability of developers to create Windows front-end applications to legacy mainframe systems.

SNA provides a level of middleware that would require additional third-party servers or complex custom middleware layers that are customized to the applications.

Other methods of connecting to mainframe code and data exist. Screen scraping can be used with the HLLAPI and 3270 libraries to read and write data from virtual terminal screens. The main disadvantage here is that the code is not very extensible. If there are any major changes to the mainframe system, the PC applications will no longer work or worse—the data will be corrupted during the transmission back to the mainframe. SNA helps to build a layer around these problems and prevent costly errors and major code changes to custom middleware.

CICS

Customer Information Control System (CICS) is an IBM communication system that was created for database access and transaction processing on mainframe systems. Most mainframe systems that deal with large volumes of data implement CICS for all transaction processing.

Microsoft SNA Server allows CICS transactions to be called as COM objects so that Windows developers can leverage legacy code that is tested and solid while porting the legacy systems to Windows platforms.

Other

Microsoft produces many other enterprise-level applications. The gratuitous "Other" category has been created to list the remaining technologies that do not fit in any prior categories but are too important to leave out.

Microsoft Transaction Server

Microsoft Transaction Server (MTS) is a middleware server that provides the capability to wrap in process COM servers in nondatabase transactions. MTS can isolate each server so that stability is increased because the process is not running within the process of the calling applications. MTS provides an additional level of security through DCOM and its internal security mechanisms.

MTS is capable of pooling object and database connections so that enterprise systems can utilize fewer database connections due to the on-demand usage of the connections; the connections are faster because the pooling aspect of ODBC is very efficient. This reduces TCO, increases scalability, and increases overall performance.

MTS should be utilized when developers want to utilize the processing power of existing servers, wrap business objects in transactions with little development effort, and isolate processes that might not be as stable as desired.

MTS is included in the NT option pack that also includes Microsoft Message Queue Server and Internet Information Server 4.0. MTS can be run on Windows 95/98 workstations, but NT Server is recommended for production applications.

As with any DCOM-dependant application, MTS should not be used over slow WAN connections because the application objects must be marshaled across the network to the MTS server. Also, for increased efficiency, state should not be used within MTS objects because state limits the capability of MTS to pool objects. MTS is designed to be used with stateless objects (objects that do not maintain property information). The reason for the stateless support is the need to create and destroy objects as quickly as possible. A stateful component is not destroyed until the application releases it. If the application utilizes a customer object that returns data and processes changes, the object can be used quickly.

If the customer object maintains state on the server, the object is used for long periods of time. Connection pooling relies on objects being used quickly. When an object is released from the application, MTS keeps the reference alive for a short time. If another application calls for the object, the open object is sent, thus decreasing processing time. Stateful objects require numerous instances in memory because the applications are less likely to pool an object in memory. By maintaining open objects with state, you are limiting the scalability of MTS-hosted components and possibly causing valuable resources (memory and available database connections) to run out.

MTS should be used for

- Maintaining critical business logic in a secure environment.
- Pooling objects and database connections.
- Isolating processes that are prone to crashing or erratic behavior.
- Creating complex object-based transactions.

MTS should not be used for

- Storing state or state objects.
- An object repository.
- Object pooling over very slow connections.
- End-user installation.

MTS cannot host out-of-process servers.

Microsoft Exchange Server

Microsoft Exchange Server is an enterprise mail and news server. Exchange provides messaging and collaboration functionality that can be used from many clients, including Windows and Macintosh clients.

The Exchange messaging abilities can be accessed from many platforms, such as VBScript, VBA, Visual Basic, Visual C++, and any other COM-enabled development language.

Exchange is capable of programmatically routing information, which is valuable when dealing with applications that require multiple levels of approval or follow predefined business processes.

Exchange can handle a large number of users and can be distributed over many servers to handle increased loads or changes in business organization.

Exchange Server only runs under Windows NT Server, but the clients run under many operating systems.

Exchange should be utilized in large organizations that need messaging, routing, collaboration, and public information storage.

KEY TERMS AND DEFINITIONS

The following terms may be encountered throughout this text, on the exam, and in many business organizations. A good source of reference for these terms and other important concepts is MSDN, which includes all the SDKs and APIs that Microsoft provides.

Term	Definition
ACID test	Any transaction must exhibit four properties that define a transaction: atomicity, consistency, isolation, and durability. All of these must be met in the ACID test to allow an operation to be marked as a true transaction:
	♦ Atomicity: All data modifications must take place or none of them can take place. This is the smallest unit of work that can be described to create a full transaction.
	♦ Consistency: A transaction is a correct transformation of the system state.
	♦ Isolation: Protects concurrent transactions from seeing each other's partial and uncommitted results.
	♦ Durability: Updates that have been committed will remain in place even in the event of a system failure.

Hotlist of Exam-Critical Concepts

Term	Definition
ActiveX	A set of technologies that enable software components to interact with one another in a networked environment, regardless of the language in which the components were created. ActiveX, which was developed as a proposed standard by Microsoft in the mid 1990s and is currently administered by the Open Group, is built on Microsoft's Component Object Model (COM). Currently, ActiveX is used primarily to develop interactive content for the World Wide Web, although it can be used in desktop applications and other applications. ActiveX controls can be embedded in Web pages to produce animation and other multimedia effects, interactive objects, and sophisticated applications.
APPC (Advanced Program-to-Program Communication)	(1) The general term that characterizes the LU 6.2 architecture and its various implementations in products. (2) Sometimes used to refer to the LU 6.2 architecture and its product implementations as a whole, or to an LU 6.2 product feature in particular, such as an APPC application programming interface. (3) A method for allowing programs to communicate directly with each other across a network or within a single system. APPC uses a type of LU called LU 6.2 and allows TPs to engage in peer-to-peer communications in an SNA environment.
ASP (Active Server Pages)	An open application environment in which HTML pages, scripts, and ActiveX components are combined to create Web-based applications.
COM (Component Object Model)	An open architecture for cross-platform development of client/server or object-based applications. It is based on object-oriented technology as agreed upon by Digital Equipment Corporation and Microsoft Corporation. COM defines the interface, similar to an abstract base class, IUnknown, from which all COM-compatible classes are derived.

Term	Definition
DCOM	DCOM (or distributed COM) is a specification that allows applications to utilize COM objects that reside on other physical computers. Traditional COM required that the object reside on the machine that wants to utilize it. DCOM allows other machines to host and process the objects within an application.
Domain	A group of workstations and servers that share a single group name. Utilizes Windows NT Server to act as a *domain controller* to centralize user accounts and security.
Dynamic Data Exchange (DDE)	A form of interprocess communications that uses shared memory to exchange data between applications. Applications can use DDE for one-time data transfers and for ongoing exchanges in applications that send updates to one another as new data becomes available. DDE is now obsolete because COM has come to the forefront of interprocess communications.
FTP (File Transfer Protocol)	The protocol used for copying files to and from remote computer systems on a network using a Transmission Control Protocol/ Internet Protocol (TCP/IP), such as the Internet. This protocol allows users to use FTP commands to work with files, such as listing files and directories on the remote system.
HTTP (Hypertext Transfer Protocol)	The Internet protocol used by World Wide Web browsers and servers to exchange information. The protocol makes it possible for a user to use a client program to enter an URL (or click a hyperlink) and retrieve text, graphics, sound, and other digital information from a Web server. URLs of files on Web servers begin with http://.

Term	Definition
InProc (In-Process) Server	A COM library that runs in the same process space as the application calling the object. InProc servers are DLL files. InProc servers are fast because Windows does not need to process the system calls across multiple processes. OutProc server uses more memory if multiple applications use the objects in the server because each calling application has its own copy of the server in memory.
ISAPI (Internet Server Application Programming Interface)	A set of functions for Internet servers, such as a Microsoft Windows NT Server running Microsoft Internet Information Server.
ISAPI extension	ISAPI extensions run within the Web server and operate on specific requests and transmissions within the server. An example of ISAPI extensions would be the FrontPage server extensions.
ISAPI filter	ISAPI filters act as a gateway for all server transmissions. Filters look at every packet of information that the server processes regardless of whether a specific action will be taken on the packet. The secure sockets layer (SSL) is an ISAPI filter that looks at all the requests to determine whether a specific level of security should be implemented. Filters adversely affect server performance because all traffic must be processed.
LU 6.2	A protocol used by two TPs (transaction programs) communicating as peers. LU 6.2 works in combination with node type 2.1 to provide APPC communications using independent LUs. LU 6.2 also works with node type 2.0 to provide APPC communications with dependent LUs.
Mailslot	A pseudofile used for one-way interprocess communications.

Term	Definition
MAPI (Messaging Application Programming Interface)	A messaging architecture and a client interface component. As a messaging architecture, MAPI lets multiple applications interact with multiple messaging systems across a variety of hardware platforms. *See also* MAPI subsystem, messaging system. As a client interface component, MAPI is the complete set of functions and object-oriented interfaces that forms the foundation for the MAPI subsystem's client application and service provider interfaces. In comparison with Simple MAPI, Common Messaging Calls (CMC), and the CDO Library, MAPI provides the highest performance and greatest degree of control to messaging-based applications and service providers.
Marshaling	The process through which operation parameters are packaged into a specific format so that they can be transmitted across process boundaries.
Named pipe	A one-way or two-way pipe used for communications between a server process and one or more client processes. A server process specifies a name when it creates one or more instances of a named pipe. Each instance of the pipe can be connected to a client process that uses the pipe name to open a handle to the other end of the pipe.
NTFS file system (NTFS)	A file system that supports object-oriented applications by treating all files as objects with user-defined and system-defined attributes. NTFS provides all the capabilities of the file allocation table (FAT) file system without many of its limitations. NTFS has the capability to compress files on the fly and implement file-level security. NTFS is only available under Windows NT.

Term	Definition
Object	A programmable software component representing an instance of one or more defined interfaces. Objects are used through COM in a Windows environment or can be a conceptual item within a system object model and diagram.
OOD (Object-Oriented Design)	The process of creating a physical diagram of all data, process, and objects that comprise a system. OOD utilizes tools for database modeling, object diagramming, and application documentation.
OOP (Object-Oriented Programming)	A system of programming that permits an abstract, modular typing hierarchy and features polymorphism, inheritance, and encapsulation.
OutProc (Out-of-Process) Server	A COM library that runs in its own process independent of the calling application. OutProc servers are created as EXE files. Information in an OutProc server can be shared between multiple applications and uses less overall memory for multiple calls because there is only one instance of the actual server in memory. OutProc servers are much slower than InProc servers because Windows must marshal the calls between different applications memory addresses.
Process	An executing application that consists of a private virtual address space, code, data, and other operating system resources, such as files, pipes, and synchronization objects that are visible to the process. A process also contains one or more threads that run in the context of the process.
RAD	Rapid Application Development.
RDBMS	Relational database management system.

Term	Definition
SAPI (Speech Application Programming Interface)	The set of functions that allows programming of voice and text-to-speech-enabled devices. SAPI can utilize both voice recognition and speech synthesis over standard multimedia devices or special voice processing hardware.
Screen Scraping	The process of using a software layer to copy data from a virtual 3270 terminal screen to memory and back again. This is used when accessing transactions on a mainframe computer. Screen scraping is an easy way to create a set of middleware objects that talk to CICS transactions without requiring extensive third-party support, re-coding, or complex middleware creation.
TAPI (Telephony Application Programming Interface)	A set of functions that allows programming of telephone line-based devices in a device-independent manner, giving personal telephony to users. TAPI supports both speech and data transmission, allows for a variety of terminal devices, and supports complex connection types and call-management techniques, such as conference calls, call waiting, and voice mail. TAPI allows all elements of telephone usage—from the simple dial-and-speak call to international e-mail—to be controlled within applications developed for the Microsoft Win32 application programming interface (API).
TCP/IP (Transmission Control Protocol/ Internet Protocol)	A protocol developed by the Department of Defense for communications between computers. It is built into the UNIX system and has become the *de facto* standard for data transmission over networks, including the Internet. Transport and address protocols; TCP is used to establish a connection for data transmission, and IP defines the method for sending the data in packets.

Term	Definition
Thread	The basic entity to which the operating system allocates CPU time. A thread can execute any part of the application's code, including a part currently being executed by another thread. All threads of a process share the virtual address space, global variables, and operating system resources of the process.
Transaction	A series of processing steps that results in a specific function or activity being completed, ensuring that a set of actions is treated as a single unit of work.

OTHER KEY TECHNOLOGY INFORMATION

We have discussed the many tools and technologies that Microsoft provides to developers; now let's compare the technologies side-by-side. These charts provide a quick reference for determining which tool or technology best fits a situation.

Development Tools Comparison

Here we compare the different development tools that Microsoft provides. Each tool is evaluated in the following categories:

RAD: Is the development tool considered a rapid application development tool?

Power: What level of flexibility does the development tool provide (that is, accessing and calling the Windows API, and direct hardware access)?

Web-enabled: Does the tool provide any Web-enabled support?

Learning curve: What is the application's typical learning curve?

Database-enabled: Does the tool provide direct database support within the environment?

COM-enabled: Can the application create and access COM components?

Client/server: Is this tool suitable for client/server development on its own?

Industry support: Is the tool widely supported throughout the industry, or is it a limited-use tool?

	Visual C++	*Visual Basic*	*Visual FoxPro*	*Visual InterDev*	*Visual J++*
RAD	No	Yes	Yes	Yes	No
Power	Very high	High	High	Low	High
Web-enabled	ISAPI, ActiveX, Active Documents	ActiveX, Active Documents, Web classes	ActiveX documents	HTML, ASP, DHTML, ActiveX, Java (usage)	Java classes
Learning curve	Very high	Medium	Medium	Low	High
Database-enabled	Some functionality	Some functionality	Tight integration	High level of integration	Some functionality
COM-enabled	Yes. Very high-level COM.	Yes	Yes	Yes. Usage and limited creation.	Yes
Client/server	Yes	Yes	Yes	Yes	No
Industry support	Very high. Development standard.	Very high. Development standard.	Medium. Strong following of existing users.	High. Web functionality widely supported, but the tool is relatively new.	Medium. Still used for some Internet programming and limited client/server use.

Database Comparison

We've compared the development tools; now let's take a look at the databases from Microsoft.

Large client/server applications: Does the database support a large number of users, and is the system scalable as the user base increases?

Stand-alone database: Can the database support local stand-alone applications, or is an additional programming language required to access the data?

Desktop database: Is the system designed to be used as a single-user local database?

Distributed database: Is the system designed to handle multiple users and reside in a central location for multiple application, and is the system scalable for multiple servers and/or processors?

Maximum users: The maximum number of users that the database can support before internal limitations on locking and file access become affected.

Record locking: The types of record locking supported by the database.

Stored procedures: Does the database support stored procedures?

Triggers: Does the system support triggers?

Cost: What is the relative cost of implementing the database system?

Ease of use: What is the general learning curve and technical skill level required to implement solutions with the database?

Ease of administration: What is the relative ease of day-to-day administration for items such as backups; maintaining indexes, tables, and queries; and adding new hardware and devices?

Industry support: What is the level of awareness and usage in large businesses?

Reporting capability: Does the database system include the capability to create data reports from tables and queries?

	SQL Server	*Access*
Large client/server applications	Yes	No
Stand-alone database	No	Yes
Desktop database	No (prior to SQL Server 7.0)	Yes
Distributed database	Yes	No
Maximum users	Unlimited	Max 255 for DAO
Record locking	Table, page, and row level. Row level was not available prior to version 7.0.	Table, page
Stored procedures	Yes	No (can use macros and VBA code)
Triggers	Yes	No
Cost	High	Low
Ease of use	Low	High
Ease of administration	High	Low
Industry support	High	High
Built-in reporting	No	Yes

Additional Terms and Concepts

This is an exam preparation book. It's the belief of the author and publisher that it's difficult to get too much practice with sample exam questions. There are other study material available—books and software—that enable you to practice extensively, and we recommend that you give strong consideration to using these in some form.

What follows in this chapter is a practice test designed to reflect the questions you'd likely be challenged with on an actual Microsoft exam. These questions tie in directly to the material covered in this book. Take note that when this exam goes to an adaptive format, the number of questions, passing score, and minutes necessary to take this exam will vary.

Note: Please see the end matter of this book for more information on New Riders TestPrep books and New Riders Top Score exam preparation software, among other New Riders certification study resources.

CHAPTER 8

Sample Scenario and Sample Test Questions

SAMPLE SCENARIO-BASED QUESTIONS

The Solutions Architecture exam brings in a new type of question—the scenario-based question. These questions provide a detailed case study that will be used for a series of questions that could range from multiple choice to an interactive data flow diagram.

When working with a scenario question, be sure to read the scenario, but not too deeply because each testlet you encounter is timed. For example, you might be given 30 minutes to complete testlet one. Later, you might get an hour to complete another testlet. Skim over the scenario to pick up the general ideas, but do not try to memorize all of the fine points of the scenario. You might only have four questions over an entire scenario. So, much of the data will not apply to the questions. If you need more information, you can go back to review the scenario during each testlet. Keep in mind that time might be short, and the scenarios are very long. You will not use most of the information contained in each scenario.

Generally speaking, questions based on the scenario can be classified into the following categories:

- **"Role-Based" question.** Here you encounter questions on user roles and their permissions.

- **One "Business Problem" question.** You are asked to select a statement that most closely reflects the problem described in the scenario. The answer to this is not always straightforward, and you might have to read the scenario carefully to answer it.

- **Questions on database design and normalization.** You are asked to connect the entities to show proper relationships between them.

- **"Process-Based" question.** Here, a series of boxes with labels have to be connected to show the proper workflow of the business.

- **Other types of questions.** Aside from these, you might see questions about tool selection and availability requirements.

The types of questions are covered in more detail in Chapter 9, "Insider's Spin on Exam 70-100."

Look at the following scenario. It shows what a typical scenario might cover. We will be using this for some of our sample questions later in section 2. This is a shortened scenario, but it gives you an idea of what to expect. A good reference for the scenarios and the interactive exams can be found at http://www.microsoft.com/train_cert/download/mcsd.exe. This sample exam is not graded, but it does give an example of each new scenario-based question type.

BACKGROUND

The Walla Walla Widget Company (WWWC) produces several different types of widgets that are sold to large manufacturing companies with a small department that sells to individuals. The majority of the users are salespeople who are on the road 90% of the time. Orders are taken offline through notes that the salespeople make to themselves. Each salesperson has his or her own tools to track sales data and client information.

After a company places the order, the salesperson returns to the office and an order-entry clerk keys in the order and processes the shipments.

PROBLEM STATEMENTS

Salesperson

My biggest problem in the sales force is that I cannot enter orders directly. I must wait until I get back to the office to have an order-entry specialist process the order. I am on the road more than anyone, and I might be out of the office for two weeks at a time. Sometimes, I fax or mail the orders to someone in the order department, but this is unreliable at best. I need to be sure that an order has been placed, but it also needs to be placed in a timely manner.

Order-Entry Specialist

We need a way to receive orders in a more organized fashion. Most of the sales force is back in the office on Friday, and we get hammered with new orders. Obviously, each salesperson's customer is the most important and needs to be processed first. We get some orders in during the week, but for the most part, the sales force gives them to us all at once. We are under some pressure and highly overloaded, and we do make errors in the orders because we are forced to work too fast. The remainder of the week is slow, and we sit around waiting for individuals to call.

Information Technology Manager

Our systems are overloaded at the end of the week. It seems like the order-entry department holds every order until Friday, and they all decide to hit the system at once. I get a lot of users complaining about slow performance and timeouts. We use an Access database for our order-entry information, and the shipping and warehouse updates get sent to a mainframe that ties into our older systems in the warehouses. We are on a 10-megabit network, and the database server is also the PDC.

CURRENT SYSTEMS

Customers

A customer places orders through salespeople for corporate accounts. Small businesses and individuals place orders with clerks at the main offices. Corporate clients have one or more salespeople with whom they deal with directly. After orders have been placed, the order is queued until a batch process updates all of the systems and sends the appropriate information to manufacturing, warehouses, and the shipping departments.

Salesperson

A salesperson has several corporate clients who are visited on a regular basis. All orders are placed with the sales force and are stored on their laptop PCs until they return to the office. When they are in the office, they print the corporate orders and send them to the order clerks for processing.

Information Technology Manager

We are currently running on several different systems. First, the warehouse management system is a mainframe-based system. This system does more than process our orders; it maintains all of the inventory-based functions of the company. This is a core system since it manages the majority of our business. We run a series of batch cycles nightly in order to process all order, shipment, and inventory changes.

ENVIRONMENTS

Information Technology Manager

Our shipping system runs on a Novell file server, and our order-processing system runs on a Windows NT 4.0 server. The warehouse and manufacturing system is on an AS/400 mainframe, and the system is written in CICS/COBOL. We are all running a 10Mb network, but we just upgraded the hubs, routers, and switches for a 100Mb network. We are in the final stages of setting up a direct Internet connection.

All workstations are P2 300 desktops with 64MB of RAM and a 6GB hard drive. We just upgraded the systems last year, and these should hold out for at least one more year. The workstations are a mix of Windows 95 and Windows 98.

Chief Information Officer

We have just finished our budget for the year, and we will have ample funds to upgrade our existing computer systems. As long as we can justify the expense, we can have it. We need to be sure that out customers are getting what they need, and we are willing to pay for the tools to make this happen.

Network Administrator

We currently run on only two Windows NT servers—one is the PDC and the other is the BDC (Backup Domain Controller). Our PDC runs the majority of our applications and is starting to have some problems processing all of the data and managing the user accounts.

ENVISIONED SYSTEM

Sales Manager

Each salesperson needs to be able to access our system from the client sites. If each salesperson could place a client's order in real time, we would sell more units and provide better service. We would also reduce the errors in order processing because the customer would be able to verify the order with the salesperson.

Order-Processing Manager

We need to reduce the amount of orders we get in at a single time. My team needs to focus on the smaller customers and all order maintenance. We need to be able to place an order in one system without being forced to duplicate data over several systems. Currently, my team enters the order in one system, updates inventory in another system, and adds some preliminary shipping data in a third system. The batch cycles take care of the majority of the work, but an error in one system sends the bill to one customer and the order to another. We need to integrate these systems.

Network Administrator

We need to reduce the load on the main servers. I would also like to see us utilize some additional servers so that we do not need to update each client machine (and salesperson's laptop) manually whenever there is a system update.

SECURITY

Sales Manager

Our current systems are not secure. You can easily make changes to orders that are not yours. I want each of my salespeople to see the other orders, but I only want the owner and managers to make changes. I also want to be sure that we do not allow employees who are not part of sales to see our contact and order information because our competitors would love to know who we are working with and what they are buying.

Order Processing Manager

My team cannot make changes to orders after they are placed. We are entering a lot of data, and when we make a mistake or the sales force gives us the wrong information, we need to find a salesperson to make changes. If we do not find one fast enough, the order gets processed incorrectly. Either the system sends it out as an error and adds at least one more day to the process, or we end up sending 1000 widgets to a customer who ordered 100 widgets.

Performance

Sales Manager

We expect to almost double our sales force in the next year due to our new product line. We can look to get about 75 to 100 new employees.

System Administrator

We need to increase our uptime because we will go international this year, and we need to be able to service Europe and parts of Asia. We currently have the luxury of having weekends and evenings for downtime, but that will change. We need to add some redundancy for maintenance.

Information Technology Manger

Five satellite offices will be opened next year. We will need to add a WAN connection to each office. Currently, we do not have a direct network connection or even a RAS bank. We have three dial-in lines for administrators and developers for off-hours, but they are only single-channel ISDN lines.

Maintainability

Network Administrator

When the developers send me a new version of our applications, we have to install the new software to each system manually. We cannot be guaranteed that each user will properly update the system. We need some system in place to push the new files to each desktop automatically. We still have a problem with the sales force because they might be out of the office, and we need to coordinate with each employee when there are system changes.

Information Technology Manager

Our current development staff is made up of experienced COBOL/CICS developers, some midlevel Visual Basic developers, two junior-level Visual C++ programmers, and a few employees who know some basic HTML. We do not have a dedicated DBA, but we have a developer on the PC as well as the mainframe side handling those duties as well as their development duties.

Availability

Order-Entry Manager

My team needs the system from 8:00 a.m. to 8:00 p.m. Monday through Friday. Orders are processed during these times.

Information Technology Manager

The batch cycles run between midnight and 3:00 a.m. every morning except for weekends.

Sample Test Questions

You might need to refer to the scenario to answer some of these questions.

1. *Draw the business flow for the sales force. Figure 8.1 is an example of the screen you will see on the exam:*

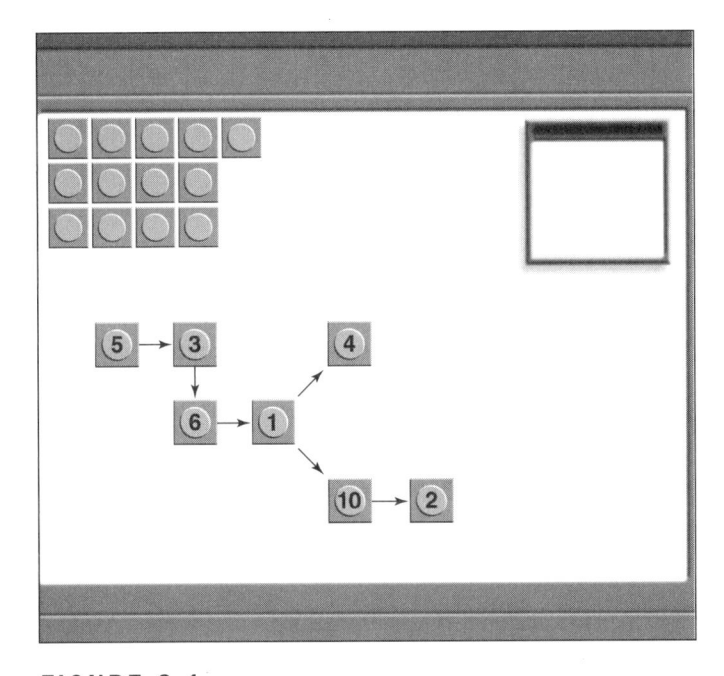

FIGURE 8.1
An example of a screen shot you might see on the exam.

2. *You want to upgrade the current system to use the most recent database technology. What data access layer would you implement?*

    A. DAO
    B. RDO
    C. ADO
    D. DAO with ODBCDirect

258 CHAPTER 8 Sample Scenario and Sample Test Questions

3. What database system would you implement in the order entry system at the main office?
    A. Access
    B. SQL Server
    C. FoxPro
    D. None of the above

4. The WWC Coffee Company is thinking about implementing a VRU (voice response unit) on the phone for touch-tone order entry and assistance. What API would be used for a VRU system?
    A. MAPI
    B. SAPI
    C. TAPI
    D. Win32 API

5. You are planning to implement some form of remote system access for the sales force. You want to minimize the total cost of implementation while maximizing flexibility for connections. What would you choose?
    A. Implement a phone bank and set up dedicated RAS servers to allow the sales force to dial in from any location.
    B. Implement a virtual private network through the Internet.
    C. Continue with the existing program.
    D. Utilize a terminal server application.

6. The CIO wants to leverage the Internet for commerce. He has asked you to start a project with the internal development teams. What development tools should you use?
    A. FrontPage
    B. Site Server
    C. InterDev
    D. Internet Information Server

7. What technologies could you use to give the Windows developers access to the mainframe data files?
    A. SNA Server
    B. SMS Server
    C. SQL Server
    D. Exchange Server

8. What are the availability requirements of the system? List the days and hours of operation.

9. The current order system uses Microsoft Access. You want to integrate the system with SQL Server as quickly as possible. The existing system uses an ODBC connection to the Access database. What steps would you take?
    1. Use the Access upsizing wizard to move to SQL Server.
    2. Update the ODBC DSN.
    3. Install the SQL Server tools on each machine.
    4. Create a device under SQL Server for the new database.
    5. Change from DAO calls to ADO in the client application.
    6. Reconfigure each machine to use the SQL Server connection libraries.
    7. Upgrade the existing system to use ODBCDirect.
    8. Import the database into SQL Server using SQL Enterprise manager.

10. In order to reduce processing costs, the company is looking to implement one of the following system changes. Review each and determine which will produce the highest return on investment (ROI).
    Note: There are eight employees in the order-entry department running at 75% capacity, which is the management target. Each clerk makes $27,000 per year. The expected lifetime of the application is two years.
    A. One application change would enable them to automatically route the shipping and order information to the shipping department and the warehouse. This would reduce the number of misshipments by 75%. Monthly orders are $75,000, and currently 10% of the orders need to be modified.

    Cost of implementation: $20,000

B. The second change would be to put a front end on the Web for the sales force. This would allow them to enter their own orders and bypass the clerks. This would decrease the overall wait time for an order, and WWC figures that sales would rise 10% due to the enhanced service. This would decrease the workload of the clerks by 25%.

Cost of implementation: $110,000

11. *You are the project manager for the WWC system modifications. What development methodology should you follow to adhere to Microsoft standards?*
    A. DNA
    B. MSF
    C. MCP
    D. Any development methodology would adhere to the Microsoft standards.

12. *Where should you implement security within a three-tier architecture? (Select all that apply)*
    A. User services
    B. Business services
    C. Data services
    D. Reporting services

13. *At what level should you validate a credit card to be sure the numbers are from a valid card type?*
    A. User services
    B. Business services
    C. Data services

14. *You are organizing the employees into groups in order to implement system security. List the groups and members that you may use.*

15. *Which of the following items are important for budgeting and feature implementation purposes?*
    A. TCO
    B. DAO

C. ROI
D. ISO
E. LCO

16. *You want the application and environment to be as stable and secure as possible. What operating system should the users be running?*
    A. Windows 95
    B. Windows NT Workstation
    C. Windows NT Server

17. *What are the three main components of an Entity-Relationship (ER) diagram?*
    A. Joins
    B. Attributes
    C. Entities
    D. Columns
    E. Tables
    F. Relationships

18. *Part of the WWC application will have an Explorer-style interface. Which of the following common controls should be included?*
    A. Tabbed dialog boxes
    B. Toolbars
    C. Progress bars
    D. Tree views
    E. Status bars
    F. List views

19. *What are the two types of help in Windows?*
    A. HTML Help
    B. App Help
    C. Standard Help
    D. WinHelp
    E. Sysinfo

20. *In a standard Windows application that has no custom menus, what should be the four menu items and the correct order of the items?*

21. *Read the following description:*

    A customer places an order with a salesperson. Each order contains one or more items. The order is then sent through the system where an invoice is generated. The invoice is generated at the end of the month for all orders and sent to the billing contact for the customer. A payment is received from the customer and is processed though the system.

    What are the entities?

22. *In order to save the customer data that has changed, you call Customer.Update. Update is a:*
    - A. Property
    - B. Event
    - C. Method
    - D. Callback

23. *You want to be able to accommodate users with hearing or vision impairments, but you want other users to be able to use the application without the special enhancements. What service would be responsible for this?*
    - A. User services
    - B. Business services
    - C. Data services

24. *In SQL Server, how would you enforce referential integrity?*
    - A. Constrains
    - B. Triggers
    - C. Views
    - D. Stored Procedures

25. *Look at the following statement:*

    "A customer must have a credit account set up before they can ask to be invoiced for the order."

    This is an example of a(n):
    - A. Business case
    - B. Data rule
    - C. Business rule
    - D. Feature
    - E. Use case

ANSWERS AND EXPLANATIONS

1. Figure 8.2 is an example of an answer that is considered correct. You can get partial credit for these answers, so you do not have to answer exactly like Figure 8.2 to get points.

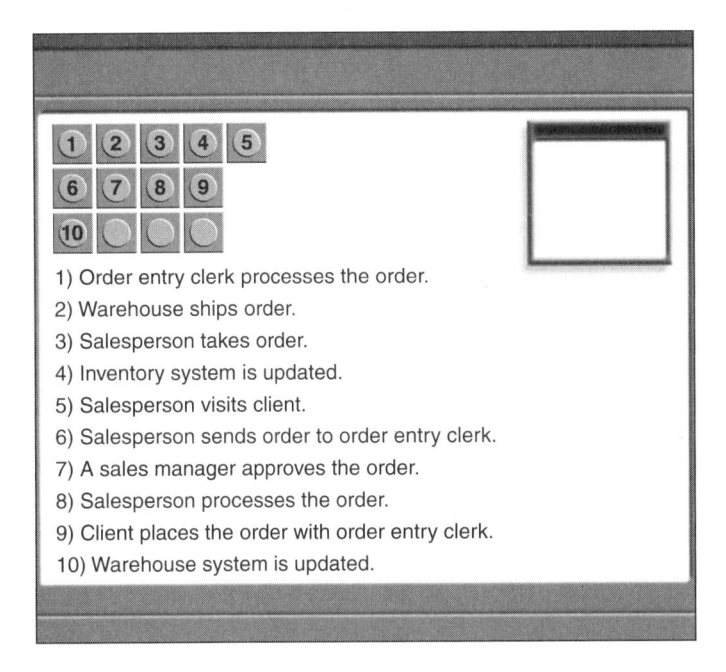

   ```
   ① ② ③ ④ ⑤
   ⑥ ⑦ ⑧ ⑨
   ⑩ ○ ○ ○
   ```

   1) Order entry clerk processes the order.
   2) Warehouse ships order.
   3) Salesperson takes order.
   4) Inventory system is updated.
   5) Salesperson visits client.
   6) Salesperson sends order to order entry clerk.
   7) A sales manager approves the order.
   8) Salesperson processes the order.
   9) Client places the order with order entry clerk.
   10) Warehouse system is updated.

   FIGURE 8.2
   An example of a correct answer for the screen shown in Figure 8.1.

2. **C** You would use ADO because ADO uses OLE DB to service data from relational database systems though ODBC and native OLE DB drivers, but it also provides access to nonrelation and nondatabase systems though custom OLE DB providers. RDO is limited in its scope and is designed to be used with SQL Server and Oracle. DAO is the JET libraries used with Access and adds an additional and unnecessary object layer to ODBCDirect. Basic DAO is designed to be used primarily with Access.

3. **B** SQL Server is the database of choice because it is the most scalable of all the Microsoft database technologies and is most suited to large systems and systems that are mission critical. SQL Server will lower the TCO of the system by being scalable, helping to separate the system into an *n*-tier application, and providing an additional layer of security. Both Access and FoxPro are geared toward smaller systems and desktop applications. Neither of these provides for triggers, stored procedures, or custom data types. Also, security with FoxPro and Access is limited, whereas SQL Server can use either its built-in security or integrated security with Windows NT.

4. **C** TAPI is the Telephony API that allows computer systems to integrate with telephone systems and switches. The MAPI library is for email integration, whereas the SAPI library is for speech recognition and control. The Win32 API is the link to the Windows system but does not have any of the TAPI engine information built in.

5. **B** The company is finalizing a direct Internet connection, and implementing a virtual private network will have the lowest overall cost. Phone banks are expensive and can host only a limited number of connections. If you have too few connections, the sales force will not be able to connect at the same time. This also increases the load on the internal phone system, possibly forcing an upgrade. On top of the hardware problems, connectivity charges may be a problem financially. A RAS server would require each salesperson to connect through a long distance connection. On the other hand, a virtual private network will allow the sales force to connect to the network though any Internet service provider (ISP). National ISPs have local access numbers in almost every major city in the country. The VPN rides on the bandwidth of the Internet connection and utilizes the large amount of bandwidth available.

6. **C** Although Internet Information Server is necessary for hosting a Web site, it is not a development tool. FrontPage, though easy, is limited in its development possibilities. Site Server is primarily for large sites that require member specific services and e-commerce. Site Server requires additional administrators and developers familiar with current e-commerce technologies.

Visual InterDev can leverage the Visual Basic knowledge of the team through VBScript. InterDev also gives some of the WYSWYG capabilities of FrontPage while allowing Web pages to access business objects and various databases.

7. **A** SNA Server provides several forms of access to mainframes. Among other things, SNA Server has the capability to link PCs to mainframe data so that Windows applications can take advantage of the data though ODBC. SNA also allows some CICS transactions to be called as COM objects from Windows applications. SQL Server is a database server, SMS is an administrative maintenance and enterprise configuration tool, and Exchange server is an email and collaboration server.

8. The system must be available between 8 a.m. and 8 p.m. Monday through Friday, as well as midnight to 3 a.m. Monday through Friday.

9. 1. Create a device under SQL Server for the new database

   2. Use the Access upsizing wizard to move to SQL Server

   3. Change from DAO calls to ADO in the client application

   4. Update the ODBC DSN

   You can argue that upgrading to ODBCDirect is faster than changing to ADO calls, and the system does give partial credit for that answer. Keep in mind that Microsoft is really pushing the ADO initiative, and you want to focus on ADO when it is an answer choice. ADO isn't always the correct answer, but when ADO and any other technology can be used, you can bet the ADO is the correct answer.

10. The ROI calculation for the first change would be as follows:

    The monthly misshipments total $7,500 ($75,00 sales × 10% misshipments). We would reduce this by $5,625 per month ($7,500 × 75%). The total amount saved would be $135,000. The ROI would then be $115,000 ($135,000 - $20,000).

The ROI for the second item would be as follows:

Sales would increase by 10%, adding an additional $7,500 per month. We would reduce the workload on the sales force by 25%, bringing utilization to 50%. The management target for utilization is 75%, so we could reduce the number of employees by two and still be below the management target. We determine this by plain algebra: eight employees × 50% = X employees × 75%. This gives just over five employees, and because we cannot have a fractional employee (I hope), we say six employees.

So, we know that each employee makes $27,000 per year, and we would save $54,000 in employee costs. We would gain $7,500 in additional sales per month. Over the life of the application, this would equate to $180,000 ($7,500 × 24 months). The total amount saved would be $234,000. The ROI would then be $124,000 ($234,000 − $110,000).

Although the second feature would not be the employee-friendly option, it is still the best option from a financial standpoint. When dealing with TCO and ROI questions, you need to focus on the math rather than the human factor. The other tip is to complete the calculations because one answer might jump out as the sure bet, but you might be surprised at the real answers.

11. **B** DNA is the new Distributed interNet Applications Architecture development model, not methodology. MCP is a Microsoft Certified Professional (what you will be when you pass this exam). MSF is the Microsoft Solutions Framework, the primary development methodology of Microsoft. More information on MSF can be found at http://www.microsoft.com/msf.

12. **B, C** You should implement security at the business object layer to validate users and authentication levels. You should also implement security at the database level to keep unauthorized users from directly connecting to your data.

13. **B** You are not attempting to validate database level data. The validation of a credit card number is a business rule because you can add and remove accepted credit cards, vendors can modify numbering schemes, and you might need to process data differently, depending on the type of credit card.

Answers and Explanations   267

14. Your answers may vary a bit. Sales for the sales force, Clerks for the order entry clerks, Managers for management and supervisors.

15. **A, C**   TCO is Total Cost of Ownership and is important in budgeting because the overall cost (not just the development cost) is a major driving force when planning an application. You must look at administration, maintenance, and training costs, as well as the initial development costs to determine the overall TCO. ROI is Return on Investment and is important in the feature implementation phases of development. Features with a high ROI will help offset a relatively high TCO because you are saving more money than you are spending. Some features might have a high price tag and an even higher ROI, whereas others might have a small price tag but a low ROI and high development cost.

16. **B**   Windows 95 is fast, but not secure. Windows NT Workstation is very secure. NTW is C-2 level compliant, which means it passes government standards for security. Windows NT Sever is too expensive for desktop use and is not optimized for end-user applications, whereas NT Workstation is designed to be an end-user operating system.

17. **B, C, F**   Two of the answers were giveaways: C, entities; and F, relationships. Attributes, correct answer B, are the properties of an entity. These will later become the columns in a table. Answers A, D, and E are all created during the physical data modeling phase of development.

18. **B, D, E, F**   A true Explorer-style window has a toolbar on top, a tree view in the middle-left, a list view in the middle-right, and a status bar on the bottom.

19. **A, D**   HTML Help is a new help system that incorporates HTML and DHTML into help files to enhance help systems with interactive and multimedia support. WinHelp is the old help system that was based on Rich Text Format (RTF) files that had bookmarks for topics.

20. The four menus and the correct order are: File, Edit, View, and Help.

21. The entities are as follows: Customer, Order, Item (inventory), Employee (salesperson is a subset of an employee), Invoice (because it can contain multiple orders), and Payment (because payments might not be complete, we need to track multiple payments to a single invoice).

    The billing contact would not be an entity; rather, it would be an attribute of the Customer entity.

22. Customer.Update is a method of the Customer object.

23. **A**   Any interface changes or modification occur here. These are not part of the system's business logic.

24. **B**   Triggers are used in SQL Server to enforce referential integrity by enabling you to view and modify data before the update or delete actually occurs. Views are stored and compiled queries. Stored Procedures are precompiled functions in SQL Server. Constraints are rules that are applied to columns for data validation.

25. **C**   This is an example of a business rule because it clearly defines the interaction between data and objects within the application. The business case would be the process that occurs but does not fully define the rule.

The Insider's Spin gives you the author's word on exam details specific to 70-100, as well as information you possibly didn't know but could definitely benefit from about what's behind Microsoft's exam preparation methodology. This chapter is designed to deepen your understanding of the entire Microsoft exam process. Use it as extra inside info brought to you by someone who teaches this material for a living.

CHAPTER 9

Insider's Spin on Exam 70-100

At A Glance: Exam Information

Exam Number	70-100
Minutes	180
Questions	Varies (4-5 testlets)
Passing Score	*
Scenarios	Yes
Single-Answer Questions	Yes
Multiple Answer with Correct Number Given	Yes
Multiple Answer without Correct Number Given	Yes
Build List and Reorder	Yes
Create a Tree	Yes
Drop and Connect	Yes
Objective Categories	6

At the time of publication, this information was unavailable.

The Analyzing Requirements and Defining Solution Architectures exam is computer-administered and is intended to measure your ability to analyze customer needs and make critical implementation decisions. This exam is essentially codeless and requires detailed knowledge of Microsoft tools and technologies. Knowledge of product integration issues and product limitations will be tested in detail.

This exam introduces a new type of question referred to as a scenario-based question. You are given a series of "testlets" that analyze a specific business scenario. You are then given a short series of questions specific to that scenario. The number and types of questions presented vary. The different types of questions are described in more detail in a moment.

One key point you need to remember with this exam is that after you complete a testlet, you cannot go back. You can review answers in the current testlet when you reach the end of the testlet, but you cannot review prior testlets. This avoids the trick of reviewing all the questions in the exam and hoping that a later question will provide the answer to a previous question.

Each testlet is individually timed. You might have 180 minutes to finish the test, but the time saved on a testlet does not carry over. Do not rush through the testlets for fear of time restraints, because the time will reset to 0 on the next testlet.

You will encounter several new types of questions on the new exam:

- Build list and reorder
- Create a tree
- Drop and connect

BUILD LIST AND REORDER

The build list and reorder questions require you to take a list of data items and order them in a specific way as outlined in the question. Read the question carefully, because a small word or phrase can change the order criteria. Note that it might have a situation where you do not use all of the data items. You will not be told to "select the four groups" or any given any other indication of the number of data items to use.

Figure 9.1 asks the user to rank from most access to least access. If you do not read the question carefully, you might accidentally rank in the opposite order.

CREATE A TREE

Create a tree questions require you to organize data points under several classifications (see Figure 9.2). You might not use all of the data points, and some of the data points are used in multiple locations. You might be told the maximum number of data items to use.

Many of the items need to be inferred from the information in the scenario. Not a lot information is taken verbatim from the text of the scenario.

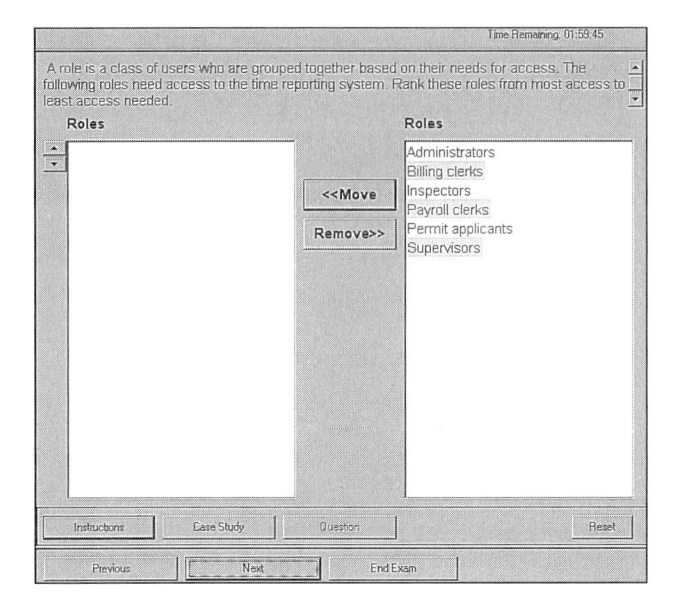

FIGURE 9.1
Build list and reorder example.

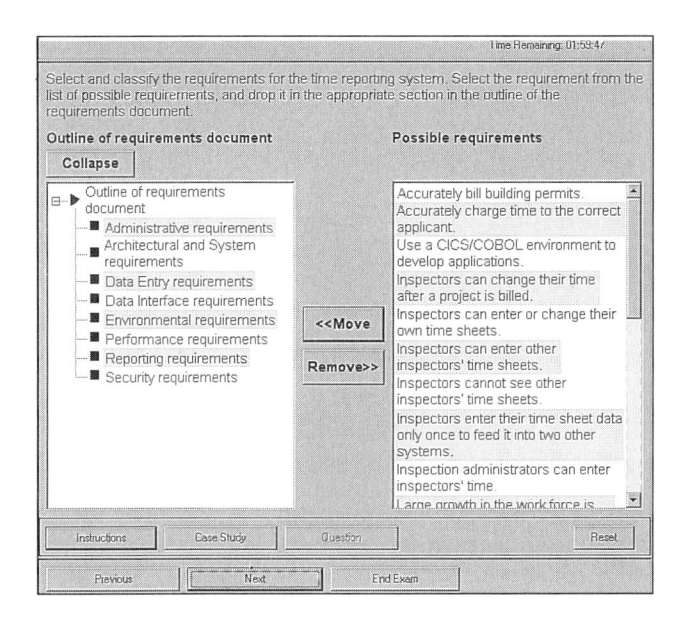

FIGURE 9.2
Create a tree example.

Drop and Connect

The drop and connect questions are used with data diagrams and process flows (see Figure 9.3). You select two data items and the connection between them. One problem many users have on the exam is being able to see the physical connections. It makes a difference which order you select when drawing data diagrams, and on smaller monitors, it might not be possible to see all the data connections for verification. You must move the data items around the screen to see whether the relationships are pointing in the correct direction. You can drag the data points all over the screen, and the layout is not important in answering the question.

Not all the data points are used in some questions, and some data points have several connections to other data points.

This exam covers every major aspect of application design, development, and analysis. Questions range from determining users and groups to implementing key technologies and order of implementation.

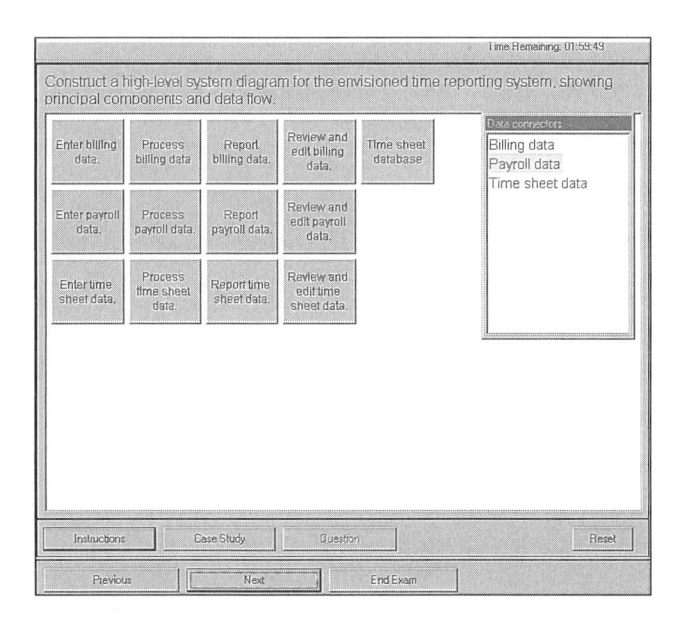

FIGURE 9.3
Drop and connect example.

Microsoft has made it clear that the new exams will be harder and more experience-based than before. The syllabus for 70-100 states that you should have two years of experience in the following areas:

- Analyzing customer needs and creating requirements specifications documents for client/server solutions in multiple business domains
- Process modeling, data modeling, component design, and user interface design
- Designing, developing, and implementing a client/server solution
- Knowledge of the functionality of both Microsoft Office and Microsoft BackOffice applications
- Integration of new systems and applications into legacy environments
- Developing Microsoft Windows and Web applications

There is no question that through the intense level of questions, new scoring scheme, and new forms of questions, Microsoft is planning on eliminating passing through the use of braindumps or rote memorization.

Although Microsoft no longer releases specific exam information, at one time they said that 85 percent of those who take a certification exam fail it. Common logic then indicates that only 15 out of every 100 people who think they know a product know it well enough to pass—a remarkably low number.

Quite often, developers who do know a product very well and use it daily fail certification exams. Is it because they don't know the product as well as they think they do? Sometimes, but more often than not, it is because of other factors, including the following:

- They know the product from a real-world perspective, not Microsoft's perspective.
- They are basing their answers on the product's previous release(s), which might be significantly different from the new version.
- They are unaccustomed to so many questions in such a short time, or they are unaccustomed to the electronic test engine.
- They don't use all the testing tools or pretest time available to them.

The purpose of this chapter is to try to prepare you for the exam and help you overcome these four issues. If you've been taking exams daily and you don't think you need this information, skim this chapter and go on. Odds are that you will still uncover some helpful tips. On the other hand, if you haven't taken many electronic exams or you've been having difficulty passing them by as wide a margin as you should, read this chapter carefully.

GET INTO MICROSOFT'S MIND-SET

When taking the exam, remember that Microsoft was responsible for writing the exam. Microsoft employees don't write the exams themselves. Instead, experts in the field are hired on a contract basis to write the questions. However, all questions must adhere to certain standards and be approved by Microsoft before they make it into the actual exam. What this translates into is that Microsoft will never put anything in an exam that reflects negatively on them. It will also use the exam for promotional marketing as much as possible.

Therefore, to successfully answer questions and pass the exam, you must put yourself into the Microsoft mind-set and see questions from their standpoint. For example, consider the following question:

1. Which RAD development tool will allow for the most flexibility with using third-party applications and will have the shortest client/server development time?

   A. Visual C++

   B. Visual InterDev

   C. Visual Basic

   D. Visual FoxPro

Although you could make a sincere argument for at least three of the answers, only one answer would be correct on the exam. Don't try to read too much between the lines, and don't think you can put a comment at the end of the exam, arguing why another choice would be better. If you answer anything other than C, you might as well write this one off as a missed question.

Also, related to this, Microsoft always promotes the new technologies within its software. When choices are given reflecting older versions of Microsoft products and newer capabilities, always choose the newer technologies over older equivalents. Consider the following question:

2. You are developing a client/server application that will access a database across all internal networks, as well as the Internet. Which database technology would you choose?

   A. RDO

   B. ADO

   C. DAO

   D. RDS

Again, arguments could be made for at least three of the choices, but because the ADO architecture represents the "new" solution to this situation, it is the correct choice.

Understand the Exam's TimeFrame

When you take an exam, find out when it was written. In almost all cases, an exam goes live within three months of the final release of the product it is based on. Before the exam is released, it goes through a beta process in which all the questions that can be on the exam are written. This exam version is then available for a short time (typically a week), during which scores on each question can be gathered. Questions that exam takers get right every time are weeded out as being too easy. Those that are too hard are weeded out also.

When you create an exam for a major BackOffice system (which will remain nameless in this example), you end up with a timeframe similar to the following:

1. The product goes into early beta.

2. A survey is done (mostly of beta testers) to find out which components of the product they spend the most time with and consider the most important. The findings are used to generate the objectives and the weighting for each.

3. The product goes to final beta.
4. Contract writers are hired to write questions about the product using the findings from the survey.
5. The product goes live.
6. The exam is beta-tested for one to two weeks. After that, the results of each question are evaluated, and the final question pool is chosen.
7. The service pack for the product is released.
8. The exam goes live.
9. Another service pack is released. It fixes problems from the first service pack and adds additional functionality.
10. Yet another service pack comes out.
11. An option pack that incorporates service packs is released.
12. You take the exam.

Now suppose that the product happens to be Windows NT Server 4, and you see a question such as this:

3. What is the maximum number of processors that Windows NT Server 4 can handle?

   A. 2
   B. 4
   C. 8
   D. 16

In the real world, the answer would be C or D, depending on how you look at it: The end-user license agreement states that 8 is the limit, but NCR and other vendors make SMP servers that can run NT on 16. When NT 4 first came out, however, the answer was B. Because the original exam questions were written to the final beta, the answer then was B, so the answer now is B. Microsoft has maintained that it will test only on core products, not add-ons. Service packs, option packs, and the like are considered something other than core product.

With this in mind, you must always answer the questions as if you were addressing the product as it exists when you pull it from the box and before you do anything else with it, because that is exactly what the exam is written to. You must get into this mind-set and understand the timeframe in which the exam was written, or you will fail the exam consistently.

GET USED TO ANSWERING QUESTIONS QUICKLY

Every exam has a different number of questions. If you run out of time, every question you haven't answered is graded as a wrong answer. Therefore, keep the following in mind:

- Always answer every question; never leave any unanswered. If you start running out of time, answer all the remaining questions with the same letter and then go back and start reading them. Using the law of averages, if you do run out of time, you should get 25 percent of the remaining questions correct.

- Time yourself carefully. A clock runs in the upper-right corner of each screen. Mark all questions that require lots of reading or that have exhibits, and come back to them after you've answered all the shorter questions.

- Practice, practice, practice. Get accustomed to electronic questioning and answering in a short period. With so many exam simulators available, there is no reason for anyone not to run through one or two before plunking down $100 for the real test. Some simulators aren't worth the code they're written in, and others are so close in style to the actual exam that they prepare you very well. If you want to save money, look for demos and freebies on Web sites. The site at http://www.MeasureUp.com is an excellent example of where you can try some sample exams online.

If you do run out of time, spend as much time as you want to on the last question. You will never time out with a question in front of you. You will time out only when you click Next to go from that question to the next one.

Taking the Test

An enormous amount of common sense is important here, and much of that common sense comes only as you get more used to the testing procedure. Here's a typical sequence of events:

1. You study for an exam for a considerable period of time.
2. You call Sylvan Prometric (1-800-755-EXAM) and register for the exam, or you register online at www.sylvanprometric.com.
3. You drive to the testing site, sit in your car, and cram on last-minute details.
4. You walk into the center, sign your name, show two forms of ID, and walk to a computer.
5. Someone enters your ID into the computer and leaves. You're left with the computer, two pieces of plain paper, and two No. 2 pencils.
6. You click the button on the screen to begin the exam, and the 180 minutes begins.

When you call Sylvan, be sure to ask how many questions are on the exam so that you know before you go in. Sylvan is allowed to release very little information (for example, they can't tell you what constitutes a passing score). This is one of the few pieces of information they can pass along.

The exam begins the minute you click the button to start it. Before that, the 180-minute timeframe hasn't started. After you walk into the testing center and sit down, you're free (within reason) to do whatever you want to. Why not dump everything from your brain (including those last-minute facts you studied in the parking lot) onto those two sheets of paper before you start the exam? The two sheets provide you with four sides—more than enough to scribble down everything you remember. You can refer to this information during the test.

When you click Start, the first testlet overview appears. Various types of questions are asked, including the type shown in Figure 9.4. Because Microsoft doesn't readily make available the capability to take screen shots of the exams (for obvious reasons), all the figures in this chapter are from a third-party emulator that closely resembles the real thing.

280 CHAPTER 9 Insider's Spin on Exam 70-100

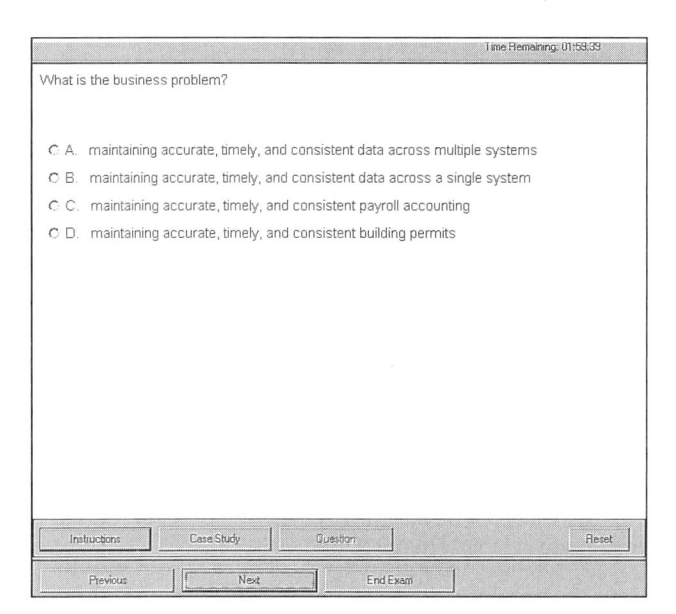

FIGURE 9.4
A sample test question.

Look at the sample question briefly, but more important, look at the information on the screen. First, you can mark this question. By doing so, you can see at the end of the testlet any questions you thought were difficult and jump back to them. (However, if you're taking an adaptive exam, you can't go back and review a question once you move to the next one.) Never mark a question and then go to the next one without choosing an answer. Even if you don't read the question at all because you're saving it for later, mark it and answer C. That way, if you run out of time, you have a chance of getting the question right.

In the upper-right corner, you see the number of the question you are on. In the real exam, you also see the time remaining. Under the question are the possible answers. The radio buttons to the left of the answers indicate that there is only one correct answer.

Although this isn't always true, many times when there are four possibilities, one is so far off the mark as to not even be plausible, and another is too much of a gimme to be true, so you are left with two possibilities. For example:

4. In NT Server 4.0, to view the Application log, what tool must you use?

   A. Application Viewer

   B. Event Viewer

   C. Event Observer

   D. Performance Monitor

In this case, choice A is the gimme of a nonexistent option that fits the question too perfectly. Choice D is the blow-off answer—so far away from what's possible as to not even be a possibility. That leaves choices B and C.

Even if you know nothing about Windows NT Server, a clue that B and C are legitimate possibilities is the similarity of their wording. Anytime you see two answers worded closely, assume that they are the ones to focus on.

The buttons at the bottom of the screen allow you to move to the next or previous question. The latter option is important, because if you come across a question whose wording provides the answer to a question you saw before, always use the Previous button to go back and change or check your answer. Never walk away from a sure thing.

When an exhibit is associated with the question, the command button for it is displayed. The problem with exhibits is that they appear on top of the question, or they can be tiled in such a way that you can't see either. Whenever you have an exhibit, read the question carefully, open the exhibit, memorize what is there (or scribble information about it on your two sheets of paper), close the exhibit, and answer the question.

Figure 9.5 shows an example of a question that has more than one correct answer, as evidenced by the check boxes next to the answers instead of radio buttons.

There are two types of these questions: one where you are told how many answers are correct (choose two, choose three, and so on), and another where you are not. In Figure 9.5, you must choose all of the correct answers. In some cases, the questions are presented in a fashion to trip you up. Sometimes there is only one correct answer, and other times all the selections are correct.

282 CHAPTER 9 · Insider's Spin on Exam 70-100

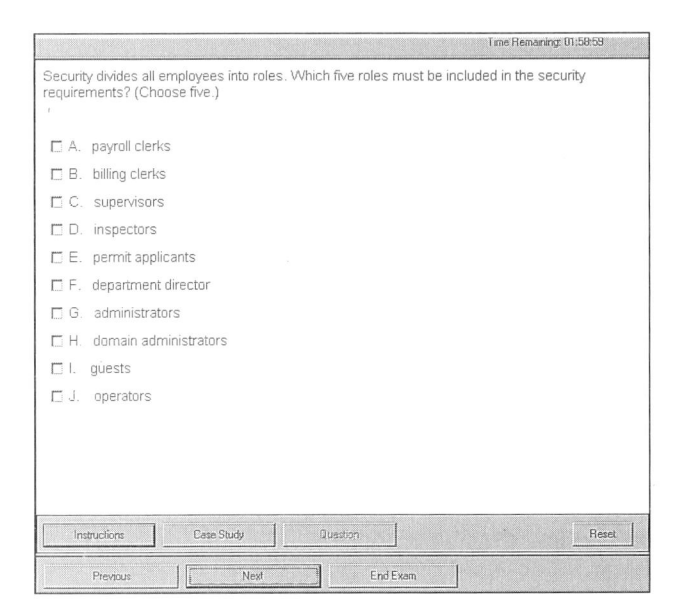

```
                                              Time Remaining: 01:58:59
Security divides all employees into roles. Which five roles must be included in the security
requirements? (Choose five.)

   □ A.  payroll clerks
   □ B.  billing clerks
   □ C.  supervisors
   □ D.  inspectors
   □ E.  permit applicants
   □ F.  department director
   □ G.  administrators
   □ H.  domain administrators
   □ I.  guests
   □ J.  operators


   [ Instructions ]  [ Case Study ]  [ Question ]              [ Reset ]
   [   Previous   ]  [    Next    ]  [ End Exam ]
```

FIGURE 9.5
Another sample test question.

In addition to the multiple-choice and single-answer questions, there are the three new question types mentioned at the beginning of this chapter.

Most multiple-answer questions offer four possibilities, meaning that you must choose one, two, three, or four, but those with more possibilities (as in Figure 9.5) are not uncommon in the 70-100 exam. With multiple-answer questions, read the question carefully and begin eliminating choices.

The biggest problem with multiple answers is that there is no such thing as partial credit. If you are supposed to choose four items, but you choose only three, the question still counts as being wrong. If you need to choose two, and you pick one right answer and one wrong answer, you miss the whole question. Spend much more time with multiple-answer questions than single-answer questions, and always come back after the exam (if time allows) and reread them carefully.

The new 70-100 question forms are graded on a different scale. There is the "correct" answer that Microsoft sees as 100% correct, and then there are multiple correct answers that give partial credit. Rumor has it that there can be many combinations that give partial credit, so try to answer these questions as best you can and move on to the next question. If you spend too much time on a single question, you might run out of time in a testlet.

At the end of the exam, you can see the questions you marked and jump back to them. If you've already chosen an answer on that screen, it remains chosen until you choose something else (the question also remains marked until you unmark it). The command buttons at the bottom of the question include an Item Review choice to let you jump back to the Item Review screen without going through additional questions.

Use the capability to mark and jump as much as you possibly can. All lengthy questions should be marked and returned to in this manner. Also note all answers that are incomplete. You can ill afford to leave questions unanswered, so be certain to go back and answer them all before choosing to finish the exam (or before you run out of time).

After you click Finish, the grading is done, and the Examination Score Report appears. Typically, the Examination Score Result you're shown has only the bar graphs and a message as to your passing or failing. A section analysis doesn't appear on the screen—only on the printed documentation you walk out of the testing center with. The pass/fail score is based on the beta of the exam and on statistics gathered from the performance of those who took it.

If you fail an exam (and everyone will occasionally), never be lulled into a false sense of confidence by the Section Analysis. If it says you scored 100% in a particular section, you should still study that section before retaking the exam. Too many test-takers study only the sections they did poorly on. That 100% in Monitoring and Optimization could be the result of the first question pool containing only one question on that topic, and you had a 25 percent chance of guessing correctly. Also note that on the real exam, you are not given the number of questions in each section. What happens the next time, when there are three questions in the random pool from that objective category, and you don't know the answers? You're handicapping yourself right off the bat.

A good rule of thumb if you do fail an exam is to rush back to your car and write down all the questions you can remember. Have your study materials in the vehicle with you, and look up the answers then and there. If you wait until later, you'll forget many of the questions.

A new Microsoft policy allows you to retake an exam you fail once without any waiting period (other than registering for it and so on). If you fail it again, however, you must wait 14 days before you can take it a third time (and 14 days from that point for the fourth try, and so on). This is to prevent people from memorizing the exam. Do your best to never fall into this category. If you fail an exam once, start all over again and study anew before trying it a second time. Make the second attempt within a week of the first, however, so that the topics are fresh in your mind.

WHERE THE QUESTIONS COME FROM

Knowing where the questions come from can be as instrumental as knowing how to prepare for the exam. The more you know about it, the better your odds of passing. Earlier, I discussed the timeframe used to create the exam, and I mentioned that contract writers are hired for the exam. The contract writers are given a sizable document detailing how questions must be written. If you want to pursue the topic with fervor, contact Microsoft and inquire about a contract writing position. Here are a few tidbits that can be gleaned from multiple-choice authoring:

- No question should have an All of the Above answer. When such a choice is available, it is almost always the correct answer, so it isn't a good representation of a multiple-choice question.

- For the same reason, there should never be a None of the Above answer.

- Scenarios should be used when they increase the value of the question.

- Subjective words (such as best and most) should be avoided.

- Negative words (such as not and cannot) should be avoided.

- Although there can be only one correct answer for the question, all other possibilities should appear plausible and should avoid all rationale or explanations.

- Single answers must be mutually exclusive (no A+C, B+C, and so on).

DIFFERENT FLAVORS OF QUESTIONS

At one time, all questions were either single-answer or multiple-answer. There is a push today to go more toward ranking and performance-based questions, as well as simulations, case studies, and adaptive questions. Older exams still have only the first two types of questions, whereas newer ones offer the latter types.

Ranking questions give you a scenario, a list of required objectives, a list of optional objectives, and a proposed solution. You have to rank how well the solution meets the objectives. This was a commonplace question type on recent Microsoft exams. Although similar questions will be on the exam, they will have a slightly different flavor.

A simulation imitates a portion of the functionality of the product being tested. The person taking the exam is given a scenario and one or more activities to complete. Although this exam has no simulation questions, many of the Microsoft exams do have questions of this type.

Case study questioning provides smaller tests ("testlets") within the exam. Each testlet provides a case study and several questions to accompany the testlet. At this point, this question type is being used only in the MCSD core 70-100 exam.

After trying adaptive testing styles, Microsoft recently revisited its traditional format. However, Microsoft makes no promises as to the type of exam you will get when you actually sit down to take it. The current format (at the time this book was written) used by Microsoft in the majority of its newer tests is a 30-question, 90-minute exam with a very high passing score. For example, at last look, the Networking Essentials exam had a passing score of 833. This new standard certainly raises the bar for those attempting Microsoft certification exams.

Not every interesting item that the instructor shares with the class is necessarily directly related to the exam. This is the case with "Did You Know?" Think of this information as an intriguing sidebar, or the interesting diversion you want the instructor to share with you during an aside.

CHAPTER 10

Did You Know?

The following are interesting items not directly relevant to the exam:

- Old mainframe applications used to run on terminals that displayed bright green characters. The application screens eventually were coined "green screens." Today, green screens are any mainframe window on dumb terminals or terminal emulators.
- Many articles that cover the material on the Solutions Architecture exam can be found at `http://msdn.microsoft.com`.
- The following books are excellent project management and project planning references "the Microsoft way":

    Code Complete: A Practical Handbook of Software Construction by Steve McConnell (Microsoft Press)

    Debugging the Development Process: Practical Strategies for Staying Focused, Hitting Ship Dates, and Building Solid Teams by Steve Maguire (Microsoft Press)

    Software Project Survival Guide by Steve McConnell (Microsoft Press)

    The Mythical Man-Month: Essays on Software Engineering by Frederick P. Brooks Jr. (Addison-Wesley)

- Wide area networks (WANs) need to run protocols that are routable to segments of the network. TCP/IP and IPX/SPX are both routable. Microsoft's NetBEUI is not a routable protocol and can only be used with local networks.
- Visual C++ is the only Microsoft development tool that enables you to write low-level items, such as device drivers.
- Microsoft Internet Information Server 4.0 requires Microsoft Transaction Server.
- Both FrontPage and InterDev use the FrontPage server extensions for communicating with Web servers during development.
- Active server pages (ASP) are supported only on Windows NT and Windows 95/98 platforms. Microsoft does not natively support UNIX with ASP.

- Access 2000 enables developers to have the opportunity to use the JET database format or the new Microsoft Data Engine based on the new SQL Server 7.0 data formats.

- Microsoft J++ can build cross-platform application, but it extends additional functionality to allow for native Windows application development, thus supporting COM components (creation and usage).

- Microsoft Transaction Server can be used for COM objects even if they do not support the MTS ObjectContext interface. MTS can still provide connection pooling and process isolation even when the components are not transaction-aware.

- SNA Server can provide ODBC access to mainframe data and can wrap CICS transactions into COM components, allowing for a gradual migration to Windows platforms.

- Microsoft Visual SourceSafe can be used with FrontPage and InterDev to manage source files and versions for remote Internet development.

- Many bug-tracking tools now integrate with Visual SourceSafe for managing source code and bug fixes. Visual Intercept is a popular bug-tracking tool that integrates with Visual SourceSafe.

INDEX

A

accelerator keys, 143
Access 2000, 225-226
  JET database format, 289
ACID test, 238
Active Data Objects (ADO), 227-228
Active Server Pages, 239, 288
ActiveX, 239
administration support staff, 61
ADO (Active Data Objects), 227-228
Advanced Program-to-Program Communication, 239
Analyzing Requirements and Defining Solution Architectures exam
  failing, 283
  questions, 271, 279-285
    "build list and reorder," 271-272
    "create a tree," 271
    drop and connect, 273-275
    Microsoft mind set, 275-276
    scenario-based, 250-256, 260, 262-270
    time factor, 278
  registering for, 279
  screen shots, 257
  time, 271, 276-278
  tips for taking, 269-271, 279-284, 289
answers to scenario-based questions, 260-268
APPC (Advanced Program-to-Program Communication), 239
applications, 104, 196. See also interfaces
  advantages, 110-111
  COM (Component Object Model), 119-120
    events, 124-126
    interfaces, 120-121
    methods, 123
    properties, 121-123
  console, 106-107
  Crystal Reports, 168
  design. See design
  development. See development (MSF)

disadvantages, 110-111
environment, 31
green screens, 288
interfaces. *See* interfaces
MDI, 105-106
models, 104
project scope, 16
review items for test, 204-207
SDI, 104
service, 107-108
third-party, 216
Web-based, 108-109
architecture
   client/server, 111-112
      n-tier, 117-119
      single tier, 113-114
      thin client/terminal,
         114-115
      three-tier, 116-117
      two-tier, 115-116
   design, 164
      business requirements, 169
      contingency plans, 169-170
      data storage, 166
      EDI (Electronic Data
         Interchange), 164
      feasibility testing, 168
      performance considerations,
         167-168
      POSIX, 164-165
      reporting, 168
      use cases, 169
   review items for test, 211-213
AS/400, 231-232
**ASPs (Active Server Pages),
239, 288**
assistance methods (interface
design), 147
   formatting input, 151-152
   input validation, 147-149
   visual cues, 149-151

attributes (ER diagrams),
73-76
   identifying, 87
auditing, 49-51
auto-complete, 144
auto-tabbing, 144
AutoNumber field, 89
availability, 63
   downtimes, 64-65
   geographic scope, 63
   operational timelines, 63-64

B

bandwidth, 54-55
   design considerations,
      167-168
   offline time, 56-57
   peak usage, 56
batch systems, 16
budgets
   project scope, 18
      benefit trade-offs, 20-22
      cost total, 19-20
      time/labor, 18-19
   projects, 197
   TCO (total cost of
      ownership), 27
bugs, tracking tools, 289
**"build list and reorder"
questions, 271-272**
businesses
   flow diagrams, 44
   logic, 128
   practices, 44
      customer needs, 46
      organizational structures,
         44-45

requirements, 22
　application environment, 31
　architecture design, 169
　business goals, 23-24
　customer requirements, 24
　infrastructure design, 30
　new technology, impact of, 30-31
　problem analysis, 24-26
　return on investment (ROI), 26-29
　review items for test, 196-203
　schedules, 32
　total cost of ownership, 26-27
rule, 128
services, 112-113, 127

C

cartesian product, 130
certification exam
　failing, 283
　questions, 271, 279-285
　　"build list and reorder", 271-272
　　"create a tree", 271
　　drop and connect, 273-275
　　Microsoft mind set, 275-276
　　scenario-based, 250-256, 260, 262-270
　　time factor, 278
　registering for, 279
　screen shots, 257
　time, 271, 276-278
　tips for taking, 269-271, 279-284, 289

characters
　representation, 38
　translation, legacy systems, 43
child entities, 80
child tables, 79
CICS (Computer Information Control Systems), 235
classification, feature-selection list, 21
client/server architecture, 111-112
　n-tier, 117-119
　single tier, 113-114
　thin/client terminal, 114-115
　three-tier, 116-117
　two-tier, 115-116
clients. *See* customers
colors
　cues for interface design, 150-151
　windows, 141
column identity, 89
COM (Component Object Model), 39, 119-120, 239
　events, 124-126
　interfaces, 120-121
　methods, 123
　objects, Transaction Server, 289
　properties, 121-123
composed keys, 78
composite keys, 79
Computer Information Control Systems (CICS), 235
connection pooling (ODBC), 166
connectivity, legacy systems, 42-43

294 CONSOLE APPLICATIONS

console applications, 106-107
contingency plans, 169-170
controls (interface), 137
   limiting number of, 141-143
   listview, 138-140
   progress bars, 140-141
   tabstrips, 137
   toolbars, 137
   trackbar, 139-140
   treeview, 138-139
costs
   project scope, 19-20
   TCO (Total Cost of Ownership)
      budgeted, 27
      minimizing, 26-27
      unbudgeted, 27
"create a tree" questions (on exam), 271
creep (feature), 22
Crystal Reports, 168
cues, interface design, 149-151
currency formatting, 38
custom keystrokes, 144
custom middleware, 42
customers
   needs, 46
   requirements, 24

D

DAO (Data Access Object Library), 228
data
   conversion, 43
   expansion, 67
   services, 112-113, 128
   sharing, Component Object Model, 39, 119-120, 239
      events, 124-126
      interfaces, 120-121
      methods, 123
      objects, Transaction Server, 289
      properties, 121-123
databases
   Access 2000, 225-226
      Jet database format, 289
   ADO (Active Data Objects), 227-228
   architecture design, 166-168
   compared, 247-248
   DAO (Data Access Object Library), 228
   design
      logical. See *logical design*
      physical, 70, 99-100
   encapsulating, 130-131
   ODBC (Open Database Connectivity), 226-227
      connection pooling, 166
   OLE DB, 229
   RDBMS (relational database management system), 243
   RDO (Remote Data Object Library), 228-229
   records, orphaned, 89
   review items for test, 203-204
   security, 48-49
   servers, 224-225
   size, 166
   tables
      cartesian product, 130
      child, 79
      join, 83-84
      junction, 83-84
      keys. See *keys*
      referential integrity, 89
   VSAM (Virtual Sequential Access Method), 40

DCOM, 240
DDE (Dynamic Data Exchange), 240
denormalization (logical database design), 90, 98
deployment, 170-171
design. *See also* development (MSF)
  application models, 104
    advantages, 110-111
    console, 106-107
    disadvantages, 110-111
    MDI, 105-106
    SDI, 104
    service, 107-108
    Web-based, 108-109
  architecture, 164
    business requirements, 169
    contingency plans, 169-170
    data storage, 166
    EDI (Electronic Data Interchange), 164
    feasibility testing, 168
    performance considerations, 167-168
    POSIX, 164-165
    reporting, 168
    use cases, 169
  availability, 63
    downtimes, 64-65
    geographic scope, 63
    operational timelines, 63-64
  business practices, 44
    customer needs, 46
    organizational structures, 44-45
  business requirements, 22
    application environment, 31
    architecture design, 169
    business goals, 23-24
    customer requirements, 24
    infrastructure design, 30
    new technology, impact of, 30-31
    problem analysis, 24-26
    return on investment (ROI), 26-29
    review items for test, 196-203
    schedules, 32
    total cost of ownership, 26-27
  client/server architecture, 111-112
    n-tier, 117-119
    single tier, 113-114
    thin client/terminal, 114-115
    three-tier, 116-117
    two-tier, 115-116
  interfaces, 136
    clean designs, 141-143
    controls, 137-141
    errors, 156-159
    menus, 144-146
    navigation, 143-144
    prototyping, 159-160
    user ease, 147-152
    user feedback, 152-154
  legacy systems, 39
    character translation, 43
    connectivity, 42-43
    data conversion, 43
    hardware, 39
    middleware, 40-42
    migration to new systems, 40
  logical, 70
    denormalization, 90, 98
    ER diagrams, 70-78, 80-89
    normalization, 70, 90-93, 95-97

maintainability, 59
   application distribution,
    59-61
   future planning, 62-63
   support, 61-62
   upgrades, 59-61
performance. *See* performance
physical, 70, 99-100
review items for test. *See*
   review items for test
scalability, 65
   expansion data, 67
   organizational changes, 66
   planning for growth, 65-66
security models, 46
   auditing, 49-51
   databases, 48-49
   fault tolerance, 51-54
   file-level, 48
   group, 47-48
   identifying roles, 49
   server, 47
   system-level, 47
   user-level, 47
development (MSF).
See also **design**
availability, 63
   downtimes, 64-65
   geographic scope, 63
   operational timelines, 63-64
business practices, 44
   customer needs, 46
   organizational structures,
    44-45
localization, 38
maintainability, 59
   application distribution,
    59-61
   future planning, 62-63

   support, 61-62
   upgrades, 59-61
MSF Web site, 196
performance. *See* performance
project scope, 12-13
   budgets, 18-22
   defining problems, 15
   existing applications, 16
   feature creep, 22
   feature-selection, 20-22
   life expectancy, 16-17
   solutions definitions, 15-16
scalability, 65
   data expansion, 67
   organizational changes, 66
   planning for growth, 65-66
security models, 46
   auditing, 49-51
   database, 48-49
   fault tolerance, 51-54
   file-level, 48
   group, 47-48
   identifying roles, 49
   server/machine, 47
   system-level, 47
   user-level, 47
TCO (total cost of
   ownership), 27
tools, 216
   compared, 245-246
   Visual Basic, 216-217
   Visual C++, 218-219
   Visual FoxPro, 219-220
   Visual InterDev, 220-222
   Visual J++, 222-223
   Visual SourceSafe, 223-224
users, 32-33
   identifying, 33-34
   local, 36-37

remote, 36-37
training, 35-36
diagrams
  entity-relationships, 70
    attributes, 73-76, 87
    entities, 71-73, 80, 87
    generating models, 85-88
    relationships, 76-78, 80-84, 88-89
  infrastructure design, 30
disks
  duplexing, 51-52
  striping, 52-53
distribution, 59-61
documentation, infrastructure design, 30
domains, 240
downtimes (availability), 64-65
"drop and connect" questions (on exam), 273-275
Dynamic Data Exchange (DDE), 240

E

EDI (Electronic Data Interchange), 164
encapsulating databases, 130-131
environments, 31
ER (entity-relationship diagrams), 70-73, 80
  attributes, 73-74, 76
  child, 80
  entities, 71-73, 80
  identifying, 87
  generating models, 85-88
  parent, 80

relationships, 76-77
  creating, 88
  keys, 77-78, 80, 89
  many-to-many, 83-84
  one-to-many, 82-83
  one-to-one, 81
errors, 156
  handling, 158-159
  messages, 156-158
events, COM (Component Object Model), 124-126
exam 70-100
  failing, 283
  questions, 271, 279-285
    "build list and reorder," 271-272
    "create a tree," 271
    drop and connect, 273-275
    Microsoft mind set, 275-276
    scenario-based, 250-256, 260, 262-270
    time factor, 278
  registering for, 279
  screen shots, 257
  time, 271, 276-278
  tips for taking, 269-271, 279-284, 289
exam, Analyzing Requirements and Defining Solution Architectures
  failing, 283
  questions, 271, 279-285
    "build list and reorder," 271-272
    "create a tree," 271
    drop and connect, 273-275
    Microsoft mind set, 275-276
    scenario-based, 250-256, 260-270
    time factor, 278

registering for, 279
screen shots, 257
time, 271, 276-278
tips for taking, 269-271, 279-284, 289
Exchange Server, 237-238
Explorer (Windows)
    toolbar, 137
    treeview control, 138
extensions, ISAPI, 241

F

failing certification exam, 283
fault tolerance, 51
    hardware, 51-54
        disk striping, 52-53
        mirroring, 51-52
        RAID, 52, 54
    software, 54
feasibility testing, 168
feature-selection process, 20-21
    creating feature list, 21-22
    feature creep, 22
fields, autonumber, 89
file systems, NTFS, 242
File Transfer Protocol (FTP), 240
file-level security, 48
files
    help, 155
        HTML, 155-156
        standard, 155
    RMS (Record Management Services), 42
    systems, NTFS, 242
filters, ISAPI, 241
first normal form (normalization), 91

flow diagrams (business), 44
foreign keys, 80, 89
formatting input, interface design, 151-152
friend properties, 123
FrontPage, 288-289
FTP (File Transfer Protocol), 240

G-H

geographic scope (availability), 63
goals (business), 23-24
graphical icons, localization, 38
green screens, 288
group security, 47-48
hardware
    fault tolerance, 51-54
        disk striping, 52-53
        mirroring, 51-52
        RAID, 52, 54
    legacy systems, 39
help
    files, 155-156
    ToolTips, 153
    What's This Help, 153
    wizards, 154
helpdesks, 61
HTML help, 155-156
HTTP (HyperText Transfer Protocol), 240

I-J

icons, localization, 38
identity columns, 89
IIS 4.0 (Internet Information Server), 234, 288

implementation, feature-selection list, 21
infrastructure design, 30
  incorporating platforms, 30
  project scope, 13
InProc Server, 241
input validation, 147-149
interaction diagrams, 33-34
InterDev, 288-289
interfaces, 136. *See also* applications
  COM (Component Object Model), 120-121
  controls, 137
    limiting number of, 141-143
    listview, 138, 140
    progress bars, 140-141
    tabstrips, 137
    toolbars, 137
    trackbar, 139-140
    treeview, 138-139
  errors
    designing messages, 156-158
    handling, 158-159
  MDI (multiple document interface), 105-106, 164, 169
  menus, 144-146
  navigation, 143-144
  prototyping, 159-160
  review items for test, 207-211
  SDI (single document interface), 104, 169
  SNA, 41
  user ease, 147
    formatting input, 151-152
    input validation, 147-149
    visual cues, 149-151
    user feedback, 152
    status bars, 152-153
    ToolTips, 153
    What's This Help, 153
    wizards, 154
  Web, 169
Internet, IIS 4.0, 234
Internet Information Server (IIS), 234, 288
ISAPI (Internet Server Application Programming Interface), 241

J++ cross-platform applications, 289
Jet database format, 289
join tables, 83-84
junction tables, 83-84

K-L

keys, 77
  composed, 78
  composite, 79
  defined, 77
  foreign, 80, 89
  primary, 77-78, 80, 89
labor budgets, 18-19
LANs (local area networks), 232
legacy systems, 39
  character translation, 43
  connectivity, 42-43
  data conversion, 43
  hardware, 39
  middleware, 40-42
  migration to new systems, 40
life expectancy, project scope, 16-17
listview controls, 138-140

local area networks
  (LANs), 232
local users, 36-37
localization, 38
location deployment, 171
logical design, 70
  denormalization, 90, 98
  ER diagrams, 70
    attributes, 73-76, 87
    entities, 71-73, 80, 87
    generating models, 85-88
    relationships, 76-78, 80-84,
      88-89
  normalization, 70, 90
    first normal form, 91
    second normal form, 91, 93
    third normal form, 95-97
LU 6.2, 241

M

mailslots, 241
mainframe computing,
  234-235
maintainability, 59
  application distribution, 59-61
  future planning, 62-63
  support, 61-62
  upgrades, 59-61
maintenance, 62, 171
many-to-many relationships,
  83-84
MAPI (Messaging Application
  Programming Interface), 242
marshaling, 242
MDI (multiple-document
  interface), 105-106, 164, 169
MeasureUp.com, 278

menus
  interface design, 144-146
  shortcut keys, 145
messages, errors, 156-158
Messaging Application
  Programming Interface
  (MAPI), 242
Microsoft
  Application Programming
    Interface (MAPI), 242
  Component Object Model.
    See COM
  Data Engine, 289
  Exchange Server, 237-238
  Message Queue, 56-57
  Solution Framework. *See* MSF
  Transaction Server. *See*
    Transaction Server
  Visual Modeler, 129
  Web site, 288
middle-tier servers, 168
middleware legacy systems,
  40-42
migration of legacy systems, 40
mirroring, 51-52
MSF (Microsoft Solution
  Framework), 12-13.
  See also design
  availability, 63
    downtimes, 64-65
    geographic scope, 63
    operational timelines, 63-64
  business practices, 44
    customer needs, 46
    organizational structures,
      44-45

NTFS FILE SYSTEM 301

feature-selection process, 20-21
   creating feature list, 21-22
   feature creep, 22
localization, 38
maintainability, 59
   application distribution, 59-61
   future planning, 62-63
   support, 61-62
   upgrades, 59-61
performance. *See* performance
project scope, 12-13
   budgets, 18-22
   defining problems, 15
   existing applications, 16
   life expectancy, 16-17
   solution definitions, 15-16
scalability, 65
   data expansion, 67
   organizational changes, 66
   planning for growth, 65-66
security models, 46
   auditing, 49-51
   database, 48-49
   fault tolerance, 51-54
   file-level, 48
   group, 47-48
   identifying roles, 49
   server, 47
   system-level, 47
   user-level, 47
TCO (total cost of ownership), 27
users, 32-33
   identifying, 33-34
   local, 36-37
   remote, 36-37
   training, 35-36
Web site, 196
MSMQ (Microsoft Message Queue), 56-57

MTS (Microsoft Transaction Server). *See* Transaction Server
multiple-document interface (MDI), 105-106, 164, 169

N

n-tier architecture, 117-119
named pipes, 242
navigation, interface design, 143-144
networks, 232
   ActiveX, 239
   AS/400, 231-232
   Internet, IIS 4.0, 234
   LANs, 232
   RAS (remote access services), 233
   speed, 232-233
   traffic, design considerations, 167-168
   VPNs (Virtual Private Networks), 37, 233
   WANs, 232, 288
      linking remote users, 36
      protocols, 288
   Windows 3.11, 229
   Windows 95, 230
   Windows 98, 230
   Windows NT, 230
   Windows NT Server, 231
   Windows NT Workstation, 230
nodes, treeview controls, 138
normalization (logical database design), 70, 90
   first normal form, 91
   second normal form, 91, 93
   third normal form, 95-97
NT (windows) RAS, 37
NTFS file system, 242

O

Object Oriented Design (OOD), 243
Object Oriented Programming (OOP), 243
objects, 243
    COM, Transaction Server, 289
    events, 124-126
    methods, 123
    models, 128-130
    organization, 126
        business services, 127
        data services, 128
        user services, 126
    process flow, 130
    properties, 121-123
    state, 121-122
ODBC (Open Database Connectivity), 226-227
    connection pooling, 166
    SNA Server, 289
offline time, 56-57
OLE DB, 229
one-to-many relationships, 82-83
one-to-one relationships, 81
OOD (Object Oriented Design), 243
OOP (Object Oriented Programming), 243
operating systems
    AS/400, 231-232
    Windows 3.11, 229
    Windows 95, 230
    Windows 98, 230
    Windows NT, 230
    Windows NT Server, 231
    Windows NT Workstation, 230

operational timelines (availability), 63-64
organization of objects, 126
    business services, 127
    data services, 128
    scalability, 66
    structures, 44-45
    user services, 126
orphaned records, 89
OutProc, 243

P

parent entities, 80
peak usage, 56
perceived response time, 58
performance, 54
    architecture design, 167-168
    bandwidth, 54-55
        offline time, 56-57
        peak usage, 56
    remote users, 36-37
    response time, 57
        perceived, 58
        physical, 57-58
        transactions, 58-59
physical database design, 70, 99-100
physical response time, 57-58
planning
    future considerations, 62-63
    scalability, 65-66
platforms, incorporating with infrastructure design, 30
POSIX (portable operating system interface for UNIX), 164-165
practicing for exam, 278

primary keys, 77-78, 80, 89
priorities, feature-selection list, 21
private properties, 123
problem analysis, business requirements, 24-26
problem definition (project scope), 15
processes, 243
  flow, 130
programming
  J++ cross-platform applications, 289
  Visual C++, 288
programs. *See* applications
progress bars, 140-141
projects
  budgets, 197
  business requirements, 22
    application environment, 31
    business goals, 23-24
    customer requirements, 24
    establishing problem type, 25-26
    infrastructure design, 30
    new technology, impact of, 30-31
    problem analysis, 24-25
    ROI (return on investment), 26-29
    schedules, 32
    TCO (total cost of ownership), 26-27
  scope, 12-13
    budgets, 18-22
    defining problems, 15
    existing applications, 16
    life expectancy, 16-17
    review items for test, 197
    solution definitions, 15-16

properties, COM (Component Object Model), 121-123
protocols
  FTP, 240
  HTTP, 240
  TCP/IP, 244
  WANs (Wide Area Networks), 288
prototyping interface design, 159-160
public properties, 123
publications, resources for taking exam, 288

Q-R

questions on exam, 271, 279-285
  "build list and reorder," 271-272
  "create a tree," 271
  "drop and connect," 273-275
  Microsoft mind set, 275-276
  scenario-based, 250-256, 260-270
  time factor, 278

RAD (Rapid Application Development), 243
RAID (Redundant Array of Inexpensive Disks), 52, 54
RAS (remote access services), 37, 233
RDBMS (relational database management system), 243
RDO (Remote Data Object Library), 228-229
read-only properties, 122-123
read-write properties, 122-123
Record Management Services (RMS), 42

records, orphaned, 89
Redundant Array of
  Inexpensive Disks (RAID),
  52, 54
redundant data. *See*
  normalization
referential integrity, 89
registration, exam, 279
relational database
  management system
  (RDBMS), 243
relationships (ER diagrams),
  76-77
    creating, 88
    keys, 77
      defined, 77
      foreign, 80, 89
      primary, 77-78, 80, 89
    many-to-many, 83-84
    one-to-many, 82-83
    one-to-one , 81
remote access services (RAS),
  37, 233
Remote Data Object Library
  (RDO), 228-229
remote users, 36-37
replication, SQL Server, 224
reporting, 168
requirement analysis, project
  scope, 12-13
    budgets, 18-22
    defining problems, 15
    existing applications, 16
    life expectancy, 16-17
    solution definitions, 15-16
resources
  Microsoft Web site, 288
  publications, 288
response time, 57
  perceived, 58
  physical, 57-58
  transactions, 58-59

return on investment
  (ROI), 26
  increasing, 27-29
review items for test
  application models, 204-207
  architecture, 211-213
  business requirements,
    196-203
  developing data models,
    203-204
  project scope, 197
  user interfaces, 207-211
RMS (Record Management
  Services), 42
ROI (return on
  investment), 26
  increasing, 27-29

S

SAPI (Speech Application
  Programming Interface), 244
scalability, 65
  data expansion, 67
  organizational changes, 66
  planning for growth, 65-66
scenario-based questions (on
  exam), 250-256, 260-270
schedules, business
  requirements, 32
scope (projects), 12-13
  budgets, 18
    benefit trade-offs, 20-22
    cost total, 19-20
    time/labor, 18-19
  defining problems, 15
  existing applications, 16
  life expectancy, 16-17
  review items for test, 197
  solutions definitions, 15-16

scraping (screen), 41-42, 244
screens
  green, 288
  scraping, 41-42, 244
  screen shots on exam, 257
SDI (single-document interface), 104, 169
second normal form (normalization), 91-93
security
  auditing, 49-51
  fault tolerance, 51
    hardware, 51-54
    software, 54
  identifying roles, 49
  models, 46
    database, 48-49
    file-level, 48
    group, 47-48
    server/machine, 47
    system-level, 47
    user-level, 47
  SQL Server, 224
servers, 224
  Exchange, 237-238
  IIS 4.0 (Internet Information Server), 234, 288
  InProc, 241
  ISAPI (Internet Server Application Programming Interface), 241
  middle-tier, 168
  MSMQ (Microsoft Message Queue), 56-57
  MTS (Microsoft Transaction Server), 49, 236-237
  SANA, ODBC access, 289
  security, 47
  SMS (Systems Management Server), 171
  SNA, 235
  SQL Server, 224-225
  Transaction COM objects, 289
  Transaction Server, 39
services
  applications, 107-108
  business, 112-113, 127
  data, 112-113, 128
  user, 113, 126
shortcut keys, menus, 145
single-tier architecture, 113-114
single-document interface (SDI), 104, 169
sites (Web sites)
  MeasureUp.com, 278
  Microsoft, 288
  MSF, 196
size, databases, 166
SMS (Systems Management Server), 171
SNA Server, 41, 235
  ODBC access, 289
software
  fault tolerance, 54
  middleware, 40-42
solution definitions (project scope), 15-16
sources, feature-selection list, 21
Speech Application Programming Interface (SAPI), 244
speed, networks, 232-233
SQL Server, 224-225
standards
  help files, 155
  POSIX, 165
state objects, 121-122

status bars, interface design, 152-153
storage, architecture design, 166-168
stored procedures, 167
support, 61-62
Sylvan Prometric telephone number, 279
system-level security, 47
Systems Management Server (SMS), 171

T

tables
   cartesian product, 130
   child, 79
   join, 83-84
   junction, 83-84
   keys. *See* keys
   referential integrity, 89
tabs, auto-tabbing, 144
tabstrips, 137
TAPI (Telephony Application Programming Interface), 244
TCO (total cost of ownership), 26
   budgeted, 27
   minimizing, 26-27
   unbudgeted, 27
TCP/IP, 244
technical architecture. *See* architecture
technology, impact on business requirements, 30-31
telephone numbers, Sylvan Prometric, 279
Telephony Application Programming Interface (TAPI), 244
testlets, 270
tests, ACID, 238
tests. *See* Analyzing Requirements and Defining Solution Architectures exam
thin client/terminal applications, 114-115
third normal form (normalization), 95-97
third-party applications, 216
threads, 245
three-tier architecture, 116-117
time
   budgets and project scope, 18-19
   taking exam, 271, 276-278
tips for taking exam, 269-271, 288-289
   questions, 271, 279-285
   "build list and reorder," 271-272
   "create a tree," 271
   "drop and connect," 273-275
   Microsoft mind set, 275-276
   scenario-based, 250-256, 260-270
   time factor, 278
   screen shots, 257
   time, 271, 276-278
toolbars, 137
tools, development, 216, 245-246
   Visual Basic, 216-217
   Visual CC++, 218-219
   Visual FoxPro, 219-220
   Visual InterDev, 220-222
   Visual J++, 222-223
   Visual SourceSafe, 223-224

ToolTips interface design, 153
total cost of ownership
  (TCO), 26
  budgeted, 27
  minimizing, 26-27
  unbudgeted, 27
trackbar controls, 139-140
traffic (network), design,
  167-168
training
  support staff, 61
  users, 35-36
Transaction Server 4.0, 39, 49,
  236-237, 288
  COM objects, 289
transactions, 58-59, 245
  batch systems, 16
Transmission Control
  Protocol/Interface Protocol
  (TCP/IP), 244
trapping, 149
treeview controls, 138-139
two-tier architecture, 115-116

U

unbudgeted TCO, 27
upgrades, 59-61, 171
use cases, architecture
  design, 169
user base deployment, 171
user-level security, 47
users, 32-33
  feedback
    interface design, 152
    status bars, 152-153
    ToolTips, 153
    What's This Help, 153
    wizards, 154
  identifying, 33-34
  interfaces. *See* interfaces
  local, 36-37
  remote, 36-37
  services, 113, 126
  training, 35-36

V

VB (Visual Basic), 216-217
Virtual Private Networks,
  37, 233
Virtual Sequential Access
  Method (VSAM), 40
vision/scope process, 12-13
  budgets, 18
    benefit trade-offs, 20-22
    cost total, 19-20
    time/labor, 18-19
  defining problems, 15
  existing applications, 16
  life expectancy, 16-17
  solution definitions, 15-16
Visual Basic, 216-217
Visual C++, 218-219, 288
visual cues, interface design,
  149-151
Visual FoxPro, 219-220
Visual InterDev, 220-222, 289
Visual J++, 222-223
Visual Modeler, 129
Visual SourceSafe (VSS),
  223-224
  bug-tracking tools, 289
  FrontPage, 289
  InterDev, 220-222, 289
VPNs (Virtual Private
  Networks), 37, 233
VSAM (Virtual Sequential
  Access Method), 40
VSS. *See* Visual SourceSafe

W-Z

WANs (Wide Area Networks), 232, 288
  linking remote users, 36
  protocols, 288
Web interfaces, 169
Web sites
  MeasureUp.com, 278
  Microsoft, 288
  MSF, 196
Web-based applications, 108-109
What's This Help, interface design, 153
Wide Area Networks (WANs), 232, 288
  linking remote users, 36
  protocols, 288

windows, colors, 141
Windows 3.11, 229
Windows 95, 230
Windows 98, 230
Windows Explorer
  toolbar, 137
  treeview control, 138
Windows NT, 230
  RAS, 37
  Server, 231
  service applications, 107-108
  Workstation, 230
wizards, interface design, 154
write-only properties, 123

New Riders Titles

MCSE Fast Track: Networking Essentials
1-56205-939-4,
$19.99, 9/98

MCSE Fast Track: TCP/IP
1-56205-937-8,
$19.99, 9/98

MCSE Fast Track: Windows 98
0-7357-0016-8,
$19.99, 12/98

MCSE Fast Track: Internet Information Server 4
1-56205-936-X,
$19.99, 9/98

MCSE Fast Track: Windows NT Server 4
1-56205-935-1,
$19.99, 9/98

MCSD Fast Track: Solution Architectures
0-7357-0029-X,
$29.99, 9/99

MCSE Fast Track: Windows NT Server 4 Enterprise
1-56205-940-8,
$19.99, 9/98

MCSD Fast Track: Visual Basic 6, Exam 70-175
0-7357-0018-4,
$19.99, 12/98

MCSE Fast Track: Windows NT Workstation 4
1-56205-938-6,
$19.99, 9/98

MCSD Fast Track: Visual Basic 6, Exam 70-176
0-7357-0019-2,
$19.99, 12/98

NEW RIDERS CERTIFICATION TITLES

TRAINING GUIDES

Complete, Innovative, Accurate, Thorough

Our next generation Training Guides have been developed to help you study and retain the essential knowledge that you need to pass your certification exams. We know your study time is valuable, and we have made every effort to make the most of it by presenting clear, accurate, and thorough information.

In creating this series, our goal was to raise the bar on how certification content is written, developed, and presented. From the two-color design that gives you easy access to content to the new software simulator that allows you to perform tasks in a simulated operating system environment, we are confident that you will be well-prepared for exam success.

Our New Riders Top Score Software Suite is a custom-developed set of full-functioning software applications that work in conjunction with the Training Guide by providing you with the following:

Exam Simulator tests your hands-on knowledge with over 150 fact-based and situational-based questions.
Electronic Study Cards test your knowledge with explanations that are linked to an electronic version of the Training Guide.
Electronic Flash Cards help you retain the facts in a time-tested method.
An Electronic Version of the Book provides quick searches and compact, mobile study.
Customizable Software adapts to the way you want to learn.

MCSE Training Guide: Networking Essentials, Second Edition
1-56205-919-X, $49.99, 9/98

MCSE Training Guide: Windows NT Server 4, Second Edition
1-56205-916-5, $49.99, 9/98

MCSE Training Guide: Windows NT Server 4 Enterprise, Second Edition
1-56205-917-3, $49.99, 10/98

MCSE Training Guide: Windows NT Workstation 4, Second Edition
1-56205-918-1, $49.99, 9/98

MCSE Training Guide: Windows 98
1-56205-890-8, $49.99, 1/99

MCSE Training Guide: TCP/IP, Second Edition
1-56205-920-3, $49.99, 11/98

Training Guides

First Editions

Your Quality Elective Solution

MCSE Training Guide: SQL Server 7 Administration
0-7357-0003-6, $49.99, 5/99

MCSE Training Guide: SQL Server 7 Database Design
0-7357-0004-4, $49.99, 5/99

MCSD Training Guide: Solution Architectures
0-7357-0026-5, $49.99, 10/99

MCSD Training Guide: Visual Basic 6 Exams 70-175
0-7357-0002-8, $69.99, 3/99

MCSE Training Guide: Systems Management Server 1.2, 1-56205-748-0

MCSE Training Guide: SQL Server 6.5 Administration, 1-56205-726-X

MCSE Training Guide: SQL Server 6.5 Design and Implementation, 1-56205-830-4

MCSE Training Guide: Windows 95, 70-064 Exam, 1-56205-880-0

MCSE Training Guide: Exchange Server 5, 1-56205-824-X

MCSE Training Guide: Internet Explorer 4, 1-56205-889-4

MCSE Training Guide: Microsoft Exchange Server 5.5, 1-56205-899-1

MCSE Training Guide: IIS 4, 1-56205-823-1

MCSD Training Guide: Visual Basic 5, 1-56205-850-9

MCSD Training Guide: Microsoft Access, 1-56205-771-5

NEW RIDERS CERTIFICATION TITLES

TESTPREP SERIES
Practice, Check, Pass!

Questions. Questions. And more questions. That's what you'll find in our New Riders *TestPreps*. They're great practice books when you reach the final stage of studying for the exam. We recommend them as supplements to our *Training Guides*.

What makes these study tools unique is that the questions are the primary focus of each book. All the text in these books support and explain the answers to the questions.

Scenario-based questions challenge your experience.

Multiple-choice questions prep you for the exam.

Fact-based questions test your product knowledge.

Exam strategies assist you in test preparation.

Complete yet concise explanations of answers make for better retention.

Two practice exams prepare you for the real thing.

Fast Facts offer you everything you need to review in the testing center parking lot.

MCSE TestPrep: Networking Essentials, Second Edition
0-7357-0010-9, $19.99, 12/98

MCSE TestPrep: Windows 95, Second Edition
0-7357-0011-7, $29.99, 12/98

MCSE TestPrep: Windows NT Server 4, Second Edition
0-7357-0012-5, $19.99, 12/98

MCSE TestPrep: Windows NT Server 4 Enterprise, Second Edition
0-7357-0009-5, $19.99, 11/98

MCSE TestPrep: Windows NT Workstation 4, Second Edition
0-7357-0008-7, $19.99, 12/98

MCSE TestPrep: TCP/IP, Second Edition
0-7357-0025-7, $19.99, 12/98

**MCSE TestPrep:
Windows 98**

1-56205-922-X, $19.99, 11/98

TESTPREP SERIES
FIRST EDITIONS

MCSE TestPrep: SQL Server 6.5 Administration, 0-7897-1597-X

MCSE TestPrep: SQL Server 6.5 Design and Implementation, 1-56205-915-7

MCSE TestPrep: Windows 95 70-64 Exam, 0-7897-1609-7

MCSE TestPrep: Internet Explorer 4, 0-7897-1654-2

MCSE TestPrep: Exchange Server 5.5, 0-7897-1611-9

MCSE TestPrep: IIS 4.0, 0-7897-1610-0

How to Contact Us

IF YOU NEED THE LATEST UPDATES ON A TITLE THAT YOU'VE PURCHASED:

1) Visit our Web site at www.newriders.com.

2) Click on Product Support, and enter your book's ISBN number located on the back cover in the bottom right-hand corner.

3) There you'll find available updates for your title.

IF YOU ARE HAVING TECHNICAL PROBLEMS WITH THE BOOK OR THE CD THAT IS INCLUDED:

1) Check the book's information page on our Web site according to the instructions listed above, or

2) Email us at support@mcp.com, or

3) Fax us at (317) 817-7488 attn: Tech Support.

IF YOU HAVE COMMENTS ABOUT ANY OF OUR CERTIFICATION PRODUCTS THAT ARE NON-SUPPORT RELATED:

1) Email us at certification@mcp.com, or

2) Write to us at New Riders, 201 W. 103rd St., Indianapolis, IN 46290-1097, or

3) Fax us at (317) 581-4663.

IF YOU ARE OUTSIDE THE UNITED STATES AND NEED TO FIND A DISTRIBUTOR IN YOUR AREA:

Please contact our international department at international@mcp.com.

IF YOU WANT TO PREVIEW AN OF OUR CERTIFICATION BOOK FOR CLASSROOM USE:

Email us at pr@mcp.com. Your message s include your name, title, training company c school, department, address, phone numbe office days/hours, text in use, and enrollme Send these details along with your request desk/examination copies and/or additional information.

WE WANT TO KNOW WHAT YOU THINK

To better serve you, we would like your opinion on the content and quality of this book. Please complete this card and mail it to us or fax it to 317-581-4663.

Name _____

Address _____

City _____ State _____ Zip _____

Phone _____ Email Address _____

Occupation _____

Which certification exams have you already passed? _____
_____
_____

Which certification exams do you plan to take? ___
_____
_____
_____

What influenced your purchase of this book?
- ❏ Recommendation
- ❏ Cover Design
- ❏ Table of Contents
- ❏ Index
- ❏ Magazine Review
- ❏ Advertisement
- ❏ Publisher's reputation
- ❏ Author Name

How would you rate the contents of this book?
- ❏ Excellent
- ❏ Very Good
- ❏ Good
- ❏ Fair
- ❏ Below Average
- ❏ Poor

What other types of certification products will you buy/have you bought to help you prepare for the exam?
- ❏ Quick reference books
- ❏ Testing software
- ❏ Study guides
- ❏ Other

What do you like most about this book? Check all that apply.
- ❏ Content
- ❏ Writing Style
- ❏ Accuracy
- ❏ Examples
- ❏ Listings
- ❏ Design
- ❏ Index
- ❏ Page Count
- ❏ Price
- ❏ Illustrations

What do you like least about this book? Check all that apply.
- ❏ Content
- ❏ Writing Style
- ❏ Accuracy
- ❏ Examples
- ❏ Listings
- ❏ Design
- ❏ Index
- ❏ Page Count
- ❏ Price
- ❏ Illustrations

What would be a useful follow-up book to this one for you? _____
Where did you purchase this book? _____
Can you name a similar book that you like better than this one, or one that is as good? Why? _____
_____
_____

How many New Riders books do you own? _____
What are your favorite certification or general computer book titles? _____
_____

What other titles would you like to see us develop? _____
_____

Any comments for us? _____
_____

Fold here and tape to mail

Place
Stamp
Here

New Riders
201 W. 103rd St.
Indianapolis, IN 46290